The Last Cowboy

The Personal Story of a Vanishing Cowboy

DAVIS L. FORD

EAKIN PRESS ◆ Austin, Texas

*Dedicated to all those cowhands, mostly anonymous,
who, through long days and nights with little pay,
carved out a piece of Americana
that will always be a
centerpiece of
our heritage.*

Cover photography by Gray Hawn

Copyright © 2002
By Davis L. Ford
Published in the United States of America
By Eakin Press
A Division of Sunbelt Media, Inc.
P.O. Drawer 90159 Austin, Texas 78709-0159
email: sales@eakinpress.com
 website: www.eakinpress.com
ALL RIGHTS RESERVED.

3   4   5   6   7   8   9

1-57168-709-2

Library of Congress Cataloging-in-Publication Data

Ford, Davis L.
    The last cowboy: the personal story of a vanishing cowboy / Davis L. Ford.– 1st ed.
        p.   cm.
    ISBN 1-57168-709-2
    1. Webb, Leroy, 1933–. 2. Cowboys–New Mexico–Santa Rosa Region–Biography. 3. Ranch life–New Mexico–Santa Rosa Region. 4. Ranch life–New Mexico. 5. Ranch life–Texas. 6. Santa Rosa Region (N.M.)–Biography. I. Title
F804.S3 F37   2002
978.9'25–dc21   2002014065

If Leroy had ever decided to focus in on rodeos, he would have been a world champion roper. It would have been hard to catch him because everything he did, he did it right. He's like a god to me. When he's gone, there won't be any more like him. He's one of a kind.

—Carlos Ortiz, cowboy and friend,
former manager of the Arnett Clabber Hill Ranch

Leroy Webb is the best cowboy that I've ever known, and I'll back that up any day! He doesn't have a big ego, doesn't use profanity, and I've never seen him lose his temper. He's never tried to be a ladies' man or big time cowboy—he's just a true gentleman.

—Donn Davies
Member, Cowboy Hall of Fame

There's something unique with Leroy and horses. He just does things with horses that I just don't think anybody else can do.

—Johnny Caldwell, cowboy, politician,
brother-in-law, and long-time friend

Leroy is one of those great American guys. He's worked hard ever since I've known him. In my opinion, he's the top quarter horse trainer in the nation. He's a superman cowboy, great bronc rider, and as an individual, no better person on earth.

—Jack Kyle
Member, Cowboy Hall of Fame

Leroy Webb is one of the best cowboys I've ever known and is one tough man. I've never seen a better roper.

—Shoat Webster, four-time
world champion roper

Leroy Webb is a wonderful man. You couldn't have picked anybody in the world better to write about.

—Harp McFarland, former manager, Bar S,
Bill Blakley and Henry Singleton, San Cristobal Ranch

"Only the past is real. Even that reality is too often lost as recollection fails us and we neglect the record of the event. We discard the accomplishments not only of those who have gone before us but also the earlier phases and occurrences of our own lives. Let us devote ourselves to the preservation of this only reality in time, that the efforts, sacrifices, and the achievements of the past are not wasted."

—J. C. "Cap" McNeill
(West Texas rancher)
Inscription on wall of
Margaret Elliot Museum,
Spur, Texas

Contents

A young Leroy Webb—
the beginning of an authentic American.

Preface

*L*eroy Webb is not the "last cowboy" any more than Larry McMurtry's Royal Theater is the "last picture show." Even so, the septuagenarian Leroy Webb, who at the time of this writing is still in the saddle from "can't see to can't see" while running a giant ranch in New Mexico, might come close to qualifying. He has spent most of the last sixty years in the saddle; broken more than 2,500 horses; slept under the stars or in a line camp for more than 15,000 nights; raised, trained, and sold world champion roping and cutting horses; attained championship status as a rodeo performer; roped bears, elk, coyotes, and antelope in addition to thousands of cattle; worked at more than twenty-five major ranches in the Southwest; flirted with the New York and Hollywood scene; and today can outwork and outperform most cowboys of any age. Leroy Webb is an American treasure, an icon of the American West.

Back in the 1980s, I wrote the following description of the American cowboy. When I met Webb a few years later, I knew I had it right.

> The cowboy is the true manifestation of the American dream and is one of our few identifiers that is uniquely American. His traits are those of self-reliance, optimism, energy, and true grit. The open range, grazing cattle, a coyote's distant call, the rugged face which has weathered the blue northers, the winter snows, the parching summer winds ... all of these reflect both the realism and imagery that Americans cherish ... the common thread which binds North, South, East, and West.... The American cowboy.
>
> The American cowboy of the 1980s is similar to his predecessors of a century ago. He is a producer more than a speculator ... an individualist, not a conformist. He prefers the outdoors to confining rooms. Generally a loner rather than gregarious, he is steeped in tradition, casually cantankerous, sometimes cynical, but always helpful ... and he would practice no other profession.
>
> Such is the taproot of this country, embellished by tabloid and song, but nevertheless real, and true to the American dream ... the cowboy.

As an environmental engineer and part-time professor, I have wondered why Leroy Webb so captured my imagination.

Maybe it was because I was inoculated with the ways of a cowboy when I worked as a boy for my father's dry land wheat and cattle operation in the western Texas Panhandle during the summers of the late 1940s and early 1950s.

Maybe it was because I was mesmerized by the John Ford classic western movies *Stagecoach*, *Fort Apache*, *She Wore a Yellow Ribbon*, and *Rio Grande*, and Howard Hawks' *Red River*. Maybe it was my Saturday afternoon tradition of being entranced with the "B" cowboy movies and serials starring Gene Autry, Roy Rogers, and Hopalong Cassidy in the old theaters of Lubbock, Texas, during the 1940s and 1950s.

It could have been due to my astonishment at the accuracy of McMurtry's portrayal of my own youth in *The Last Picture Show*, or an increasing attention to my father's library that included books by such authors as Ben K. Green, J. Evetts Haley, Walter Prescott Webb, and J. Frank Dobie.

Maybe it was because of my grandfather and namesake, G.C. Davis, who recorded his memoirs in *Over My Shoulder*, depicting his early life as a cowboy in Archer County, Texas, during the early 1900s. I've read and reread his accounts of working cattle on the 66 Ranch, meeting and marrying a beautiful schoolteacher who had just arrived in the small community of Holliday (my grandmother), and spending many of his later years selling ranches in that county to a local rancher named Will Taylor (most of which later developed oil).

Maybe it was because of these same grandparents, who later moved to Amarillo and befriended a local citizen in the 1920s named Cal Farley, who, in the 1940s, took waif boys off the streets, and along with Lee Bivins created a Boys Ranch in the ghost town of Old Tascosa and turned problem youngsters into cowboys and good citizens.

It might have been derived from my more recent epiphany that many of our American virtues of hard work, ethical behavior, and entrepreneurship evolved from this heritage.

Or maybe it came from my understanding of an old African proverb, loosely translated, that when a person of history, knowledge, and wisdom dies an unrecorded death, it's like burning down a library.

When I got to know Leroy and his wife, Nora, the confluence of all these "maybes" made it obvious that this book had to be written.

—Davis L. Ford
Austin, Texas, 2002

Introduction and Acknowledgments

*I*t was a cold, blustery May morning as I drove north from Santa Rosa, New Mexico, to the Bar Y Ranch to meet with Leroy Webb and his wife, Nora, at the ranch headquarters. A good rain had preceded me, and I had to put my old Suburban into four-wheel drive to make it through the slippery red clay of the ranch road. Once I passed the Bar Y gate, I drove about fifteen miles to the headquarters, where Leroy and Nora waited with a full pot of hot coffee. The ranch office was filled with priceless memorabilia such as photographs, articles, trophies, and family artifacts I wanted to review, a portion of which I would select and memorialize in the book. I was overwhelmed by this remarkable history of ranching and cowboying.

The Bar Y Ranch division which Leroy currently manages is unique, incorporated into 600,000 acres split into five divisions, each under separate management, ranging from Tucumcari to Las Vegas, New Mexico. This ranch, combined with another 600,000 acres in the western part of the state, was put together by a Texan, Henry Singleton, a brilliant engineer who started Teledyne and led one of the nation's largest conglomerates for three decades. He was known for his prowess on Wall Street and as a merger guru, but he loved the beauty and landscape of New Mexico and rolled a significant amount of his fortune back into the land to preserve it. Leroy was one of his favorite people, and they maintained a personal and professional relationship until Singleton's death in 1999. One of his last acts was to retain Leroy to manage his Bar Y Ranch.

As I navigated through the New Mexico mud, trying to decide whether to enjoy the beauty of the rain-refreshed grassland or maintain control of my vehicle, I was thinking what a magnificent pairing it was: Leroy the cowboy and Singleton the owner and preservationist. I doubt if our successors will ever witness such a combination.

I made my selection of photographs and articles, drank a couple of cups of strong, black coffee, promised Nora that I would protect these irreplaceable items with my life, and worked my way to Albuquerque to get them scanned for printing. This book, therefore, comprises my own research and narrative, transcribed tapes from Leroy (who, from his hand-held Dictaphone, would record his memories from the saddle, the corral, or the pickup) as well as his friends, and photographs interspersed where appropriate. Leroy's words and those of others I've interviewed are italicized.

The chapters are arranged chronologically, beginning with Webb's serious cowboying as a ten-year-old and progressing through his career today as the manager of the Bar Y. He has worked or leased more than twenty-five ranches in his professional life:

WS/Vermejo Ranch, Raton, New Mexico
CS Ranch, Cimarron, New Mexico
UU Bar Ranch, Cimarron, New Mexico
Red River Y 7 Ranch, Springer, New Mexico
Fort Union Ranch, Watrous, New Mexico
Circle Dot Ranch, Maxwell, New Mexico
Reynolds Long X Ranch, Kent, Texas
Frank Burk Ranch (Cimarroncita), Ute Park, New Mexico
One Thousand Acre Dude Ranch, Stony Brook, New York
Matador Ranch, Matador, Texas
Sawyer Cattle Company (Bar S), Big Lake, Texas
San Cristobal Ranch, Lamy, New Mexico
Trigg Ranch, Logan, New Mexico
Hampton Ranch, Logan, New Mexico
McCarty Ranch, Logan, New Mexico
Mitchell Ranch, Mosquero, New Mexico
Chappell Spade Ranch, Tucumcari, New Mexico
Clabber Hill Ranch, Conchas, New Mexico
Conchas Ranch, Conchas, New Mexico
CA Ranch, Las Vegas, New Mexico
Latigo Ranch, La Querva, New Mexico
Bar Y (Singleton) Ranch, Santa Rosa, New Mexico
Shelly Hays Ranch, Cline's Corners, New Mexico

These ranches represent a broad cross-section of the major ranching operations that evolved in Texas and New Mexico during the nineteenth century, many of which are still operating today.

The evolution of the major Texas ranches, such as the Matadors, XIT, Pitchfork, Four Sixes, King, Waggoner, Lambshead, Schriener, JA, and Halffs, was different from those in New Mexico. These Texas ranches originated not through Mexican land grants but through European and American investors, primarily in the 1880s, attracted by the immense profit potential of marrying the vast Texas grasslands to the growing American demand for beef. Unlike New Mexico, which was a territory until statehood was attained in 1912, Texas had been an independent republic from the time of its successful revolution against Mexico in 1836 until its statehood in 1845. Following the 1848 Guadalupe Hidalgo Treaty and U.S. statehood status, both before and after the Civil War, these investors had safer title protection from the Texas legislature. These historical events in the American Southwest enhanced the opportunity for the working cowboys to flourish and subsequently become an inherent part of our American culture.

I have researched the history of major ranches for background information and have interviewed numerous individuals. Moreover, I have included a bibliography of published material enumerating these sources as well as notes from personal interviews of more than thirty cowboys and relatives and acquaintances of the Webbs. I have donated many of those tapes to the Southwest Collection on the Texas Tech campus in Lubbock. With the help of Leroy and Nora, I have attempted to identify the individuals in the photographs as well as the approximate dates.

There were many friends in New Mexico during the period I was leasing the Atmore and Ute Creek ranches at Ute Park, New Mexico. It was at the Atmore Ranch, then owned by Dick and Doris Atmore and their sons, Frank and John, that I met Leroy and Nora Webb in 1988. John Atmore, married to Leroy's sister, Shirley, made the introduction, describing Leroy as "an authentic, old-time Christian cowboy." Many other family and Texas friends who have a sense of western history have provided invaluable assistance. I would like to acknowledge the following:

Research and Informational Sources

Ms. Pam Arthur (my talented secretary, transcriber, and editor)—Austin, Texas

Ms. Lucile Davis Ford (my mother, friend, and source of family history)— Lubbock, Texas

Ms. Gray Hawn (world-class photographer and great friend)—Austin, Texas

Ms. Hope Coslett Pees (Nora Webb's niece)—Seguin, Texas

George M. Cowden (ranching family, Sunday school teacher, good friend)— Austin, Texas

Ms. Evelyn Marsh (Count Caldwell's daughter)—Austin, Texas

James O. Collins (long-time friend)—Gunnison, Colorado

Ms. Janet Neugebauer (associate archivist, Southwest Collection)—Lubbock, Texas

Dr. Isabelle Howe (friend)—Lubbock, Texas

Senator Joe Tydings (historian and friend)—Washington, D.C.

Ms. Kate Clark (friend and editor)—Washington, D.C.

Dr. Susan Ford Wiltshire (friend, sister, and editor)—Nashville, Tennessee
Dr. Charles Backus (friend, literary resource, director of Texas A&M Press)—College Station, Texas
Ms. Veryl Goodnight (artist and great friend)—Santa Fe, New Mexico
Roger Brooks (military historian, airline pilot, good friend)—Santa Fe, New Mexico
Jim McGowan (farmer, rancher, business partner)—Hereford, Texas
Ms. Lucy Green McGowan (ranching family and wife)—Hereford, Texas
Mrs. Howard Hampton (widow of Howard Hampton, rancher and philanthropist, now deceased)—Lubbock, Texas
Claytie and Modesta Williams (great friends, philanthropists, benefactors of Texas A&M, and ranching family)—Midland, Texas
Rich Anderson (cattleman, historian)—Gail, Texas
Jan Hays (education coordinator, American Wind Power Center)—Lubbock, Texas
Dr. Earnest Gloyna (mentor, educator, great friend)—Austin, Texas
Joe Hiram Moore (benefactor of A&M Press, long-time friend)—Austin, Texas
Dr. Noel Parsons (literary source and advisor, director of the Texas Tech University Press)—Lubbock, Texas

Institutions

Raton Public Library—Raton, New Mexico
Philmont Museum—Cimarron, New Mexico
Texas Cattle Feeders Association—Amarillo, Texas
American Quarter Horse Association—Amarillo, Texas
Rough Rider Museum—Las Vegas, New Mexico
Old Grist Mill Museum—Cimarron, New Mexico
Cowboy Hall of Fame—Oklahoma City, Oklahoma
Bob Bullock Texas State History Museum—Austin, Texas
St. James Hotel—Cimarron, New Mexico
Southwest Collection, Texas Tech University—Lubbock, Texas
Texas A&M Press—College Station, Texas
Old Fort Sumner Museum and Billy the Kid Museum—Fort Sumner, New Mexico
National Ranching Heritage Center, Texas Tech University—Lubbock, Texas
Nita Stewart Haley Memorial Library and J. Evetts Haley History Center—Midland, Texas
The Gene Autry Museum of Western Heritage—Los Angeles, California
American Wind Power Center—Lubbock, Texas
Panhandle-Plains Museum—Canyon, Texas
Kit Carson Museum—Taos, New Mexico

Personal Interviews
(Conducted between December 2000 and March 2002)

Leroy Webb (cowboy)—Santa Rosa, New Mexico

Nora Caldwell Webb (cowgirl, wife, and partner)—Santa Rosa, New Mexico

Carlos Ortiz (cowboy)—Tucumcari, New Mexico

Albert "Sucker Rod" Osborne (cowboy)—Maljamar, New Mexico

Harp McFarlane (cowboy)—Stanley, New Mexico

Paul Engler (feedlot executive)—Amarillo, Texas

Charles Ball (retired TCFA executive director)—Amarillo, Texas

Jack Kyle (cowboy)—Yukon, Oklahoma

Shoat Webster (cowboy)—Lenapah, Oklahoma

Tammy Garrison (director of Customer Service, American Quarter Horse Association)—Amarillo, Texas

Sam Arnett, III (rancher)—Lubbock, Texas

Don Webb (cowboy)—Raton, New Mexico

Donn Davies (cowboy and historian)—Taos, New Mexico

Johnny Caldwell (cowboy)—Clayton, New Mexico

Rob Chappell (artisan and rancher)—Tucumcari, New Mexico

Jim Payne (cowboy)—Logan, New Mexico

Jimmy Rockinfield (friend, hunting guide, firefighter)—Ute Park, New Mexico

Frank Atmore (hunting guide and friend)—Ute Park, New Mexico

Steve Zimmer (Philmont Ranch historian, rodeo announcer)—Miami, New Mexico

Bill Hemphill (cowboy)—Roaring Springs, Texas

Frank Chappell (retired rancher)—Essex, Connecticut

Robert S. Allen (long-time resident of Raton, rancher, great friend, and average golfer)—Raton, New Mexico

Rick, Dennis, and Diego Romo—Anton Chico, New Mexico

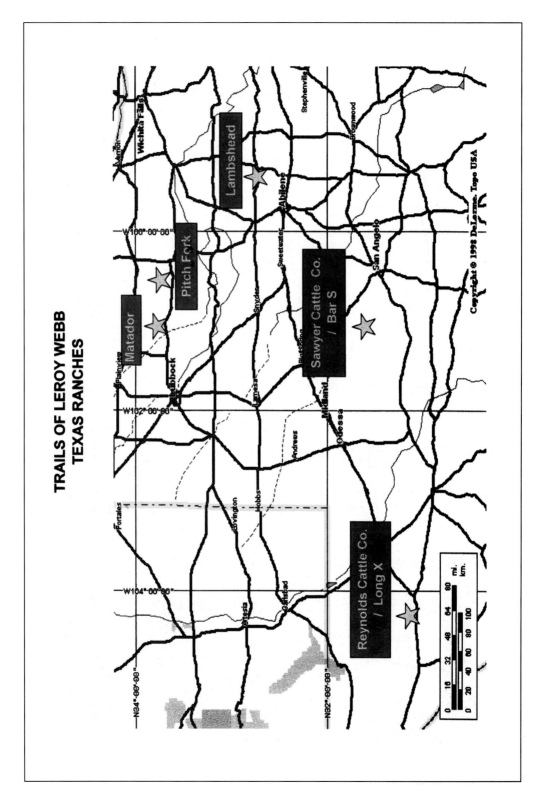

TRAILS OF LEROY WEBB
TEXAS RANCHES

Lambshead

Pitch Fork

Matador

Sawyer Cattle Co. / Bar S

Reynolds Cattle Co. / Long X

Copyright © 1998 DeLorme, Topo USA

Vernon
Wichita Falls
Stephenville
Brownwood
Abilene
Sweetwater
San Angelo
Snyder
Plainview
Lubbock
Big Spring
Lamesa
Midland
Odessa
Andrews
Portales
Hobbs
Lovington
Artesia
Carlsbad

W100°-00'-00"
W102°-00'-00"
W104°-00'-00"
N34°-00'-00"
N32°-00'-00"

mi.
km.
0 16 32 48 64 80
0 20 40 60 80 100

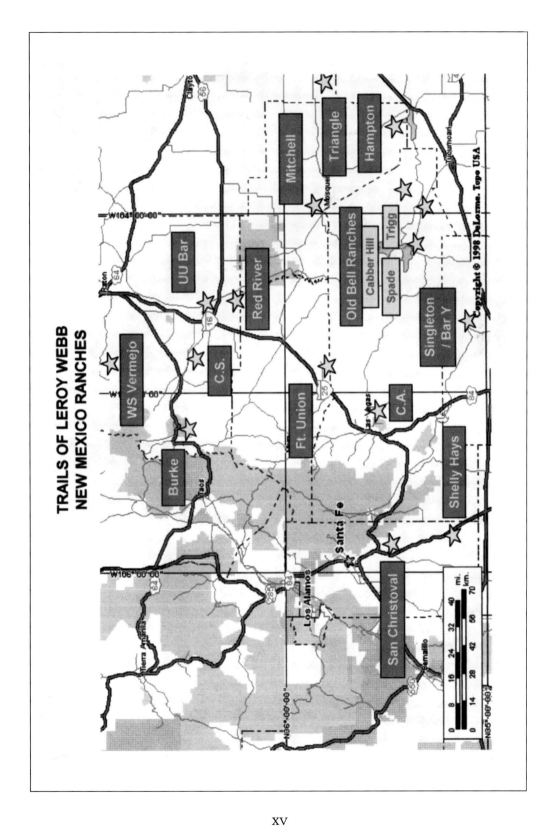

TRAILS OF LEROY WEBB
NEW MEXICO RANCHES

LEROY WEBB TIMELINE

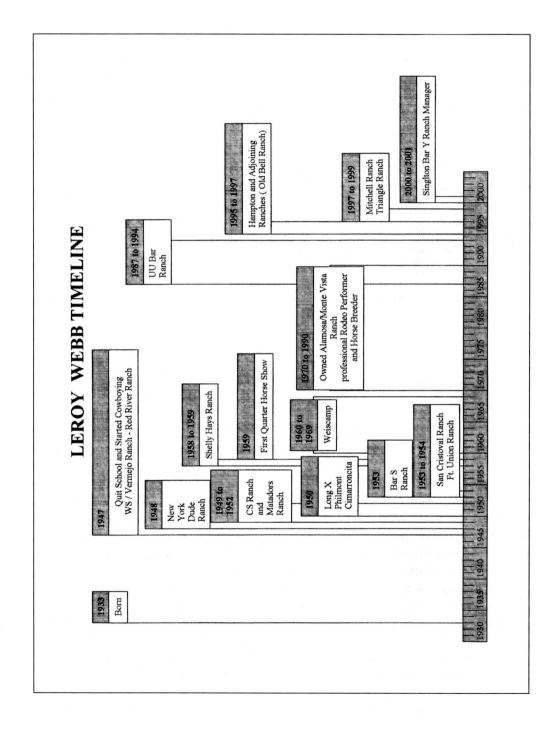

1933 Born

1947 Quit School and Started Cowboying
WS / Vermejo Ranch - Red River Ranch

1948 New York Dude Ranch

1949 to 1952 CS Ranch and Matadors Ranch

1950 Long X Philmont Cimarroncita

1953 Bar S Ranch

1953 to 1954 San Cristoval Ranch Ft. Union Ranch

1958 to 1959 Shelly Hays Ranch

1959 First Quarter Horse Show

1960 to 1969 Weiscamp

1970 to 1990 Owned Alamosa/Monte Vista Ranch professional Rodeo Performer and Horse Breeder

1987 to 1994 UU Bar Ranch

1995 to 1997 Hampton and Adjoining Ranches (Old Bell Ranch)

1997 to 1999 Mitchell Ranch Triangle Ranch

2000 to 2003 Singlton Bar Y Ranch Manager

1930 1935 1940 1945 1950 1955 1960 1965 1970 1975 1980 1985 1990 1995 2000

xvi

CHAPTER 1

What's Past Is Prologue

*A*s the ancestral histories and lives of Leroy Webb and his wife, Nora Caldwell Webb, revolved so much around Texas, New Mexico, and the cattle industry, it seems appropriate to first establish the background for this biography. As Shakespeare wrote, "What's past is prologue." The histories of New Mexico, Texas, and the ranching industry are a prelude to the ranching and cattle era that Leroy and Nora Webb have experienced.

The ranching and cowboy evolution over the past two centuries can be predicated on several major events: the influence of the railroads, the slaughter of the buffalo (which ironically enhanced the availability of native grasslands), the availability of foreign capital, the advent of barbed wire fences and windmills, political influence, legislative and judiciary decisions, ranch transportation improvements, the introduction of grain sorghums and feedlots, and the evolving American demand for quality beef. These and other factors set the stage and demand for ranch cowboys such as Leroy Webb and his friends.

As I researched the backgrounds of the Leroy Webb and Nora Caldwell Webb ancestors, I was amazed to discover that so many familiar names appeared within these two families.[1] Such names included Kit Carson (whose son married Leroy's great aunt), Davy Crockett (whose son was a friend of Nora's grandparents), Jesse James and Cole Younger (whom Nora's grand-

parents met near Missouri on their way in covered wagons to New Mexico),
the Ketchum gang (Sam and Tom "Blackjack" Ketchum, some of whom were
apprehended by U.S. marshals near Cimarron, New Mexico, along with
the help of a Springer deputy sheriff named Berlin Caldwell, Nora's father),
and Billy the Kid's killer, Pat Garrett (who had a business relationship
with Nora's grandfather, James M. Caldwell). Others were Clay Allison (a
local character and gunfighter well known to Nora's parents) and Fred
Lambert (a prominent lawman, author, historian, and close friend and con-
fidant of Nora's father, Berlin Caldwell, Colfax County sheriff; Lambert
was the grandson of Henri Lambert, U.S. Grant's cook, Abraham Lincoln's
personal chef, and the founder of the St. James Hotel in Cimarron in 1880).[2]

Historical Setting:
New Mexico (Statehood, 1912)
and Texas (Statehood, 1845)

New Mexico and Texas have common historical roots, although they followed distinctly different pathways toward statehood. The early history of
New Mexico was subject to the Spanish exploration and conquest of the early
sixteenth century. Having defeated the Moors in the reconquest of the
Iberian Peninsula, the Spaniards' interest turned toward the New World in
search of "God, Glory, and Gold." (Beck, 1962) The expedition of Coronado
through the American Southwest and his interaction with the native Indians
is well documented. (Dobie, 1964) As the lure of gold and wealth in New
Mexico was not apparent, Spain's interest in the area lagged throughout the
seventeenth century.

The first governor of New Mexico, Don Pedro de Peralta, founded the
new capital of Santa Fe in 1610. Santa Fe had easy access to the area pueb-
los, availability of water, and arable land, making it a logical choice. The century was one of conflict between the church and the state, and the succession of Spanish governors had difficulty in administering these conflicts. The
Pueblo Indians openly revolted against Spanish rule in 1680, resulting in
partial freedom from their Spanish masters. The early part of the eighteenth
century was characterized by conflicts between the Spaniards and the
Indians, with concurrent battles between the Comanches, Apaches, Utes,
and Navajos. As the nineteenth century approached, Spain was losing its
control of New Mexico.

The Anglo encroachment from the east, with the frontier spirit of seeking land for security and enrichment, was in direct conflict with the Spanish philosophy of subordinating the individual to the state. The Pike expedition in 1806 and the intrusion of American trappers and traders into New
Mexico in the 1820s changed the metrics of the area, which Mexico inherited once it attained its independence from Spain in 1821 by the Treaty of

Cordova. A trader named William Beckwell was surprised to learn that the Mexican soldiers encouraged trade between the Indians and the American Midwesterners, which led to the opening of the Santa Fe Trail. (Martin, 1972) Thus, from the early 1820s until the 1840s, New Mexico became more *"gringo*-ized." This was a prelude to the long anticipated war between Mexico and the United States, which became reality in the spring of 1846. The Anglo migration was undoubtedly a cause, but Mexico's inability to maintain a stable government was also a factor. (Beck, 1962)

U.S. President James K. Polk had expansion plans to capture New Mexico because it served as a convenient route to California. (Beck, 1962) Watts Kearny and his soldiers left Fort Leavenworth in Kansas for Bent's Fort in eastern Colorado, then through Raton Pass and into Santa Fe without firing a shot. (Jenkins and Schroeder, 1974) Governor Armijo had vacated the capital for the safety of Albuquerque and ultimately of Chihuahua. The Americans, when entering Santa Fe, generally scorned the local population for their "race, religion, poverty, and military weakness." (deBuys, 1985) There were inevitable conflicts among Anglos, Indians, and Mexicans, whose ethnic and cultural differences were acute. The Treaty of Guadalupe Hildalgo in 1848 ended the war between the United States and Mexico and secured Mexican recognition of Texas as part of the United States with the Rio Grande as the boundary. Additionally, the United States acquired California, most of New Mexico, Arizona, and Nevada, as well as portions of Colorado and Utah. (Robinson, 2000)

Polk had become the nation's eleventh president in 1844, advocating the annexation of the Republic of Texas. The Polk presidency, so vital to the future of New Mexico and Texas, is well documented in part because of his meticulous diaries. (Polk, 2001) The Mexican-American War conducted by Polk was a tenuous era in United States history. Polk was feeling the ire of Great Britain over territorial ambitions in the West and was criticized by many for his disputes with the U.S. military in the conduct of war. His legacy, however, has been matched by few U.S. presidents. By virtue of the Treaty of Guadalupe Hidalgo, the U.S. territory doubled during his term. Moreover, his administration had faced down Great Britain during the negotiation of this treaty and founded the Smithsonian Institution as well as the U.S. Naval Academy at Annapolis. (Polk, 2001)

This treaty, however, obligated the United States to give "full faith and credit to the existing laws of Mexico." The requirement led to mass confusion, exploitation, grants and land title authenticity disputes, and possession claims that were frequently settled by lawlessness and gun battles instead of the courts. This set the stage for the Colfax County Wars and the Maxwell Land Grant conflicts, which lasted all the way through New Mexico statehood in 1912 and which led to the origins of many of the New Mexico ranches on which Leroy Webb would do his cowboying some four decades later.

The events that led up to the Texas fight for independence from Mexico somewhat paralleled those in New Mexico. Moses Austin, a British subject and speculator from Connecticut, arrived in Texas in 1820 because Spain was seeking settlers and Austin wanted land. (Robinson, 2000) Following his death in 1821, his twenty-seven-year-old son, Stephen F. Austin, took over his father's Texas endeavor. Stephen was a high-energy but reclusive individual. He spent most of 1822 and 1823 in Mexico City trying to resolve disputes revolving around his Spanish land grant, now under the control of an independent Mexico. The title dispute, combined with Indian wars in Texas, slowed migration to the area. However, the United States believed that part of Texas was included in Thomas Jefferson's Louisiana Purchase and proposed to purchase parts of Texas from Mexico in 1825. The offer was $1 million with a Rio Grande boundary or half of that for a more northern Colorado River boundary. Mexico became more alarmed with this expansion, and the relationship with Austin's Anglo settlers began to deteriorate. These disputes culminated in the Texas War for Independence, and following the fall of the Alamo, where Jim Bowie, William B. Travis, Davy Crockett, and others lost their lives, Gen. Sam Houston defeated Mexican President Santa Anna at San Jacinto on April 21, 1836.

It should be noted that Sam Houston played a significant role, albeit indirectly, in the evolution of these Texas ranches. As president of the Texas Republic (1836-1845) and U.S. senator from Texas following annexation, he was a forceful senatorial voice in formulating U.S. policy during the Mexican-American War and negotiating the Treaty of Guadalupe Hidalgo in 1848, insisting that the Rio Grande be the southern border during the presidency of James K. Polk. As governor of Texas in 1860, he unsuccessfully opposed the state's secession from the Union to join the Confederacy. Sam Houston clearly left his footprints on Texas and New Mexico history.[3]

The evolution of the Texas ranches was somewhat different from those

Texas in the Confederacy had an impact on the Texas-New Mexico landscape. Henry Hopkins Sibley was a West Point graduate and became a Confederate general. His volunteer army marched up the Rio Grande toward Santa Fe, hoping to take New Mexico, then secure the Colorado gold fields for the Confederacy. They were met by Union soldiers, mostly Colorado miners who had traveled down through Fort Union toward Glorieta Pass. A battle there in March of 1862 resulted in a defeat for the Texans, the remnants of which retreated toward Galisteo and the San Cristobal area, finally escaping back to Texas. (Edrington, 1998) Following the battle, many of the Union soldiers headed east to fight during the remaining years of the Civil War, leaving the New Mexico settlers relatively unprotected against the Indians. Kit Carson was retained by the U.S. government to suppress this threat. By 1868, Anglos came in great numbers to the area, as did the railroad, and the Americanization of this country was in full swing. However, there was a lingering adverse effect between the Mexicans, Indians, and Anglos during and following these years of turbulence. (Henderson, 1955) (Thompson, Frazier, 2001) (Larson, 1993)

of New Mexico. These ranches primarily originated not through Stephen F. Austin's grants but more on an open market. The independent Republic of Texas era inserted a discontinuity in the lingering Spanish land grant disputes which were experienced by New Mexico. Following the Civil War and fall of the Confederacy, Texas was a legislatively controlled state, which minimized previous grant disputes and paved the way for a more open market system. This attracted both European and American investors, especially during the 1880s, who saw the profitable combined factors of vast, ungrazed Texas grasslands (due in part to the demise of buffalo), the availability of rail transport, and a growing American demand for beef.

The Railroads

The history of the American railroad is epochal. Few studies, however, focus on the integral role the railroads played in replacing the long and inefficient cattle drives with cattle rail transport and linking the supply (American Southwest) to the demand (American East and Midwest).

The railroad from the Atlantic east reached the Mississippi River in 1854, many observers at that time having been alive when George Washington was president. The influx of European immigrants which expanded the eastern U.S. populace was pushing westward, primarily along the waterways, but the future in pushing toward the Pacific Ocean and the lure of the vast western plains led to the era of the rail.

Following the Civil War, the great race began, with the Central Pacific heading east from California and the Union Pacific, having bridged across the Mississippi River, heading west across the expansive prairie lands. Following years of intensive labor, primarily by Chinese and European immigrants, and fighting Indians along the way, the Central Pacific's *Jupiter* and the Union Pacific's *No. 119* met nose to nose at Promontory, Utah, on May 10, 1869. The first transcontinental railroad had been completed. Ingenuity, avaricious bankers, stock manipulators, land speculators, and engineering excellence were all by-products of this accomplishment.

Branch and parallel railroads followed, and the impact on the country was profound. More than 155 million acres were given by the government to the railroad magnates, Indian tribes were decimated, and the buffalo herds fell prey to commercial hunters. (Brown, 1977) The introduction of these branch railroads in the Southwest also ended the era of the Santa Fe Trail. (Martin, 1972)

Railheads of the Kansas Pacific were established at Abilene, Ellsworth, and Hays City, Kansas, to receive cattle drives from Texas, New Mexico, and Oklahoma. The Abilene railhead came into focus as the primary recipient of southwestern-raised cattle because it bordered a river "full of water for thirsty cattle, and a sweeping sea of grass for miles around for holding and fattening stock at the end of the overland drives." (Brown, 1977, p. 80) Thousands of cattle in the later 1860s and early 1870s traversed the various trails, crossing the shallow waters of the Washita, Red, Canadian, and Cimarron rivers to the newly constructed pens at Abilene for subsequent rail shipments to Chicago and East Coast markets. The expansion of railheads and stockyards such as the ones at Abilene created additional jobs for "stock-yard cowboys," who had to provide "interim" service such as receiving, sorting, and loading cattle for transfer to their ultimate points of distribution. (Carlson, 2000)

It was a significant turning point in American history. The proliferation of cattle and rough-and-tumble, thirsty cowboys displaced Indians still on the warpath but subdued by treaties and the U.S. Cavalry. An infrastructure now in place for the development of big cattle ranches created a demand for ranch cowboys such as the predecessors of Leroy Webb and his friends. One can say that the Kansas Pacific Railroad played an integral role in the creation of the romantic folk creatures of the New World—the American cowboy. Without the railroad, the trail town, and access to beef marketplaces, the formulation and imagery of the American cowboy, a major component of American history, may not have occurred.

The New Mexico Land Grants and Colfax County

The most famous grant that shaped the history of northern New Mexico was the Beaubien-Miranda grant, which included more than two million acres of northern New Mexico, just east of the Sangre de Cristo range. In 1841 Mexican governor Manuel Armijo approved the petition submitted by Charles Beaubien, a classics-trained Canadian entrepreneur and successful

The famous Santa Fe Trail had its beginnings in the 1820s, opening a conduit for the vast and lucrative trade between the American Midwest and Santa Fe. The history of the 800-mile trail is filled with names of those who pioneered its development, contended with Comanche and other tribal hostilities, and provided the early conduit of commerce and migration of American immigrants and "gold seekers" to New Mexico and the American West. Such names as William Becknell, Missouri's Senator Thomas Benton, William Bent, Kit Carson, Charles Bent (the first U.S.-appointed governor of the New Mexico Territory), Col. William Kearny, "Wild Bill" Hickok, William "Buffalo Bill" Cody, and "Uncle Dick" Wootton are but a few names of those individuals who left footprints on this trail. (Lavender, 1954) Millions of dollars of trade and commerce were realized from this famous trail, which ended around 1876 with the construction of the branch railroads to the area. (Martin, 1972) The fifty-year saga of the Santa Fe Trail era followed by the railroads provided a historical prologue to the birth of the American cowboy.

Taos merchant, partnering with Guadalupe Miranda, the Santa Fe secretary of government. Beaubien selected Miranda as a partner for rather obvious political, ethnic, and citizenship-related reasons. (Beck, 1962) The two had petitioned Governor Armijo for the grant on the basis that the area was undeveloped, backward, but potentially developable because of its natural resources. The petition approval, over the opposition of the majority of Mexican citizens in the area, was an event of historical importance. Beaubien and Miranda took control of the area in 1843 and immediately began to develop its resources. The next year, they built a cabin on Ponil Creek near Cimarron. Famous Indian scout Kit Carson also built a house in the area before joining John Fremont on his third expedition to California.

Charles Beaubien married Marin Lobato, this union resulting in a daughter, Luz, and a son, Noreisco. While still in her teens, Luz married an ambitious emigrant from Illinois, Lucien Bonaparte Maxwell. Maxwell was a peripatetic and ambitious individual, having made several transcontinental expeditions with John Fremont and having developed a close friendship with Kit Carson. Maxwell moved from Taos to Rayado in 1849, where he built a large home with the help of Kit Carson. Maxwell had a contract with the army, providing food, lodging, and supplies to troops that were positioned along the Santa Fe Trail to serve as protection against the Indians. There were serious Indian attacks during the 1850s, but by 1857, most Indians had left the area. In that year Maxwell sold his Rayado interests, which were eventually acquired by his brother-in-law, Jesus Abreu. Maxwell moved to Cimarron, where he was appointed Indian agent and postmaster. Following the death of Charles Beaubien in 1864 (Miranda having fled from a revolt in Taos) and the untimely demise of Beaubien's son, Noreisco, Maxwell, through his marriage to Luz, was suddenly and propitiously the sole heir to this vast tract of land. (Murphy, 1983) Maxwell managed to purchase more acreage to add to that inherited from his father-in-law. With Dick Wootton facilitating travel over Raton Pass, the mountain branch of the Santa Fe Trail brought more commerce to the area. Then gold was discovered at Baldy Mountain, and the area was booming. Elizabeth Town ("E" Town) and Baldy Town grew up overnight, and Maxwell became exceedingly wealthy through leasing his land to miners. Colfax County was formed in 1869, with "E" Town becoming the county seat (later moved to Springer, then to Raton).

By 1870, Maxwell had seen it all, was the largest single landowner in the United States, and decided to sell out. He sold almost two million acres to an English company fronted by Colorado investors and moved into the buildings of a former military post in Fort Sumner, about 150 miles south of Cimarron. He went into retirement and died at Fort Sumner on July 25, 1875. He is buried there, close to the grave of Billy the Kid. The inscription on Maxwell's tombstone is interesting (probably written by Maxwell himself):

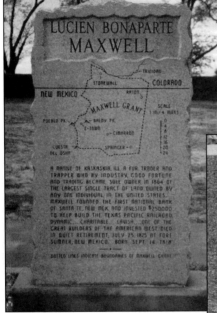

Gravesite of Lucien Maxwell, Fort Sumner, New Mexico.

Gravestone of Luz Maxwell (Lucien Maxwell's wife), Fort Sumner, New Mexico.

A native of Kaskaskia, Ill. A fur trader and trapper who by industry, good fortune and trading became sole owner in 1864 of the largest single tract of land owned by any one individual in the United States. Maxwell founded the First National Bank of Santa Fe, New Mex. And invested $250,000 to help build the Texas Pacific Railroad. Dynamic ... Charitable ... Lavish ... One of the great builders of the American West. Died in quiet retirement July 25, 1875, at Fort Sumner, New Mexico. Born Sept. 14, 1818.

It was to the Maxwell era, an autocratic and controversial period, that the northern New Mexico ranches can trace their origin.

Another vast area of eastern New Mexico was similarly developed through the grant process. In 1824 more than 656,000 acres just west of Tucumcari was awarded to a Mexican citizen by the name of Montoya. Through a long succession of ownership by Montoya's heirs and various American speculators, the great Bell Ranch empire was formed.

A third significant land grant near Las Vegas, New Mexico, was the Anton Chico grant, encompassing about 400,000 acres of prime grasslands. This grant had its origin in the early and confusing years following Mexico's independence from Spain. The grant's intent was to provide for the needs of its inhabitants and to enable them to be useful citizens of the Mexican Republic. However, following the annexation of this land by the United States as a territory, the titles of original grantees became clouded by nefarious transactions, even though protected by the terms of the Treaty of

Guadalupe Hidalgo. Litigation followed, and through a series of court decisions, reversals, and appeals, attorneys were able to secure a large portion of this land as attorney fees. Over one-third of the Anton Chico grant lands ended up in the hands of the lawyers, including 35,000 acres to Thomas Catron, an early U.S. senator from New Mexico, whose political influence was a factor in the final settlement.

The incorporation of these three grants into the United States following the Treaty of Guadalupe Hidalgo (through which the U.S. paid $15 million to Mexico for all of the Mexican territory north of the Rio Grande, an area larger than Europe) set the scene for vast American-owned cattle ranches in northern and eastern New Mexico. These New Mexico ranches would employ many range cowboys, such as Leroy Webb, dating from the latter part of the nineteenth century until today.

The Maxwell Land Grant area primarily falls within the confines of Colfax County, New Mexico. The complex history of this area is important to understanding the biographies of Leroy and Nora Caldwell Webb and their ancestors, as well as the ranches on which they lived.

Following the Civil War, the Territory of New Mexico underwent a commercial revolution that drew people from all backgrounds and professions pursuing virtually unlimited opportunities. Immigrants from many countries (including many of Leroy and Nora's ancestors) poured into northern New Mexico, which was governed by Washington, D.C. appointees. Although bound by treaty to honor "a priori" Mexican land grants, much land was still in the public domain and thus open to homestead and preemption claims. Rich mineral deposits were being discovered, so opportunities abounded. Accompanying these opportunities, however, were ethnic disruptions following the transition from Mexican ownership to U.S. territorial status, legal complexities of land tenure and title, and economic and political turmoil. This was particularly true in the Maxwell Land Grant area comprising much of Colfax County, which was in a virtual state of war in the 1870s. (Taylor, 1979) This war was far more complex than the concurrent Lincoln County War to the southern part of the Territory (involving Pat Garrett and Billy the Kid), which was basically an economic battle mixing cash scarcity with the lure of Indian and government contracts. (Fulton, 1997)

The New Mexico land tenure policy for Spanish settlers which prevailed for more than 200 years followed a far different policy from those developed for the Anglo frontiersmen. Many of these grants were made hastily, and probably illegally, by Governor Armijo in the waning days of Mexican ownership. (Taylor, 1979) A new pattern of private ownership emerged with U.S. territorial possession in 1848. Claims of all kinds and from numerous sources were made in the 1850s, many of which were quickly approved by Congress. This maelstrom lasted over twenty years, with land ownership being the lightning rod. The Maxwell Grant was the centerpiece, simply because it was the largest (1.7 million acres) and under the control of Lucien Maxwell, with

Dutch investors later taking control. Those who defended the integrity of the land grant patent were those in control, as well as railroad interests (Atchison, Topeka and Santa Fe), ranchers, developers, and individuals who had purchased large segments of the Maxwell grant. Settlers of the area opposed this as a "land grab" by special interests and claimed it was illegal under Mexican law (legally binding the United States under the terms of the Treaty of Guadalupe Hidalgo, which limited each grant to no more than 96,000 acres). Thus developed a recipe for war: two groups diametrically opposed with respect to land title, exacerbated by Mexican, Indian, and Anglo ethnic disputes.

This was the setting for the Colfax County transformation during the next thirty years, an era uniquely combining development, progress, law, lawlessness, corruption, legal maneuvering, Catholicism, Protestantism, bravery, cowardice, respect, and disrespect. In the middle of this dispute evolved a little-known Methodist circuit minister named Oscar P. McMains. An activist and controversial intellectual, he worked his way into the Maxwell Land Grant dispute, taking the side of the settlers. (Taylor, 1979) McMains moved from Colorado to Cimarron in 1875. Upon arrival he found the Utes and Jicarillo Apaches receiving rations and annuities from Maxwell's mill, a scattering of Federal soldiers from nearby Fort Union, which anchored the Santa Fe Trail, gold seekers from nearby Baldy City, miners from Elizabeth Town ("E" Town, then county seat of Colfax County and now a ghost town in the Moreno Valley), rowdy cowboys from nearby Maxwell-purchased ranches, and an assortment of outlaws and gunfighters.

McMains championed the settler's cause against the "grantor" interests for the next fifteen years. This tenure was highlighted by the murder of his close ministerial friend, the Reverend Franklin J. Tolby. Tolby was much more concerned about the spiritual welfare of his "flock," particularly the local Indians. He even purchased a large tract of land on the Vermejo River (his title ironically derived from Lucien Maxwell), which he dedicated as an Indian reservation. Tolby was murdered while riding down Cimarron Canyon (he is buried in the Cimarron Cemetery). This tragic event invigorated McMains to champion the cause of the settlers and to fan the flames of anti-grant fervor.

Clay Allison, a rather unsavory and idiosyncratic character, assisted McMains in trying to find Tolby's killer. Allison had served in the

It was the Atchison, Topeka, and Santa Fe (AT&SF) Railroad and other small competitors that provided local railheads for shipping the cattle Leroy, his father, and brother gathered in the early to mid-1900s. It is interesting to note that the AT&SF and the Denver and Rio Grande Western (D&RG) Railroad had arrived in Colorado about the same time in the winter of 1878. Both were racing toward Raton Pass to open up the northern New Mexico markets. Both companies sent line crews to the little town of El Moro on the Colorado side of the pass. Late in the night, the AT&SF crew met with "Uncle Dick" Wootton, who controlled the pass and "cut a deal"—much to the chagrin of the D&RG. (Mednick, 1996)

Confederate army and had traveled to New Mexico as a trail hand for Oliver Loving (Charles Goodnight's partner), settling in Cimarron after working a trail drive over Raton Pass. Allison had purchased a tract of land on the Vermejo, close to that purchased by Tolby for his Indian reservation (and probably illegally grazed his stock on Maxwell land). He appreciated men of the cloth like Tolby and McMains and was a religious man with good manners. However, he had a ruthless side to his personality, particularly when drunk. After a few drinks at Henri Lambert's St. James Hotel, he outdrew and killed Pancho Griego, who was allegedly involved in the murder of Tolby. This period is well described in McMains' biography (Taylor, 1979).

The culmination of these disputes and this era of conflict came to closure by a decision of the U.S. Supreme Court on April 18, 1887. The majority opinion, expressed by Justice William A. Kehler, stated, "The Indians, early Mexican and Spanish-American settlers, early American pioneers, the latter seeking homesteads and settling on what they believed to be free land, each in turn, discovered in the end, that they had no rights superior to Grant Rights." This decision asserted that Congress, in its sovereign power, had actually created its own grant (a grant "de novo," or new grant), an opinion that made the Maxwell patent virtually unassailable, if not indubitably correct. (Taylor, 1979) Thus, in many of the abstracts of New Mexico ranches today, one will find "Maxwell" in their contents.

Grave markers of Rev. F. J. Tolby and Henry (Henri) Lambert, Cimarron Cemetery.

Barbed Wire Fencing, Windmills, and Mechanical Ranching

The era of working cowboys in New Mexico and Texas, well established by the latter part of the nineteenth century, experienced additional transformation by the introduction of barbed wire in the late 1800s. Barbed wire provided an ingenious and inexpensive way to confine livestock, paving the way for the advent of "mechanical" ranching in the late 1940s.

The open range, free grass, and cattle drives began to see their sunset for reasons previously described. By making it possible to isolate and segregate cattle and to manage access to water, the invention of the barbed wire fence effectively ended the open range era. A dramatic demonstration of barbed wire in the Panhandle in 1887 by its inventor, J. F. Glidden, was very successful, and sales boomed. (Robertson, 1981) In an extreme example of conversion of livestock management and control from "nonconfinement" to "confinement," 6,000 miles of barbed wire was installed around the famous XIT Ranch (formed after the 16th Texas Legislature in 1882 appropriated three million acres in the Texas Panhandle as payment to a British syndicate that constructed the magnificent State Capitol in Austin). (Duke, 1961) Once barbed wires were used to partition off the wide-open range, better herd management was immediately apparent, and the range cowboy's lifestyle correspondingly changed. The number of cowboys required in isolated line camps was reduced because the daily jobs of "holding" cattle on a ranch's border and keeping out neighboring or stray brands were effectively eliminated. The XIT fencing endeavor, however, added new chores for the range cowboy. Now they were responsible for constructing and relocating fences, riding them for maintenance and rustling control, and building and repairing windmills and tanks so that each fenced pasture had convenient water for livestock.

Windmills, another invention in the late nineteenth century, had a significant impact on cattle management, allowing the wind-driven pumping of water in strategic locations. The first windmill patent was recorded in 1854 by a New England machinist, Daniel Halladay. Many of the early windmills were the old "eclipse" style with offset fans made up of a complex and somewhat fragile web of cypress blades. Competition and design improvements then flourished over the next hundred years. (Baker, 1984) (Haley, 1995) The gear assembly of the original mills had no oil bath, and early cowhands would constantly have to climb the windmills to maintain and repair them. In 1901 the "open" gears were replaced with self-oiling, enclosed gear boxes, significantly improving windmill reliability while reducing maintenance and upkeep. (Kelton, 1989)

The impact of windmills on the early cattle industry was monumental. It opened up grassland in semi-arid areas that previously provided no water for livestock; allowed farmers to live on land devoid of rivers, streams, and lakes; and gave railroads access to underground water. Windmills became symbols of American pioneers. Few paintings or movies about the American West exclude the windmill as a backdrop. (This history is preserved and documented by the American Wind Power Center in Lubbock, Texas.)[4]

Many of the old range cowboys eschewed this work with fences and windmills, as they preferred the "real" cowboy tasks such as gathering, roping, cutting, branding, castrating, dehorning, and shipping. Such fencing and windmill tasks were normally relegated by the old hands to the new hands.[5]

Mechanical ranching—the use of pickups and stock trailers to move feed, horses, equipment, and livestock—began during World War II. As most of the young cowboys had traded a cowboy hat for a helmet and chaps for military fatigues, the few older ranchers and cowboys who were left at home were short-handed and had to help each other. This necessitated making long drives from ranch to ranch in order to help out. Following the war, pickups and stock trailers became a ranching way of life, albeit slowly. Leroy's brother, Don, said that when he arrived at the Pitchfork Ranch in 1954 there was only one old pickup and a stock trailer on the whole place. Bill Hemphill, an old Matadors cowboy and former "wagon boss," remembered that when he arrived at the Matadors in 1942, "There was one truck and no stock trailers on the whole ranch."[6] It is rare for ranchers today to move livestock around without the benefit of large, four-wheel-drive pickups and modern stock trailers. The mechanical age also brought submersible pumps, which

*A working windmill today on the wintry High Plains of
Deaf Smith County, Texas.*

Windmills on display.
(Photo taken at the American Wind Power Center, Lubbock, Texas)

eventually would replace windmills, so symbolic of the American Southwest. The saga of the range cowboy would undergo an even greater transformation.

Grain Sorghums and Feedlots

In the mid-1950s, another cattle industry was emerging which would alter the method of beef production forever. Before that time, Americans grew up on range-fed beef, courtesy of ranchers and their range cowboys. The mother-cow outfits produced the weaned yearlings, which were then brought to maturity on native grass, or possibly winter wheat, then sent to the packing houses. The "saga of the sorghums," the availability of underground water for irrigation, and the relatively mild winters of the Texas Panhandle compared with those of the Corn Belt in the American Midwest were the ingredients for the emergence of a new industry. (Robertson, 1981) (Neugebauer, 1991) Concurrently, mass merchandising was having a major

*The spangled bowl of a prairie sky
I know I shall love until the day I die.
And always since my life began
I have loved the grace of a windmill's fan.*

—Ada Bates

impact on the type of beef sold at the retail level. Supermarkets used beef as a traffic builder and guaranteed its quality. Consequently, primarily fat carcasses graded USDA "Choice Beef" were ordered from the packers. Grass-fattened cattle could not meet this specification, and the feedlot concept began to flourish. (Neugebauer, 1997)

The availability of "finishing feed" was the first criterion for this emerging industry. In the early part of the twentieth century, byproducts from sugar mills, distilleries, and cottonseed oil mills were used to feed cattle. This supplemented the basic staple of grass, but not on a large scale. The "spread" in cattle productions (sale price per unit weight less the cost of producing, handling, and feeding cattle to maturity) was a closely observed financial parameter throughout the history of beef production. However, this became a much more sophisticated and optimized control factor in the 1950s and 1960s. ("Optimizing" and "control of variables" are today very much in the vocabulary of environmental engineers, as they are with cattle producers.) The most significant variable in this equation is the cost of feed and its convertibility to saleable beef. Cattle nutrition research, breeding improvement, and weight-gain dynamics became major aspects of agricultural research at major universities such as Texas A&M, Texas Tech, and New Mexico State. This, combined with the improvement of feed grains such as corn, milo, sudan, and hegari, gave a good scientific base for the developing feedlot industry. (Ball, 1992) Feed grain farming in the Panhandle of Texas (with an adequate supply of underground water from the Ogallala formation) and venture capital from banks, local individuals, and out-of-state entrepreneurs came together in the new feedlot epicenter of Hereford, Texas, and contiguous areas, resulting in a spectacular industry growth. More than 300,000 head in the Texas Panhandle were fed to "fats" in 1958, and by 1973, almost 5,000,000 head were in feedlots. (Ball, 1992) Today, in Texas, New Mexico, and Oklahoma alone, it is a multibillion-dollar industry. Two key individuals who catalyzed this growth were Paul Engler and Charles Ball. Engler arrived from Nebraska in 1960, sought investors (including my father, J. Frank Ford, Sr., who, still recalling the Dust Bowl days, was too conservative to invest), and built one of the most successful feeding operations in the country.[7]

Charles Ball, retired executive director of the Texas Cattle Feeders Association, is an excellent source of information about the industry. He also defined a new term: "The Feedlot Cowboy."[8] Unlike the Leroy Webbs of range cowboy lore, these "pen riders" make the rounds on horseback, look for cattle illness, take inventory, and manage the herd within the feedlot confines. (The eradication of the screwworm in the 1960s was a major breakthrough in minimizing death loss, both on the range and in the pens.) Feedlot cowboys must be unusually observant—able to spot a single animal in a pen of 100 that has a running nose or might have fever—and they must be unusually patient. Once they spot a sick animal, they must ease it out of the pen

Scientists focused in on the monogamous nature of the female screwworm fly using male sterilization techniques. The screwworm "dope kit" was standard fare on a cowboy's saddle prior to the successful implementation of this program. George M. Cowden was a member of the Texas legislature in the 1960s when the "fly factory" bill was passed. He remembers then governor Dolph Briscoe lobbying for the bill and discussing it in detail with him. This bill was designed to eradicate the screwworm. Cowden was raised on a ranch and had worked "wormy cattle" as a boy. He said, "I will vote for this bill, but it will never work—there is no way to get rid of the screwworm problem." It did work and reduced the work of many cowboys in the spring and summer.

and drive it slowly and cautiously to the hospital pen. There, "cowboy doctors," who have been trained by the consulting veterinarian, make a diagnosis and administer treatment. If the illness is rare or uncertain, the cowboy doctor calls in the consulting veterinarian.

Corporate or contract nutritionists, veterinarians, and financial and marketing specialists complete the staff of a very complex and sophisticated business. The feedlot cowboys generally use their own horses and ride two or more horses a day. They do not carry a rope, are vigilant, do nothing to disturb the cattle, and open and close a lot of gates. The "slow and methodical" nature of their job permits patient and calm training of a horse, as opposed to old ranch cowboys who "broke" horses and trained them for more rugged duties such as gathering cattle in rough terrain, cutting, and roping.[9] The feedlot cowboys normally sleep at home, drive to work, and have a more structured day as compared with the old range cowboys. With the exception of keeping cattle as calm as possible (a proverb for all cowboys), one can see the contrast between the feedlot cowboys and the range cowboys of Leroy's era.

It has been against this backdrop of geography, political history, and the changing era of ranches and working cowboys that Leroy Webb, an enduring old-time cowboy, has lived his extraordinary life.

CHAPTER 2

Roots and Beginnings

*I*t would seem incongruous to write about a cowboy who had spent a good portion of his life understanding the bloodlines and genealogy of horses and cattle without some effort to document the history of his predecessors. In this quest, I was most fortunate as Leroy, Nora, and his family have a fine paper trail on his ancestry.

The Leroy Webb family tree starts with William G. Richards, who arrived in the little settlement of Trinidad on the Purgatoire River, Colorado Territory, in 1864. He was born in Indiana in 1838, and around the age of twenty, he struck out on his own toward the Denver area, where "gold fever" allured the masses from all parts of the country. About the same time, a Spaniard named Andres Lujan put his wife and children in a covered wagon and headed toward Trinidad, similarly drawn to the area in a quest for gold.

Born in Spain in 1791, Andres Lujan had been brought to California at the age of two by two well-to-do aunts. Three ships made the arduous voyage around the Horn together, bringing the two women and the little boy, among others, to the town of Los Angeles in the Spanish king's empire. A short time later the boy's parents came over, and the family group, sometime prior to 1810, made the slow journey inland from California to New Mexico. Andres' father sent him all the way back to Spain at the age of nineteen to find a bride, but he returned, much to this father's chagrin, without one. It

17

Family Tree of
Leroy Webb

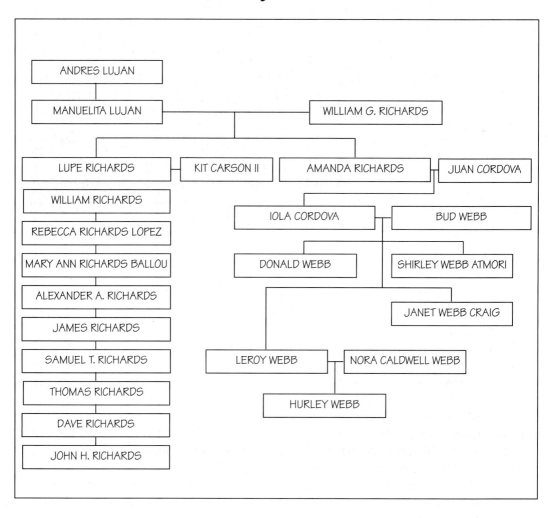

was the young man's opinion that if the Taos country were good enough for him and his people, it certainly was good enough to provide him with a wife, which subsequently occurred. Little is known about Andres' wife except that she was from New Mexico.

The vast Southwest was detached from the Republic of Mexico and became a part of the United States when war was concluded by the Treaty of Guadalupe Hidalgo in 1848. In the same year, Andres Lujan was drawn from New

Andres Lujan, great-great-grandfather of Leroy Webb. Born in Spain, 1791.

Mexico back to California by the gold rush. He left his wife and family in New Mexico and headed westward with a little train of four burros. His trip was a financial failure, and he returned to New Mexico. It was about then that a daughter, Manuelita, was born to the Lujans. Still attracted by the call of gold, Andres Lujan put his wife and children and belongings in a wagon, sometime in 1860, and headed north for Denver, but success evaded him for a second time. The Lujans then started south again and arrived at Trinidad about the time of young William Richards' appearance. (Taylor, 1964)

Manuelita Lujan and William Richards thus converged in Trinidad, courted, and were married on March 11, 1866. She was sixteen and he was twenty-eight. To this marriage eleven children were born, seven boys and four girls. The oldest girl, Lupe Richards, married the son of Kit Carson, the famous Indian scout and frontiersman.[1] A second daughter, Rebecca, born in 1872, had a profound influence on her younger sister, Amanda. When William Richards went to vote in the 1892 election between Grover Cleveland (Democrat) and Benjamin Harrison (Republican), Rebecca had to

To be ignorant of what occurred before you were born is to remain always a child— For what is the worth of human life unless it is woven into the life of our ancestors by the records of history?

—Cicero

*Marriage photo of Juan Cordova and Amanda Richards
(Leroy Webb's grandparents).
La Junta, Colorado (early 1900s).*

spur her horse for seventeen miles in order to take care of Amanda and the other siblings so their father could get there before the polls closed. Amanda, five years younger than Rebecca, married a Colorado cowboy of Spanish descent, Juan Cordova. It was through this union that a daughter, Iola Cordova, Leroy Webb's mother, was born.[2]

Juan Cordova was a handsome, dashing cowboy and bronc rider who worked in the Trinidad area in the early 1900s. Individuals from the Trinidad, Colorado, area who personally knew him or his reputation describe him as an exceptionally skilled horseman and cowboy. Leroy has a vivid recollection of his grandfather, who undoubtedly had a strong influence on his grandson, particularly in the ways of a cowboy.

In one of my initial interviews with Leroy and Nora in December of 2000 at our lodge in northern New Mexico, Leroy was browsing through my library and randomly selected a book entitled *The American Cowboy* by Kristine Fredriksson, published by Texas A&M Press. By chance he recognized his grandfather, Juan Cordova, sitting among a group of cowboys in an old photograph identified as "Riders at the Trinidad, Colorado, Fair—1910." (Fredriksson, 1989) This was my first insight into the genealogy of Leroy Webb.

Juan's daughter Iola was courted by, then married a professional range cowboy named Bud Webb. Webb was born and raised in La Junta, Colorado, and came from a family of farmers along the Arkansas River. Perennial floods in the Arkansas River valley probably convinced them that cattle might be preferable to crops, so he started a career of "range cowboying," going from ranch to ranch as a hired cowhand. After a wide circle through Oklahoma, Eastern New Mexico, and the Texas Panhandle, he returned to Colorado, where he met Iola Cordova, who was going to school and boarding with Bud Webb's sister. Iola and Bud were married shortly thereafter in Colorado.

This union first produced a son, Don, then Leroy, followed by sisters Shirley and Janet. Aside from my extensive interviews with Leroy, I had the opportunity to meet the older brother, Don, now living in Raton, New Mexico. Don is a retired cowboy with a historical and professional reputation similar to that of Leroy. He still breaks horses and rides daily. He has been an excellent source of history, particularly with respect to the Webb history and his experiences at the Pitchfork and Matador ranches. Throughout their lives he and Leroy have been good friends and cowboy pals. Earlier I had met the younger sister, Shirley, through her husband, John Atmore, and his brother, Frank. I had leased the Atmore ranch and the adjoining Ute Creek Ranch (owned by Bob Allen of Raton) for hunting purposes since the early 1990s, and had gotten to know them well. Through these acquaintances, interviews, and family memorabilia, the "roots" part of my research on Leroy Webb fell into place.

In a broad sense, this one family's saga illustrates the heritage mosaic that produced the early pioneers and cowboys in the American West before and during the turn of the twentieth century. The catalysts of gold, grass, space, and opportunity drew people from a wide spectrum of backgrounds, ethnicity, and ambitions into the recently purchased territories of New Mexico and Colorado. The severity of the times influenced this population, enhanced the family unions, and equipped the following generations of American cowboys who evolved through the century. Leroy Webb is such a product.

Leroy was born September 4, 1933, in Swink, Colorado, moving to Cimarron, New Mexico, four years later. Leroy was born fifteen months after his first-born brother, Don. Bud and Iola Cordova Webb, like all the "range people" in the area, were rather poor. The depression was upon them, and the cattle market was at its nadir. Only four years earlier, the average price for a steer was almost $70 but had dropped to around $23 in 1933, or a loss in value of over 65 percent. (The price would again rise above $45 in 1940 as the advent of World War II created somewhat of a boom.) The ranches were hiring few cowboys; there was little commerce in the area which depended largely on livestock. So, times were tough and wages were meager or nonexistent.

At a very early age, Leroy and his siblings lived on a ranch near the small New Mexican town of Colmor on the Colfax-Mora county line, east of Cimarron and about fifteen miles north of Wagon Mound. Now a ghost town, the place was thriving in the 1930s. The Atchison, Topeka, and Santa Fe

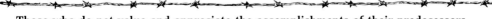

Those who do not value and appreciate the accomplishments of their predecessors will likely not accomplish anything to be remembered by their successors.

—Winston Churchill

Top: *Riders at the Trinidad,
Colorado, Fair in 1910
(Juan Cordova is seated
fourth from left).*
(Courtesy of Texas A&M
University Press)

Middle: *Bud Webb and Ray
Bosley (early 1920s).*

Bottom: *Some old-time cowboys (Bud Webb, second from
left).*

Railroad had been built in the area in 1879, and Colmor was a railhead for shipping cattle. The Ocate River flows about a half-mile south of the village and provided adequate water for citizens and cattle. The area surrounding the town is one of beautiful rolling prairies bordered on the west by stretches of flat-topped mesas and farther to the west and north by the snow-capped Sangre de Cristo Mountains.

The grasslands, predominantly gramma, bluestem and clover, which surround Colmor as well as all of Colfax and Mora counties, even today are said to be some of the best grazing lands in the Southwest. Cattlemen have praised its thick, solid turf and the ease with which it flourishes, even with scant rainfall. Being a fairly flat domain, the land soaks up most of

Leroy, the yearling (1935).

the moisture from rain and snow clouds which form over the western mountains and move easterly over the plains, leaving in their paths livelihood for the grasslands.

Nearby Wagon Mound, where Leroy spent many of his early days, was then and still is a small town, located on the old AT&SF railroad and what is now Interstate 25. According to history, the earliest name for Wagon Mound was Santa Clara. Around 1876-1877, there was a post office there by the name. It was probably called Santa Clara until about 1881, when it acquired the name Pinkerton and even had a post office under that name from 1881 to 1882. Some early history claims the little town was called Wagon Mound by the stockmen as early as 1859, and in 1882 it acquired a post office under that official name. The name was chosen because the dominant peak just east of town looks like a covered wagon or prairie schooner. Located on the old Santa Fe Trail, this was a significant landmark for the early wagon trains using the trail. (Martin, 1972)

The beginnings of this cowboy were thereby shaped and formed by the era (1930s), by hard times (the depression), by the country (the relatively undeveloped but abundant grasslands of northern New Mexico), and by the love of horses (attributable to his grandfather, father, and other cowboy mentors). All of these threads were to weave into a life which truly reflects the mid-century evolution of the American cowboy. The evolution might have first been defined by the nineteenth-century American dependency on beef and the ranges and men who provided that commodity, bridged by the twentieth-century cowboy exemplified in Leroy Webb's life, then into the twenty-first century, which most likely will end the era of the working range cowboy as we now know it. As Leroy has told me several times, "I was almost born too late." His comments are reflective of most of his cowboy friends I interviewed. The ranks of his cowboy reunions, whom he classifies as the real "ol' timers," are thinning. All agree good cowboys are replacing them, but none will ever experience the histories they've shared.

Leroy describes the "beginnings" in his own words:

> *My beginning. The life of a cowboy. I can't ever remember a time when I didn't just want to be a cowboy. As far as I can remember I always wanted to be a cowboy. That's it. My dad was a cowboy and worked on ranches always. I grew up hearing the stories of all the ranches he'd been on, worked on, traveled around on horseback with his pack horse, going from ranch to ranch, back in the '20s.*

Leroy's father, Bud, had been born and raised in the Arkansas Valley along the Arkansas River near LaJunta. His family members were farmers in the valley, which was subject to flooding. Bud recalled a major flood in 1916, when the Arkansas River washed out the whole area. Houses, pigs, chickens, and other livestock went floating down the creek. That event had a major impact on young Bud, who said it was the scariest thing he had ever seen. It ended Bud's desire to ever become a farmer. He wanted to be a cowboy and ride horses. The Webb family had some horses, cattle, and other livestock on the farm. Therefore, as a teenager, he hooked up with a friend of his, Ray Bosley, and they decided to take off and become hired cowboys. They saddled up their horses, loaded up a pack horse, and just headed out, not knowing what their final destination would be.

They did some day work on Oklahoma ranches, worked for a while, collected their pay, and moved on. From Oklahoma, they drifted down through the Texas Panhandle, as far south as Lubbock. Then they would circle back around and come up through New Mexico, working from ranch to ranch. The practice was very common during those days as many ranch tasks for young cowboys were short-term. The workers would "drift" from task to task and ranch to ranch, thus the term "drifters."

Leroy remembers that his dad talked a lot about working on the Diamond A Ranch in New Mexico at Wagon Mound before going back up through northeastern New Mexico, around the areas of Cimarron, Springer, Raton, and back into Colorado.

> *I believe they made about three trips around doing that. They took a year or two each trip, just riding around. Boy! I thought that was the deal. I thought that would be great doing that. But I guess I was born a little too late for that. Too many fences.*

Bud had met Iola Cordova on one of his ventures to Colorado. Iola had lost her mother at childbirth and was raised by different members of the Cordova family. She was going to school and boarding with Bud's sister when they met. After they married, Bud worked in southern Colorado for a while, then took his new bride south toward Springer, where he celebrated his twenty-first birthday and put their horses in a livery stable. He had developed a strong affinity for the Springer-

Iola and Bud Webb with Don, Shirley, and Leroy (1939).

Cimarron area of New Mexico as a young drifting cowboy and wanted to raise his family there. In these hard depression years, jobs were scarce, and the family had to move constantly from ranch to ranch to find work. One that Leroy remembers specifically was the WS at the "Coach House Camp." (Each large ranch had "camps" located in strategic areas within the ranch to facilitate livestock management by controlling pasture use and water access.) The WS was located close to Cimarron, and the Coach House Camp was located on Ponil Creek.

> *My brother, Don, and I started school about 1939. We had to first get from the camp to the ranch headquarters which was right on the Cimarron-Springer highway. It wasn't paved but it was the main road anyway. So, the best way for us to get around was to go horseback. Dad was able to get the ranch to give us a horse to use—we'd ride double from*

Ten-year-old Leroy on the first horse he broke (1943).

the Coach House Camp where we lived to the ranch headquarters, then catch a car that was going on into the school in Cimarron. So my brother and I rode double on this ol' horse called Happy Hooligan to the headquarters. The boss let us use it, and we used it a lot.

Leroy had developed a strong love for horses and had an extraordinary rapport with them as a boy. He speaks fondly of "Happy Hooligan" to this day.

In addition to his father and grandfather, Leroy developed some other early cowboy mentors on the WS. One of the first was Tokahanas Choctaw "Tok" Harp (whose name will later reappear). Both Bud and his sons worked for Tok, who was a tough "all work-no play" kind of cowboy.

Leroy and Don spent their early school days in Cimarron. They helped with ranch chores at the WS, and commuted to school on horseback. Happy Hooligan knew the route well between the WS line camp and Cimarron Elementary. Doubling up on ol' Hooligan, they would make the round trip to school. It was fun for a while, but the cold winter ride seemed a little harsh. They would saddle up in the morning (both boys not yet eight years old), hunker down on Hooligan, follow a brushy creek covered with ice, then spend the first few minutes in the classroom trying to thaw out.

Shortly thereafter, Bud left the WS and moved over to the Red River Ranch (Y7) near Springer, some thirty miles east of Cimarron. This meant a schoolhouse change from Cimarron to Colmor. The Red River Ranch was owned by Johnny Wootten, who lived in Clayton, New Mexico, and owned additional ranch country in that area. The Springer Ranch foreman was a tough old cowboy named Slim Cantrell. The Red River Ranch had lots of horses, and Slim was an expert at raising colts. Leroy would take the bus to and from school in Colmar, giving him more free time because the bus, even in 1942, could get a kid to school quicker than could old Hooligan. As soon as the nine-year-old Leroy got off the bus, he would jump out of his "good school clothes," jump into his boots, and go catch horses. He would head for the horse pasture, find the remuda, catch a gentle horse that he had broken, then jump on the colt with no halter, no saddle, no nothing. The colt would hightail it toward the grainery, knowing that his youthful rider would reward him with a bucket full of gourmet oats. While the colt was feasting, Leroy would bridle and saddle him and ride until the horse or its rider gave out.

Slim Cantrell and a local cowboy named Roy Milligan worked many horses under the close observation of the Webb boys, who would try to assist, probably hindering the process more than they helped. It was there that Leroy began his horse-breaking days (which continue to this day, some sixty years later). The first one he broke was a black colt.

I loved that colt. We'd get them colts broke—just gentle, gentle. I mean we could crawl under them, around them, over them. They'd follow us around. They'd do anything for us when they were little. By the time they got big enough to ride, we'd be on them bareback—and rode them and rode them. I must have been about ten years old. Anyway, it was the first horse I ever broke completely by myself—from scratch—nobody was ever on him. I would go out in the pasture with nothing, get on him, and ride him to the corral. My brother, Don, had one doing the same thing. We had these colts broke. Nobody ever fooled with them but us.

Don and Leroy breaking milk cows (1937).

Although young Leroy was euphoric about breaking his first colt, other things occupied

Don and Leroy with Dad, Phillips Ranch (1939).

his time. He had to perform many chores around the ranch before and after school. He was somewhat less enthusiastic about milking the cows and doing other trivial chores, such as carrying the dope bucket around and providing menial support for the grownup cowboys during the time for branding, castrating, dehorning, and doctoring young calves. He was too small physically to handle the calves by "flanking them" or holding them. Still, he was in his element—outdoors, way out in the country, around colts, calves, and cowboys—and he remembers his youthful experience as "a good life." Only school interfered with the ranching activities he loved.

About this time in the early 1940s, Leroy's parents, Bud and Iola, divorced. Leroy and Don decided to stay with their father, while their two sisters stayed with their mother. The choice was easy for Leroy. He wanted to be a cowboy like his father. Although the split was an obvious personal disruption in their lives, it did not distract Leroy from his cowboy ambitions. Living with his drifting cowboy father only enhanced them. Bud Webb took his two little cowboy helpers to eastern New Mexico and found work at the JE Ranch near Clayton. The three of them lived in a small line camp and continued to "punch" cows.

Leroy continued his education at a one-room country school with a notable lack of enthusiasm. Then, for the first time, he found a mentor in the schoolhouse. His teacher was a twenty-one-year-old cowboy named Virgil Miranda, whose avocation was bronc riding. He happened to be the nephew of a famous band of bronc-riding brothers from Colorado—the Like brothers.

For the first time, Leroy liked school and probably learned more that year than all his previous schooling combined. "He was a good man, good teacher, great bronc rider, and a big influence in my life," Leroy remembered. While still a young man, his new mentor was totally paralyzed in a rodeo bronc-riding event and spent the rest of his life in a sedentary state, eventually passing away in a nursing home at Trinidad, Colorado. Leroy idolizes his memory to this day and ranks him high on the list of the cowboy mentors who significantly influenced his early life.

Leroy's early transient life continued as Bud accepted a job back on the WS Ranch near Cimarron. Bud and his two boys moved into a different line camp called the Heck Place. It was just a two-room shack with no electricity or conveniences—just a woodstove and a coal oil lamp in each room. Leroy vividly remembers the wintertime, which gets severely cold in northern New Mexico. He recalls getting up well before dawn every morning as his father saddled up for work, and everything inside was frozen. It was a hard existence. But at least he and Don could ride a school bus into Cimarron and didn't have to saddle up ol' Hooligan as they did a few years earlier. Leroy didn't like school; his teachers there weren't bronc riders like the one he had back in the two-room schoolhouse. Fortunately, for Leroy, there was a country store near the Cimarron school owned by an old retired bronc rider named Van Price. Leroy loved to be around bronc riders like Van, who let the errant school kids have some "free soda pop" and play a game of pool or two.

> *My brother and I, we were supposed to get up and get ready and get to school; walk up to the highway and catch the bus. Sometimes we would and sometimes we wouldn't. We didn't want to go to school anyway. We'd get up and sometimes I would go to school and spend a half a day or whatever—maybe at noon might just take off and walk around the hills around Cimarron. You could just walk and be plum out of sight in the woods by yourself in just a little bit. Sometimes I would do that. I just would think about being on a ranch. All I wanted was to be on a ranch with a bunch of cows and cowboys.*

It was obvious where Leroy's life was heading, with his long list of cowboy mentors, his love of the outdoors, horses and cattle, and his lack of enthusiasm for school. He had developed an extraordinary mental and physical toughness through the first fourteen years of his life. His work ethic started when he first learned to walk, and the outdoor life sharpened his physical endurance and an extraordinary resistance to pain that even his old cowboy friends marvel at today. His mentors were hardened cowboys who were energetic, tough, and honest, the genre of ranch hands so typical of the range cowboys at this time and so integral to the development of the American cattle industry. Such were his "beginnings." The "grownup" phase of his life was about to start.

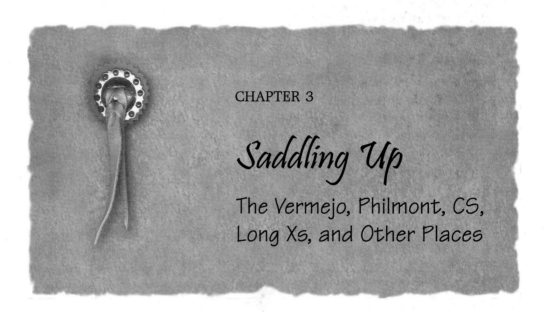

CHAPTER 3

Saddling Up

The Vermejo, Philmont, CS, Long Xs, and Other Places

The allure of horses, cowboying, and the open range exceeded that of the classroom for Leroy, which was quite typical for boys in the rural communities of the American Southwest in the 1940s. He figured it was time "to leave the nest," so at the age of fourteen, having just finished the eighth grade, he began his career as a professional cowboy. His first job was at the famous WS Ranch near Raton (later incorporated into the Vermejo Ranch, which was owned by Pennzoil and subsequently purchased by Ted Turner). In 1947 the cattle business was flourishing as America was entering a period of the post-World War II boom. The peacetime economy was on the rise, there was an insatiable appetite for beef throughout the country, and, thus, jobs for range cowboys increased. These were the pre-feedlot days, with cattle fattened on the open range, perpetuating a demand for the old-fashioned cowboy's skills.

With the innocence and energy of a fourteen-year-old, Leroy was in his glory, drawing $75 a month plus room and board. But the best job benefit was having the privilege of working with horses and cattle from 2:00 A.M. until long past dark. In his words:

> When summertime hit at the end of the eighth grade, I was fourteen years old and figured it was about time for me to leave the nest. As soon as

school was out I got a job on the WS Ranch and went to work for that ranch steady that summer. They paid me $75 a month and board and room. I worked there all summer. I learned a lot there. Ol' Jud Knight was the cow boss. I mean they work from before daylight to dark. That spring we moved the cattle to the hills, up to the Ring and Van Houghton camps. After they branded the calves, we'd take them up into the hills and just spend the summer. The summer was nice—just lookin' at the cattle, riding around the hills taking care of things, riding some colts. Just having a good time. That was the good part of it. Dad and ol' Jud went back a long way. They were the same age and worked together at both the WS and CS ranches back in the late 1920s. However, Jud pretty well stayed put while Dad drifted around.

It is hard to describe adequately the beauty and expansiveness of the WS/Vermejo country. It is full of mesas covered by piñon and ponderosa pines, mountains towering above 12,000 feet, spring-fed creeks, aspens as far as the eye can see, and lush grass in the lower plateaus and valleys. The area is ideal for fattening cattle during the late spring, summer, and early fall. A good portion of this country is now public, called Valle Vidal. The government obtained title to it in a land swap several decades ago. As Leroy described it, "Big, big country, wild and rough but beautiful."

The toughest and most mundane jobs of cowboying are normally relegated to the beginners. In the 1940s (and in some rare instances today) the working day began by gathering the cowboys' horses. The common term is to "jingle" in the working horses. This meant the day started for Leroy at 2:00 A.M., giving him an hour or two for gathering the horses that had been peacefully grazing in the open pastures during the night and preparing them for the workday. Once the horses were jingled, the older hands would fire up the stove or a campfire, over which Dutch ovens or grills were placed, and cook breakfast. Leroy, as a returning jingler, would then join them. After breakfast they would all pitch in, do the dishes, clean up camp, saddle up, and ride toward the herd that was to be worked.

Jud would get us up at two o'clock in the morning and me and the other young guys would take turns to go jingle the horses. They didn't keep any-thing in the corrals but a night horse—the jingle horse. One of us would have to saddle him and we'd take turns—go bring these horses in the mid-dle of the night. Man, it was black up there in those hills and timber. I had one horse fall on me. One time they had a mule in that camp—a mule for a jingle horse. He wasn't good for nothing. He wasn't even good for that, a no-good sucker. Saddle him up there in the dark, and he'd take out of there and run to the back side, make a little circle and run back. You just hoped there's something in front of you. You didn't know for sure until you got to the corral if you had any horses. He was a no-good sucker.

On occasion it took several hours just to ride to the workplace. The cow boss set the pace on getting to work. Jud Knight knew of just one way to get there—a long trot. He was cognizant, as were most cowboys of that era, that you don't raise beef while in transit. You had to get to the cattle in a hurry in order for a ranch to be productive and profitable. The cowboys would just stand up in the stirrups, put the horse into a fast trot, and keep that pace until they arrived in the area where the cattle might be. If it were still dark, they would wait for the first crack of dawn and go to work. Leroy commented that that was the first time he liked to see a gate. While it was being opened, he could sit down in the saddle and take the pressure off his legs for a minute or two.

No stock trailers were used as they are today, and it made for a long day. Following arrival at the herd, the cowboys would gather the cattle and move them to different country for fresh grass and water. Once that was done, as the sun was disappearing over the mountainous horizon and the chilled mountain air set in, they would head back to camp in a long trot. An older cowboy, "ol' Everett Burton," told Leroy that he had been on the job for weeks and still had never seen the line camp in daylight.

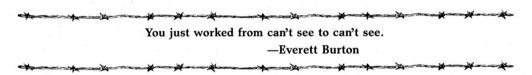

You just worked from can't see to can't see.
—Everett Burton

Leroy's first accident resulted from that "sorry ol' jingle mule." He was out jingling early one fall morning, and the frost had left the ground somewhat slick. As the jingle mule made one of his unprogrammed turns, his feet came out from under him, and he fell, pinning Leroy's leg under the full weight of the mule. Leroy's ankle began to swell and became extremely sore. He couldn't walk on it at all, so a companion cut a branch off a tree, made a makeshift crutch for him, and told him to go soak his ankle in hot water and Epsom salts at the camp.[1]

An immobilized Leroy sat there for a week soaking his ankle in Epsom salts. Saturday night he thought it might be a little better, and he wanted to go to town and do a little dancing. Ol' Jud mentioned that while he was in town, he might get it x-rayed. Leroy did so, and found that it was cleanly broken. The doctor put it in a cast just in time for Leroy to hobble over to the dancehall. It took him more than a month to get back in the saddle, and it was the first of many broken bones that Leroy would suffer in his career. Most likely, this was the beginning of his unique ability to endure and manage physical pain.

As winter approached, the work slowed, and Leroy had experienced his first season as a real cowboy, still only fifteen years old. The WS Ranch had been a magnificent starting place.

The WS Ranch, which hired Leroy as a fourteen-year-old "green broke" cowhand, can be traced back to 1880, when two Englishmen, Harold Wilson and Matague Stevens, met on a hunting trip in Wyoming. Their infatuation with the American West led to a second trip two years later and prompted them to buy a small tract in northwestern New Mexico. They partnered with an independent hunter and guide, Jim Cook, and started a makeshift cattle operation, consisting mostly of open range and unclaimed Texas longhorn and Mexican cattle. These rather poor-quality animals carried the WS brand, the surname initials of the original two owners. Stevens left shortly thereafter, and Wilson became an absentee owner by returning to England, leaving Cook to run the operation. On one of Wilson's trips back to America, he met an aristocratic Irishman by the name of William French. Captain French, a professional soldier, took leave from the Royal Irish Regiment, settled in New Mexico, and along with Wilson, leased 80,000 acres on the Ponil River in Colfax County from Maxwell. They then purchased the property from the Maxwell Land Grant Company in 1899.

Captain French retired in 1921, and Harold Wilson's son, Brownlowe, managed the ranch until he was called into service by the British Navy in 1939. Following the death of his father in 1940, the ranch was put up for sale, but during World War II, there were few buyers around. At the war's end in 1945, a Texan from Fort Worth, William J. Gourley, purchased the WS Ranch. An old cowboy, Tokahantas Choctaw Harp, ran the WS for Mr. Gourley and would mentor a young cowboy hired two years later by the name of Leroy Webb. Webb speaks affectionately of "Tok" Harp until this day as an "authentic old-time cowboy."

Gourley formed a new corporation entitled the "WS Ranch Company" and tried to purchase the adjacent Ponil Ranch from the Maxwell Land Grant Company. The deed, however, was tied up in Holland, still under German occupation, and it was not until 1956 that Gourley was able to obtain title. He had previously purchased the contiguous Heck and Bartlett ranches. The Bartlett Ranch, which he purchased in 1948, was owned by W. H. Bartlett of Chicago. Bartlett had "cornered the grain market" in the early 1900s and bought the Colfax County ranch with some of his proceeds. He built several large stone "mansions" on the place and entertained extensively. After his death in 1919, and once the estate was settled, a group of wealthy Los Angeles men, headed by Norman Chandler of the *Los Angeles Times*, purchased the ranch. From 1926 until 1947 it was known as the "Vermejo Club," which was an exclusive ranching and hunting retreat for movie stars and other notables including Will Rogers, Mary Pickford, Douglas Fairbanks,

---

Sifting through Texas and New Mexico ranch histories, one notes how many received their initial financing and ownership from European individuals and syndicates. Europe always has been fascinated with the American West. Fictional accounts of the West written more than a hundred years ago by the German author Karl May are continuously available in European bookstores today.

Herbert Hoover, Cecil B. DeMille, and Andrew Mellon. During this period, a U.S. Forest Service wildlife specialist, Elliot S. Barker, left the Service and worked for the ranch in charge of game, fish, and predator control. He was the consummate wildlife manager and preservationist, and his contributions laid the foundation for the perpetuation of abundant wildlife and conservation that is the trademark of the Vermejo today. Barker continued to enhance and expand this conservancy for the State of New Mexico, serving as the state game warden for twenty-two years. (Baker, 1945)

Gourley's purchases of the WS, the Ponil, the Heck and the Bartlett ranches consolidated his empire—all except a small tract in the middle that was owned by the Santa Fe Railroad subsidiary, the Cherokee and Pittsburgh Coal and Mining Company (now leased by the Kaiser Steel Company). Gourley had thus completed this ranch mosaic, now known as the Vermejo Ranch. Following Gourley's death in 1970, his widow sold the entire ranch to Pennzoil, which in turn formed a subsidiary named the Vermejo Park Corporation. (Murphy, 1991) Ted Turner and his wife at that time, Jane Fonda, purchased Vermejo in the 1990s as well as the Kaiser Steel tract, completing the last chapter to date of this fascinating chronological history of a beautiful 578,000-acre tract of land in northern New Mexico and southern Colorado. (Robertson, 1983)

Of the footprints left on this ranch by the rich and famous, none are deeper than those made by its working cowboys, such as Leroy Webb, Jud Knight, and Tokahantas Choctaw "Tok" Harp, and wildlife preservationists such as Elliot S. Barker.

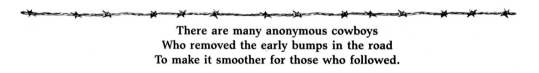

There are many anonymous cowboys
Who removed the early bumps in the road
To make it smoother for those who followed.

After Leroy's first major job at the WS, which would later evolve into the magnificent Vermejo, he drifted back down to the Cimarron area and looked for his next ranch:

I called and got a job at the Red River Ranch with a guy we knew over there—Slim Cantrell. He gave me a job although I was pretty young (fifteen). He knew me, knew I'd been around, could do a little something. So, I loaded up my stuff, which didn't take long. All I had was a bedroll and a few clothes I had rolled up in the bedroll, a saddle, riding blankets, that kind of stuff. That's it. My dad gave me a ride, took me from Cimarron over to the ranch. We went out to the Red River Ranch about fifteen miles from Springer. I went to work there—had a few colts to break, and then just feeding the cows, feeding from the feed wagon. I got these colts started, got to ride them a little, started feeding, go out in the morning, harness up these mules, hook them up to the wagon, back out to the cake house—they had cotton seed cake hauled in there in 100-pound burlap sacks—all they had then. Back that wagon up and load it up with cake, and get one of them colts, saddle one of them colts and tie it upside these mules, tie it on the hames of one of these mules and then we'd take off. We'd leave there. Them mules was kind of like that jingle mule we had— wanted to run off mostly. We'd get to the feed ground, tie these mules up, get on that colt, go around, make a pretty good circle, bring these cows in to the feed ground, and tie the colt back on the mule, get in the wagon and put out some cake and go to the next place and do the same thing. So, I spent the winter doing that and riding colts.

The Red River Ranch, where Leroy, as well as his brother and father, worked from time to time, allegedly had its origins in the nineteenth century, the active time of the Santa Fe Trail. Richard L. "Uncle Dick" Wootton built the famous Raton Pass toll road and would charge the Santa Fe Trail riders a fee for assisting the wagons and stock up and down the precipitous south-ern slope of Raton Pass during the period following the Civil War. However, the Wootten family who purchased the Red River Ranch around 1915, just southeast of Springer, New Mexico, might have been a different family and not the one of Raton Pass fame.[2] The ranch is still intact today, consisting of 35,000 acres in Colfax and Mora counties. Steve McClure, along with his wife, Karen, a Wootten descendant, took up residence and management in 1983. They raise cattle there today and "take great pride in preserving it for the next generation." (Robertson, 1983)

The "Red River" name is actually a misnomer, as the Canadian River forms its eastern boundary, miles away from the Red River. McClure traces this back to an earlier geological survey mistake that assured the Canadian and Red rivers were one and the same, but because of tradition and history there have been no plans to rename the ranch. (Barrett, 1997)

Leroy worked his way back to Cimarron following the WS experience and started to work for the CS Ranch in the spring (a busy time at a mother cow outfit). He moved in at the Crow Creek Camp and went to work for a cow boss named Joe McLaughlin. He described McLaughlin as a "tough ol' man, good cowboy, and one of the true ol' timers." Such men were good, honest fellows but rather tough on "men, livestock, and their women."

The CS remuda at that time had a reputation of including some "real bad horses." McLaughlin pulled the fifteen-year-old cowboy to the side and asked Leroy if he could ride some of the worst steeds of the bunch. Ol' Joe McLaughlin didn't mince words. He told Leroy, "If you can't ride 'em, I'll send you back to town and find someone who can!" Leroy mentioned the challenge to his father, and Bud advised him not to try: "Son, you can't ride them horses."

I was bound and determined to try. I was fifteen years old, and I thought I was tough. Anyway, I went out there and sure enough he gave me one of the bad horses. He gave me ol' Fud—an ol' sorrel horse—he really wanted

*to buck. I would first watch ol' Joe. He had his bluff in on them horses.
He'd cheek one up and kick him in the belly and get on him and spank
him down his hind leg, and they'd just kinda duck their tails and go. So, I
thought that was the thing to do. I didn't know if I could ride him or not if
I give him an even break. So I thought I better not give him an even
break, and I'd do like Joe and pull him around, kick him in the belly and
get on him and bust him down the leg—and sure enough that's what I did
and the ol' horse didn't buck. I got along with him all fine. Ol' Joe really
came to like me. From then on I got along with Joe, who was really good to
me. We got along real good.*

The CS Ranch at that time was a couple of hundred thousand acres or
more, consisting of lots of high country and expansive prairie land. They
would move cattle up to the high country in the summer, then move them
back down in the fall to a railhead located at Colfax (now a ghost town).
Colfax was located between Cimarron and Raton, and cattle were loaded on
railcars there and shipped to the markets. This working pattern at the CS
opened up the doors for Leroy to do all kinds of cowboy chores, namely gathering, cutting, roping, branding, loading, and shipping. Moving cattle over
twenty to thirty miles was not uncommon on the CS. Cattle, of course, had
to be moved slowly and carefully to minimize any weight loss.

The CS cowboys used several camps in moving the cattle. The Zastro
Camp was located at the base of the foothills and was shared by several large
ranches in the area contiguous to the CS, such as the UUBar and the Phillips
ranches (now Philmont Boy Scout Ranch). After gathering at the Zastro Camp
the cowboys would move the CS stock down to the Martinez Camp and let
the mother cows and their calves settle for a while. It was quite a chore to
settle the cattle down, as the workers were tired from the gathering process,
mothering-up all the young calves, and keeping the herd intact. They also
would manage the cattle by moving them through adjoining ranches to various other CS pastures, weaning the yearling calves, then moving them to the
railhead or the fattening pastures.

Leroy particularly enjoyed sending cattle out on the rail. The cattle were
pretty wild, having summered in the remote mountain country before being
moved over the wide open ranges. Pens and bystanders made them nervous
and difficult to handle. The cattle were sold when they hit the pens, so it was
a major task to avoid any losses as the cowboys moved them into the pens,
up the loading ramp, and into the railcars. When the train and cattle left the
railhead, it was a happy time for the cowboys who had taken weeks and
months to get them there. At a small store and bar in Colfax the cowboys
would relax some before saddling up for Crow Creek to repeat the process.[3]

All the horse miles required to accomplish these activities necessitated
taking good care of the horses and replacing their shoes on a regular basis.
(Horses cannot go "barefoot" in such rugged country.) One time, Don and
Leroy had a scare while trying to shoe a horse that went out of control, pin-

ning Don between the thousand-pound horse and a barbed wire fence (an occupational hazard). Don was injured but fell short of a major disaster.

> *Some of those ol' horses were bad enough to ride, a lot of them sure enough bad to shoe. Keeping shoes on them was a constant chore. We would get them all reshod at the Zastro Camp before we set out together. A bunch of them horses you'd have to tie down—tie them plum down— tie all four feet together—have them up on their back. You just cannot do a good job putting shoes on them that way, but there was no other way to do it. They wouldn't stand; they would kick and jump on you and you just couldn't shoe them. So then, those kind of horses you couldn't do a good job with as they were the most apt to lose shoes. You'd have to do it again—to shoe those kind of horses was twice as hard as it was to shoe a good horse.*

Leroy had grown up on these three ranches and loved what he was doing. He was becoming particularly adept in critical skills necessary for any range cowboy.

> *I thought I was a man back then. I thought I was a grownup. Doing just what I always wanted to do. I must have been sixteen by then. That fall after all the calves were shipped and everything put up, they sent me to the CS headquarters. At that time Raymond Porter was breaking horses and training the race horses. CS raised them some good race horses— thoroughbred horses. Raymond was a good hand—a sure enough good horseman. He was a bachelor—lived in the bunkhouse at headquarters— so they put me over there with him. I stayed in that bunkhouse with Raymond and helped him break them colts. Lot of them were thoroughbred colts, gonna try to run. Then they also had just regular ranch horses. So anyway I stayed there a while doing that and then I decided I wanted to see some different country (although I would return to the CS Ranch many years later).*

The CS Ranch, truly an American epic, can be traced to the 1870s. Frank Springer, an Iowa lawyer, moved to New Mexico at the request of his University of Iowa roommate, William Morley. Morley was a young engineer with the Santa Fe Railroad and contacted Springer that the "new frontier" had too many engineers and not enough lawyers (as an engineer, I would pro-

---

The primary working horses throughout the ranches in the area were American quarter horses. (The American Quarter Horse Association was organized in 1940, with clearly defined rules on what constitutes a quarter horse and what is necessary for registration.) Some ranches use breeds such as thoroughbreds, Arabian, and more recently, paints, although quarter horses are the most accepted for working cattle. Leroy would develop significant skills in training and breeding quarter horses later in his career.

pose that the opposite is true in 2002). Springer responded by traveling to Cimarron, and on his arrival before the sun had set, he purchased from the Maxwell Land Grant Company a tract of land along the Cimarron River. (My research revealed that many ranches in New Mexico were spawned by purchases from the Maxwell Land Grant Company.)

Cimarron, New Mexico, was a rough-and-tumble town in 1883 but had settled down somewhat, according to a Las Vegas, New Mexico, newspaper, because "no one had been killed there in over three days." Frank Springer transported a herd of Hereford cattle from Iowa to the CS Ranch which, over a century later, is still noted for its reputation for top quality whiteface cattle.

Although young at the time, Frank Springer was a precocious and brilliant lawyer, making his reputation doing legal work for the Maxwell Company. He won a highly contested court case, two decades in duration, over a title dispute evolving from the original Mexican land grant. The case was ultimately decided in the U.S. Supreme Court following Springer's acclaimed arguments and firmly entrenched him as one of the finest lawyers in the land. Springer was an expansive and versatile individual, serving as an attorney for the Atchison, Topeka and Santa Fe Railroad for thirty years, becoming president of the Maxwell Land Grant Company, founding the New Mexico Normal University in Las Vegas (now New Mexico Highlands University), and initiating the Art Museum in Santa Fe. Moreover, his brother, Charles Springer (his initials from which the CS Ranch derives its name), was also a very accomplished individual and one of the state's most respected citizens. (Barrett, 1997)

The CS Ranch, for which Leroy worked on at least two occasions, is quite generational. Charles Springer's son, Ed, ran the ranch from 1920 until 1946. His nephew (and the grandson of Frank Springer) played a crucial role in the perpetuation of the family ranch (now encompassing more than 200,000 acres). His name was J. Leslie Davis, born in 1919, and the son of a Philadelphia physician. After graduating from Dartmouth College in 1941, Les visited the family-owned ranch for six months and fell in love with New Mexico and ranching. He decided to abandon his earlier ambition to become a doctor. World War II then intervened, and Les served with the 4th Armored Division in Europe, receiving three Purple Hearts for injuries received in battle. Following the war he returned to the CS and ran its operations until his death in May of 2001. (Associated Press, May 2001)

He had been married for many years to the daughter of another prominent New Mexico ranching family, Albert K. and Julia Lundt Mitchell, a por-

**I was raised to work hard, be honest,
and have a commitment to the land and our heritage.**
—Linda Mitchell Davis

The best fertilizer for any ranch is the footprint of the owner.
—Claytie Williams

tion of whose ranch Leroy Webb would subsequently lease. Linda Mitchell Davis was an equal partner during the CS-Davis era.[4]

The saga of Les and Linda Davis has impressed me in many ways. First, everyone I've known in the northern New Mexico area since the late 1980s has nothing but good things to say about these two individuals. Their ability to have perpetuated the ranch from its origination with Frank Springer to its prospering operations to this day underscores that they possess the knowledge, commitment, and skills necessary to make the tough cattle business successful. However, the most impressive credential to me was the fact that they both worked hard in keeping it viable as a working cattle unit. They weren't residing in some distant suburb enjoying the leisurely life of absentee ranchers while others did the work, but were actively involved in the unromantic and arduous day-to-day labor of raising beef.

In 1949 Leroy left the CS and made his way toward Arizona by bus, kind of tracking his father's way of going from ranch to ranch. He found excitement in new country and different ranches. He had heard a lot about Arizona ranches. So, off he went.

> I rolled my bedroll, packed my saddle, and about that time I picked up a big canvas bag, a saddle bag, just for saddles. I could fold my saddle up and all my slickers and bridles, blankets, that type of stuff, put it all in this bag, big ol' bag with handles, and I had what clothes I had rolled up in this bedroll, had some good straps. So, these two bags were my total belongings. That's all it took me to move. I didn't have a car. I traveled on the bus. I would love to have gone horseback, pack horse, like Dad did— but too many fences by then, highways and fences. It was hard to travel across country. I just gathered my saddle and rode on buses.

Getting off the bus in Phoenix with his saddle and meager belongings, he found that few ranch jobs were available, probably because the late 1940s had undergone a severe drought and cattle prices were depressed. However, a feedlot operation had just started up, and he took a job there. He had to live in an abandoned chicken house and work in the feedlot, neither of which he liked. He headed out for northern Arizona, but it was still thirty days or so before the spring cattle work. So, out of money and raring to get back on a ranch, he boarded a Texas-bound bus and headed for the Big Bend country.

On a stop in Phoenix he traded his saddle for a "Porter saddle," which he treasured. Having committed his remaining funds on the trade for that saddle, he was one broke teenager when he got on that bus heading toward El Paso. Leroy arrived in El Paso and transferred to another bus and got off in Van Horn. He was out of bus tickets and out of money, but he had a fine Porter saddle.

> *I got off the bus and hawked my saddle, got some money. I think they loaned me $60 for this $160 saddle. Anyway, now I had $60, but I wasn't going to go leave that saddle. So, I went checking around the ranches, and I called the X's—the Long X's, one of the ol'-time Texas ranches, whose headquarters was in Kent, a small ranching town not too far from Van Horn. Sure enough their work was just starting and their wagon was just pulling out [a wagon "pulling out" means the range work is just beginning]. In fact, their wagon was out already. So they came and got me and advanced me enough money to get my saddle out and hauled me to the wagon, and I went to work for the Long X's out of that wagon.*

Leroy again was in his element: no chicken house, no feedlot, but one fine ranching outfit. He was fitted with good horses ("rock" horses, he called them) and teamed with good cowboys. Leroy quickly noted how different the Davis Mountains around Kent, Texas, were from the northern New Mexico Sangre de Cristo southern range of the Rockies. The Texas terrain was rugged with barren mountains—good mule deer and quail country, but if you're going to raise cattle there, you'd better know what you're doing. Webb was amazed the horses could handle that country so well. He commented that they could traverse those mountains like billy goats.

His work included "following the wagon," gathering cattle and branding the calves in the early spring. The weather was rough, and he slept outside all the time. It rained, the wind blew, there were flash floods, and the days were long, but Leroy loved the job. To add to the severity of the job, the wagon food wasn't too good.

> *The ol' wagon cook—he wasn't the greatest cook I ever saw. You'd get all you wanted to eat but it was pretty greasy and sandy. The sand would blow down there, fill them ol' Dutch ovens up. They just stayed half full of grease and half full of sand most all the time. It would keep your teeth floated pretty good.*

The Long X Ranch, which Leroy drifted toward after getting off the bus in Van Horn and hocking his Porter saddle, has an illustrious history. About the time Leroy started gathering cattle and branding in the early spring of 1949, the ranch consisted of approximately 225,000 mountainous acres in Jeff Davis and Culberson counties.[5]

The country is rugged, rocky, and subject to seasonally extreme weather. The terrain necessitates the avoidance of driving cattle with their calves long

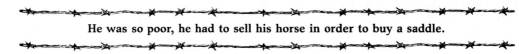

He was so poor, he had to sell his horse in order to buy a saddle.

distances to branding pens as baby calves weaken and drop out on the trail. After branding, hungry and thirsty mother cows head for the open range and tend to abandon their calves if they drop out for any length of time. (*West Texas Livestock Weekly*, 1960) When this pair separation occurs, cowboying becomes much more difficult. This rugged West Texas ranch, therefore, would prove a major testing ground for a seventeen-year-old, broke-but-energetic New Mexico cowboy named Leroy Webb. The Long X cowboys had to be able to cut cattle out of a herd during roundup with the least amount of disturbance (chousing), then accurately rope and drag the calves to the branding fire at the right speed and in coordination with the flankers. Leroy learned much at the Long X from the older and more seasoned cowboys who had to "stand in" while many of their younger counterparts were taken off the ranges to the battlefields of World War II. (J. Evetts Haley, 2001)

The Long X, a part of the Reynolds Cattle Company, had its origins in the early 1880s through the efforts of the entrepreneurial Reynolds brothers, George T. and William D. (Will), along with a trail-driving friend, John A. Matthews. Two large ranches were pur-

Windmills such as this, located in far West Texas near the Long X Ranch, revolutionized the cattle business.

> **I feel sorry for any person who spends their life
> doing something they don't enjoy doing.**
> **—Watt Matthews**

chased, one in Jeff Davis County, known as the Long X, and the other some 300 miles to the northwest on the Clear Fork of the Brazos River near Albany. The latter was called the Lambshead Ranch, named after an English immigrant who had settled in the area. The Reynolds and Matthews families had a long and interesting relationship. There were five intrafamily marriages which enhanced and perpetuated the two-ranch axis over the next one hundred years. (Matthews, 1982) Two of the key unions can be traced to the marriage of George T. Reynolds to the sister of his partner, John A. Matthews, Bettie Matthews, who settled and developed the Long X Ranch. In turn, John A. Matthews married Sallie Ann Reynolds, George T.'s sister, who developed the Lambshead Ranch. (Holden, 1982) (Neugebauer, 1997)

There was a lasting synergism between the Reynolds and Matthews families, both socially and in beef raising. The Long X and Lambshead ranches produced quality cattle throughout the twentieth century, even exporting yearlings to distant locales such as Portugal and Hungary. Watt Matthews, the son of John A. and Sallie Reynolds Matthews and a 1921 Princeton graduate, was a creative and expansive successor to his father. Watt and his brother, Joe B., worked in concert with their double cousins at the Long X over several decades in enthusiastically promoting and enhancing the beef industry in Texas.

Leroy also worked on two other interesting ranches during this era: the Phillips Ranch (now the Philmont Boy Scout Ranch) and the Frank Burk Ranch (Cimarroncita). Both of these unique ranches were made to fit for this teenage cowboy, and merit some discussion as to their historical background.

The Philmont Ranch, owned by the Boy Scouts of America, currently encompasses over 100,000 acres of prime New Mexico range land and mountainous grandeur. A good starting point in tracing its history would be to discover the origins of the Uracca Ranch. Peter Joseph, a Portuguese immigrant, had traded with both Lucien Maxwell and Kit Carson. He later bought a tract of land along the Old Santa Fe Trail just south of Cimarroncita. In 1880 Joseph sold out to Frank Sherwin, a Massachusetts-born speculator who acquired adjoining lands and then sold the ranch to an English-born entrepreneur named Francis Clutton. Clutton took possession of this ranch and obtained a large lease from the Maxwell Land Grant Company. He introduced modern livestock techniques to the area by purchasing prime Hereford bulls, irrigating fields, and upgrading the quality of produced beef.

Clutton prospered during the 1890s, but after a series of financial shortfalls and personal tragedies, he committed suicide in 1901. It was about this time that the generation of pioneer ranch men, who had driven off

Indians and wolves, built fences, and installed windmills, began to disappear. (Murphy, 1991) The following generation of ranch owners in the area included Stanley McCormick (son of the famed reaper manufacturer, Cyrus McCormick), who purchased the Clutton-owned Uracca Ranch. In 1910 George H. Webster, the ranch manager, was able to purchase the property. He was a builder and promoter and was instrumental in the construction of dams and irrigation canals throughout the area. The most significant accomplishment at the time was the construction of the Eagle Nest Dam, financed by Charles Springer, which harnessed the waters of the Cimarron River for the use of ranchers and farmers in the area.

Webster sold his holdings in 1923 to a Tulsa, Oklahoma, oil man, Waite Phillips (who would form Phillips Petroleum Company). Phillips began adding additional tracts of land along the Rayado Creek from owners such as Paul Zastrow, a Russian immigrant, and the Sauble brothers. Waite Phillips, whom Leroy would later work for and get to know, rose from humble beginnings in Iowa to become one of the wealthiest men in America. He began buying up oil leases around Okmulgee, Oklahoma, and became a millionaire virtually overnight when the area produced high yields of petroleum crude. He became increasingly interested in adding to this Uracca Ranch purchase for "recreational and investment" purposes and bought additional farms and ranches over the next three years. Named "Philmont," combining "Phillips" and "Mountain," he entertained such celebrities as Will Rogers and Wiley Post at his New Mexico "showplace." In the late 1930s, Phillips became less content with leisure and guest entertainment, embracing a pronounced philanthropic philosophy. Benevolence became a distinguishing characteristic of Waite Phillips, who donated his vast holdings to the Boy Scouts in November of 1938. (Murphy, 1991) Many boys and young men became better citizens, directly attributable to their experience at Philmont Ranch, because of Waite Phillips. Currently, more than 20,000 Scouts each year from all over the world spend their summers at Philmont learning scouting skills and nature preservation and enhancement.[6] These teenagers are given the opportunity to experience a different perspective of life, out in nature and away from their normal routines.

The Philmont was still a big-time working-cattle ranch in the 1950s in order to produce revenue for the Scouts, thus providing Leroy and other cowboys at the time the chance to work the cattle and get to know Waite Phillips as well as the Boy Scouts, scouting officials, and their staff.

The Frank Burk Ranch (Cimarroncita), located in nearby Ute Park, was

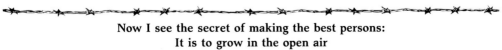

Now I see the secret of making the best persons:
It is to grow in the open air
And to eat and sleep with the earth.
—Walt Whitman

*Jimmy Rockenfield,
Frank Atmore, and
John Atmore
(December 2001).*

*Robert S. Allen
and the Ute
Creek Ranch
(September
2001).*

*The Ute Creek
Valley (Ute Creek
and former
Atmore ranches),
with Mt. Baldy
in background
(now a part of
Philmont).*

> I believe in helping others outside our own family circle
> from whom no thanks is expected or required.
> —Waite Phillips

another operation in the 1900s that gave Leroy, Frank Atmore, Johnny Caldwell, and other young cowboys an opportunity to work with and get to know horses. As background, the Burk Ranch is just south of New Mexico Highway 64, east of the village of Ute Park, and is the locale where Ute Creek joins the Cimarron River. Ute Creek is fed by numerous springs around the base of Mt. Baldy and winds several miles through the Atmore Ranch, the Ute Creek Ranch (owned by Robert S. "Bob" Allen), finally terminating its confluence with the Cimarron. It is a beautiful valley, full of deer, elk, bear, and turkey and steeped in history. (My old Lubbock High School friends and I leased both the Atmore and Ute Creek ranches for hunting during the late 1980s and 1990s. It was through our friendship with John and Frank Atmore, Bob Allen, and the son of one of Frank Burk's long-time employees, Jimmy Rockenfield, that I became aware of the area's rich heritage.)

Jimmy Rockenfield is a hunting guide with an encyclopedic knowledge of flora and fauna in the area. He recites the history of his father and how it led to the Rockenfield association with Burk's Cimarroncita Ranch.[7]

> *My dad was born in 1923 in Taylor Springs, New Mexico, at the family homestead. They had a dugout house at the time, and he was the third surviving child at that point. The two others didn't make the cut just by virtue of being so far out in the boondocks. They stayed in Taylor Springs until they starved out during the Dust Bowl, at which time my grandfather did some work for the state highway department. Most of the work at that time was still being done with teams of horses and horse-drawn equipment. It was shortly thereafter that he was able to get on at Philmont. Dad spent a significant amount of his life there at the Philmont Ranch—same time that Waite Phillips had purchased it, but before he donated it to the Boy Scouts of America. When Phillips donated it to the Boy Scouts, he sold off the cattle operation and areas he thought were suited for cattle to the McDaniel Brothers, who were truck farmers out of Arizona.*
>
> *My dad had grown up out at the Philmont Ranch because long before Waite Phillips had donated it to the Boy Scouts, my grandfather, George Rockenfield, was Waite Phillips' farm manager—and over the course of the years they lived in a variety of the ranch camps, some of which Leroy also lived at or worked out of when he was working cattle at Philmont. So, my father spent a great part of his childhood there at Rayado camp, and they lived in the buildings downstream from the little chapel that is still located out there. He also lived for a while out at the Sweetwater camp and then over at the Cimarron place, which is on the highway between Cimarron and Springer, just upstream from the CS Ranch headquarters.*
>
> *My dad started working for the Burks at Cimarroncita in 1953. Dad had a job for a while over at Los Alamos, but he decided that he liked this*

*country and wanted to be closer to his parents, who were living over at
Springer at the time. He decided to take what was supposed to be
a temporary job at Cimarroncita, taking care of the horses for one winter,
and that worked out to finishing up thirty-nine years later when he
passed away in 1992.*

*The ranch itself originally traces back to Henry Lambert, who started
the St. James Hotel in Cimarron, became a U.S. marshal, and ended up
buying a section of property from Lucien Maxwell up here in Ute Park,
and he used the property initially as a cattle ranch. There were already
several of the buildings present on the location because the St. Louis-Rocky
Mt.-Pacific Railroad, which was originated in 1911, was trying to create a
draw for tourists to come from Raton and points north to Ute Park. So,
they built a big dance hall pavilion; they had a hotel up here, and it was
just kind of a sideline thing to try to encourage traffic on the railroad in
addition to shipping mining-related equipment to and from the gold mine
at Mt. Baldy as well as other mines in this part of the country.*

*Minnette Thompson originally was a Houston girl and director of the
summer Camp Mystic down in Texas. She decided that she wanted to
start her own operation, get in a little bit better climate than what she
was subject to down there. So, her family owned a farm in what is now
the River Oaks section of Houston, and they sold that piece of property in
order to finance purchasing Cimarroncita from the Lamberts. She and her
sister bought one section of land in 1929 and started the construction of
all the cabins, incorporating the old remaining St. Louis Railroad buildings
into the new camp.*

It was actually at this railroad terminal, which later became Cimarroncita, that the Atmore brothers' paternal grandfather, Rodney Atmore, became station master in the early 1900s, responsible for stagecoach and rail
traffic as well as mail. Some of his five children were born at Cimarroncita,
although the nearby Atmore Ranch was the settling place for generations of
Atmores. (Bridget Jackson, Frank and John Atmore's great-grandmother, and
her husband, John Jackson, came off the Santa Fe Trail by ox-cart in the late
1860s and in 1870. Bridget started a boardinghouse in Baldy City, a booming gold town at the time, located halfway up the dominant Baldy Mountain.
She later homesteaded an area on downstream Ute Creek, which ultimately
became the Atmore family ranch.)

Jimmy Rockenfield, who currently lives in Ute Park with his wife,
Gretchen, and daughter, Elizabeth, continues with his historical narrative of
Cimarroncita:

*I think it was around 1933, if I remember correctly, that Frank
Burk started working for Minnette as wrangler over at the girls' camp.
At the time he also had property leased from the Maxwell Land Grant
Company to put cattle on—and that is where the Ute Park summer home
area is located right now. That particular portion of it hadn't been divided
up into home lots yet. It was just pasture land, and Frank had that leased
from them. So, he ran cattle on that during the year and then worked for*

Minnette during the summer. After a couple or three years, they decided they liked each other and got married and wasn't too long after that that they were able to buy three more sections from the Maxwell Land Grant Company, which finished out the total property area of the Frank Burk Ranch called Cimarroncita, taking in a major portion of the Ute Park Valley.

Once Frank and Minnette were married, they made a very good team. Minnette was definitely the business side of it, and Frank was an exceptional promotional person. In that respect they did extremely well with the camp operation. During the '40s they went ahead and expanded it considerably in size for two reasons. One was because many of the parents in the coastal areas during the 1940s were concerned about the possibility of military invasion from Japan or Germany; so, they liked the idea of getting the kids away from these areas and sent them to Cimarroncita. It was kind of an "Axis" scare, and they requested that Minnette expand the size of the camp to accommodate more children. The girls' camp essentially doubled in size at that time. Following World War II, it continued to grow in popularity, and girls from all over the United States came there.

Then in 1945 Minnette and Frank started the boys' camp. They had a good friend of theirs from Houston, Sally Scurry, who was recently widowed, had two boys of her own, and a daughter, and they decided that Sally would be the perfect partner to go ahead and start up the boys' camp. So, initially, during the first year of operation, the boys' camp was actually located over at the Ute Creek Ranch in the old buildings that are still out west of the headquarters across Ute Creek. This was kind of a ranch hand house for camping season, and calving season, and times like that. Then in 1946 they finally finished getting enough of the cabins constructed over at what became the boys' camp site to go ahead and move operations over there. So, from that point, they could accommodate both brothers and sisters at the same basic location even though the camps were separate in most aspects of operation.

Minnette Burk passed away in 1978; her husband, Frank Burk, died in 1981, and their son, Mike, and his wife ran the camp until it closed down in 1995. It was the end of an era of a premiere camp that provided a wonderful outdoor experience for five generations of campers.

As a youngster, Leroy Webb frequented the Atmore Ranch just on the other side of Highway 64 from Cimarroncita, where he and Frank Atmore could practice roping the milk cows. Then, as teenagers, they got a job working for Frank Burk. Frank Atmore[8] recalls their early days at Burk's Cimarroncita (Atmore, 2001):

My first recollection of actually working for wages with Leroy was at Cimarroncita. The first task in the spring was to shoe around 75 head of horses—somewhere between 75 and 100 head of horses. These were all, of course, dude horses. These horses had been shod by everybody in the world, and most of them would try to kick your head off as soon as you walked up to them. So, a lot of them had to be tied down.

Anyway, we shod horses and wrangled horses—and broke some. Frank Burk and Minnette Burk at that time had a variety of horses, and some of them were sort of wild mustangs that they had pastured on Red Lake Mesa and there was some kind of a broom tail stud horse up there. Anyway, they ended up with several of those colts. Leroy and I trained those horses. During that summer Leroy and I traded off staying at each other's houses. We'd rope and tie our milk calves to practice tying calves. Leroy was a tremendous bronc rider from the time he was just a boy, but he was just beginning to get into roping. This was about 1949.

Johnny Caldwell, who also worked with Frank and Leroy at Cimarroncita, recalls another Webb story during their employment at the Burk Ranch. Burk knew of some horses that had wintered in the high country and stayed up there in the spring. He told Leroy he would pay him a set amount of money for each horse he could bring back. So, this seventeen-year-old took off by himself with two riding horses and two pack horses and spent days and nights in the mountains, bringing back a reasonable remuda that he had gathered by his lonesome. Leroy vividly recalls the experience:

I shod a lot of horses on the Cimarroncita for fifty cents a shoe. Brother Don was supposed to go up in those mountains looking for these horses. They had wintered up in the Vermejo Park country and could go as far as they wanted—plum up to Colorado. Don couldn't go because he broke his leg in a rodeo. He had just won the bareback riding, and the pickup man ran over him when he dismounted. Anyway, I wound up with the job to go look for them horses. I left Cimarron in May 1950, with two saddle horses and two pack horses with my bedroll and gear and headed for the hills. I knew the country, the cow camp, and the cowboys that lived in those camps. I went from camp to camp looking for horses. If there was nobody in a camp, I'd just make myself at home and stay as long as I wanted. I stayed at No. 1 camp on the Vermejo for a while with an ol' buddy, Nick Mitchell, and with ol' Jud Knight for a while near the headquarters. I gathered what horses I could find and trailed them back to Cimarron, then Ute Park. Man, I wish I could do that again, right now! It was a great experience.

I can appreciate how many cowboy skills are required to accomplish the task of gathering wild horses solo, having read the accounts of a similar venture by one of my favorite cowboy authors, Ben K. Green. (Green, 1972)

Leroy also worked for Frank Sauble on his Circle Dot Ranch about this time. The Circle Dot was northeast of Springer at Rayado and at one time was part of the Maxwell Land Grant. Kit Carson had built his home on this tract in the late 1800s. Frank Sauble later sold the Circle Dot to Waite Phillips. Leroy thought Sauble was a great man who deserved admiration and respect.[9]

CHAPTER 4

New York and Time with the Dudes

*D*uring his stint at various ranches, Leroy, now seventeen years old with almost four years of hard ranching experience behind him, heard about a job opening in Stony Brook, New York, for a cowboy who could teach dudes how to ride. He thought that just might be an experience. He had never been to a big city before and never east of the Texas Panhandle. The dude ranch owners told him to show up in May with a saddle and start to work. Leroy slung his saddle over his shoulder, wrapped up his few belongings in his bedroll, asked his friend Johnny Caldwell to join him, and boarded the bus in Springer.

One can imagine two teenage cowboys carrying nothing but saddles and bedrolls rolling into New York City on the Greyhound and transferring to the local bus headed for Stony Brook. Leroy and Johnny were met at the bus stop in Stony Brook by dude ranch representatives, who saw two green-broke cowboys, their saddles over their shoulders and bedrolls under their arms.

It turns out that the Stony Brook dude ranch, called the "Thousand Acre Ranch," was owned by a man named Jack Earhart and catered to a broad range of clients, primarily from New York City. This was in 1949, a time when many of the "eastern dudes" were getting on horses for the first time and acting like they were in the cowboy movies. It was a thriving business, and Leroy and Johnny were having the time of their lives. Both were

Country cowboy in the big city (1948).

authentic cowboys by this time, handsome young men in their late teens, red blood flowing through their veins. The young girls and older women were most interested in these two cowboys from way out west. The ranch featured a large pavilion where western dances were held, a remuda of some sixty horses to accommodate the dudes, and an abundance of western-themed activities. About two to three hundred guests were there for various times throughout the summer.

The clientele included nurses, secretaries, and various celebrities. Joe and Dom DiMaggio visited with a variety of cousins, sisters, and girlfriends. Many singers and entertainers from New York City also frequented the place. Although Leroy is reticent to tell much about his summer in New York, particularly in front of his wife, Nora, his brother and his brother-in-law, Johnny Caldwell, filled in some blanks. These cowboys did a lot of dancing with the eastern-bred girls—square dancing, country and western, and the like. Leroy had a lot of girlfriends there who had never been around a real cowboy. He taught them how to ride, how to care for horses, and probably regaled them with a few stories of his cowboy experience on the open ranges of West Texas and New Mexico. Leroy and Johnny were extremely popular with the guests and received good tips in the form of money and Scotch. (Those were his wilder days, long since gone.)

The admiring female guests would believe anything Leroy and Johnny told them, such as the story that cockleburs were actually porcupine eggs. When the newly arrived girls would suit up for horseback riding, many would buy Levis at the dude ranch store and put them on backwards, with the buttons in the back. Leroy and Johnny diplomatically tried to tell them that it would be more comfortable to turn them around because those rear-end buttons might be uncomfortable when they got in the saddle.

Leroy and Johnny lived in a bunkhouse provided by the dude ranch and spent their spare time at a nearby roadhouse or bar. Sometimes they would ride the ranch horses to and

*Red Madiole (left) and Leroy (right) with a
New York "urban cowboy"?*

Leroy likes to recall that he took a subway over to New Jersey to see a rodeo, then spent hours on the subway on the way back to Manhattan, not knowing where to get off. I think he discovered Brooklyn for the first time and was still amazed that he went under the same river he had ferried across a few hours earlier. He and Johnny knew they were a couple of real hicks in the big city. As they stopped in Philadelphia, heading southwest, they took advantage of the layover to get a haircut. The barber began cutting Leroy's hair, then started manicuring his fingernails, at which point Leroy hightailed it out of there. He said he was worried they would take off his boots and start working on his toes. Enough of East Coast haircut parlors.

from their destinations along the New York highways, giving motorists a rare look at a mini-version of the old trail rides.

One young man who was learning how to ride was particularly fond of Leroy and his cowboy tutoring skills. Leroy would always pick a palomino that the young boy preferred. Little did Leroy know that his client, who was always accompanied by two or three rough-looking characters, was the son of a big-time New York Mafia figure. When the father came to pick up his son at the end of camp, he drove up to Leroy in a large black limo, complete with bodyguards, and profusely thanked Leroy for taking such good care of his son. After he hugged young Leroy a few times, New York-style, he invited him to come visit the "family" in New York, stating, "The town will be on me." It was a tempting offer that Leroy and Johnny never accepted.

At the end of the summer, Leroy and Johnny were ready to get back to the real world of New Mexico and Texas ranches. They stopped in New York City on the way back. As they walked toward Times Square, dressed like the cowboys they were, a few young toughs confronted them with some taunts. The tough guys put up their fists and asked Leroy if he was a "real cowboy." Leroy's response was: "Get one inch closer and you'll find out." Off they went.

About four or five days later, Leroy and Johnny stumbled off the bus in Raton, dead tired and probably nursing a mild hangover. After being called a "sheepherder" near the Raton bus station, another small altercation occurred, but they made the last leg to Springer safely. Both were ready to get back to some real cowboying.

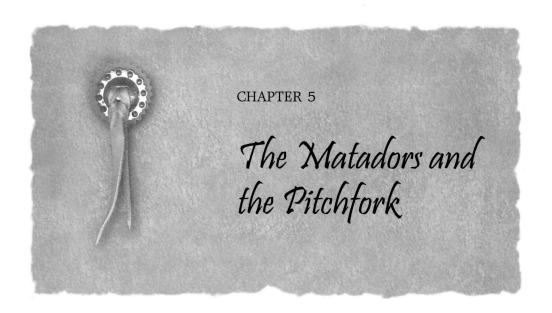

CHAPTER 5

The Matadors and the Pitchfork

The Matadors

Now recovered from his New York summer, Leroy had a treasure trove of stories about dudes and dudettes and his escapades in New York. He and brother Don found some seasonal work back at the Red River Ranch, primarily breaking colts. Evenings after work were filled with stories from fellow cowboys about big Texas ranches, particularly the ones called the Matadors and the Pitchfork. The year was 1949; Leroy was almost seventeen years old and Don a year older. Intrigued by this camp-fire talk, they piled their saddles and bedrolls in Don's old Dodge car, picked up Johnny Caldwell, and headed toward Texas and the Matadors. Awaiting Leroy, Don, and Johnny was the Matador Land and Cattle Company—one of the most interesting of the giant Texas ranches.

The unique saga of the Matadors began in the 1870s, the "bonanza era" of the range cattle industry in America. European investors had taken a keen interest in this phenomenon, and venture capital, particularly in the United Kingdom, was in great supply. Scottish interests purchased the holdings of a small Texas outfit in 1882 and transformed that investment into one of the greatest cattle empires in North America.

The Scots' interest in the U.S. cattle market probably had its genesis in the fall of 1871, when Capt. Clarence Mauck, a U.S. cavalry officer serving under Col. Ranald Mackenzie, reconnoitered the Texas Panhandle area between the upper Brazos and Red rivers. This land, known as the Llano Estacado, was long inhabited by the Comanches and probably had been traversed by Coronado. The consensus reached by Coronado, the Comanches, Captain Mauck, and later by a Scot migrant named Thomas Lawson was the same: It was a lush sea of grassland, topsoil, and sufficient rainfall to support the growth of bluestem, buffalo, and gramma grasses. When Mackenzie's vigorous campaigns of 1872 and 1874 had removed the Comanches from the area, followed by buffalo hunters who completed the slaughter of the great herds which frequented the area, the grasslands of the Llano Estacado and contiguous areas were dormant and unused.

Cheap Texas cattle, abundant grass, ample water, and high demand for beef in Chicago, Denver, and other commercial centers were the perfect ingredients for a profitable cattle venture in this area. British capitalists began to pour money into the American West during the 1870s and 1880s. However, it was the Scots, probably spurred on by Thomas Lawson, who led the way in catalyzing the Scottish entrepreneurs' interest in American markets for "growing beef." In his *The Matador Land and Cattle Company*, W. M. Pearce observes that the volume of risk capital poured into foreign land for the purposes of raising cattle by the small region of Scotland, known for their parsimony, is probably "one of the great paradoxes in the history of nineteenth century commerce." (Pearce, 1964, pp. 9-10)

These Scottish capitalists incorporated the Matador Land and Cattle Company in 1882, holding more than 100,000 acres of fee simple ownership in Motley, Cottle, and Dickens counties of Texas. Moreover, the Scottish-owned company secured the rights of range privileges on an additional 1.5 million acres. Forty thousand shares of stock were issued with the initial capitalization in the range of $1.5 million.

This area, just east of the High Plains, was broken by draws and modest canyons, allowing the construction of small dams to lessen the dependence on water from windmills. All the elements seemed in place for an enormous return on investment. However, the first decade of ownership during the 1890s fell short of expectations. Drought, blizzards, lower cattle prices, and the rapid disappearance of free grasslands forced many of the foreign-

Col. Ranald Mackenzie of the 4th U.S. Cavalry was an aggressive and efficient officer whose mission was to systematically destroy the Comanches and Kiowas on the Llano Estacado (Panhandle of Texas) by destroying Indian camps. Mackenzie's command came from Fort Clark at Brackettville. He picked up reinforcements at Fort Concho and marched to his staging area in the upper reaches of the Brazos River and into the Panhandle. A decisive battle took place in the Palo Duro Canyon near Amarillo, forcing the Indians to reservations, opening the High Plains of Texas to Anglo settlement. (Kelton, 1989)

owned cattle companies out of existence. The Scot owners and managers hung tough and worked their way through the first ten years, even though the stockholders grumbled about small dividends.[1]

Murdo Mackenzie (no relation to Ranald Mackenzie), born in County Ross, Scotland, in 1850, was to become one of the most dominant individuals associated with the Matadors and the development of the American cattle industry. In 1885 the Mackenzie family emigrated from Scotland to Trinidad, Colorado, where they maintained a home for the next twenty-six years.[2] In 1890 Mackenzie became manager of the Matadors, and promptly moved the company's office from Fort Worth to his hometown of Trinidad. By coincidence, the first manager of the Matadors operated out of Trinidad, Colorado, about the same time Juan Cordova, Leroy's grandfather, was learning the cattle business in the same town—and whose grandson would work on the Matadors then run by Mackenzie's son some sixty years later.

Mackenzie, in the early years of Matadors management, developed long-range business plans and cattle management principles that would ensure the success of the Matadors through the subsequent decades. Selected leasing, selected feeding practices, transfer management, the practice of holding steers until they were three years old, and optimizing sales under fluctuating market prices were just a few of the managerial techniques developed by Mackenzie that would serve as a model for future generations of ranch managers. As manager/board member of the Matadors for thirty-five years, Mackenzie was called by President Theodore Roosevelt "the most influential of all Western cattlemen." The consummate manager and businessman made necessary trips between the U.S. and Dundee, Scotland, reporting to and answering questions from stockholders. In 1912 he decided to leave the Matadors. He was sixty-one years old, had an established home in Trinidad, which was the social center for friends and family, and owned a small getaway at Stonewall, thirty miles west of Trinidad on the Purgatoire River. However, he was offered an unbelievable five-year contract for $50,000/year from the Brazil Land, Cattle, and Packing Company. After a brief visit to Scotland, he left for Sao Paulo, leaving the management position to another Scot, John McBain.

McBain guided the Matadors throughout the next decade, managing an ever-expanding operation. Under Mackenzie, the owned acreage had expanded from 100,000 acres to greater than 750,000 acres, including the Alamocitas Division in the Texas Panhandle near Channing. The Alamocitas tract, purchased by the Scots from the XIT holdings in 1902, consisted of around 300,000 acres, much of it bordering the New Mexico-Texas state line. Various other properties were purchased in Texas, Wyoming, Montana, and the Dakotas.

As typical in Texas, cyclical periods of drought and rain forced Matadors management constantly to adjust. A severe drought in 1913 caused McBain to seek more grass and to expand efforts for securing leased pastureland.

Profits ebbed and flowed accordingly. Oil discoveries on Matador properties in the 1920s, two world wars, taxation complexities, floods and droughts, and fluctuating cattle prices all influenced its operational decisions throughout the first half of the twentieth century.

In 1922 John McBain died, and Murdo Mackenzie, now seventy-one years old and living in Chicago, agreed to rejoin the board and again assume managerial duties. His return was most fortunate for the Matador Land and Cattle Company, as the stock market would crash seven years later, cattle would lose over half their value, and someone like Murdo Mackenzie would be

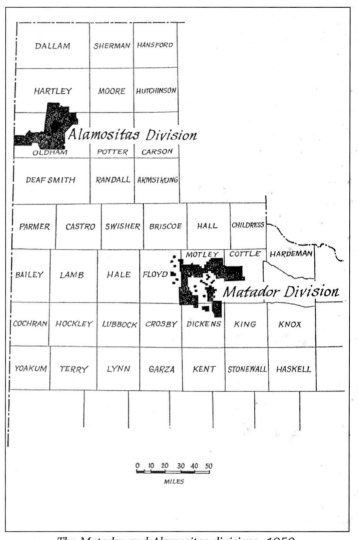

The Matador and Alamocitas divisions, 1950.

needed to guide the company through those tortuous years. In 1937, at the age of eighty-seven, Murdo again relinquished his managerial duties, to be assumed by his son, John Mackenzie, who had been only six years old when his father first became manager of the ranch. Properly schooled and with extensive experience "in the field" at various Matador Ranch divisions, John was perfectly qualified to assume his father's position. He was to become the last general manager in the seventy-year era of the Matadors, which was sold to New York investment bankers in 1951.

Leroy Webb cowboyed at the Matador Ranch out of the Matadors Division for two years, leaving before its sale. As a working cowboy in the field, he was most likely unaware that preliminary financial intrigues between Dundee and New York were being conducted. Fortunately, the ranch was intact and in full operation during his 1949-1950 tenure.

As they arrived at the ranch town of Matador, Texas, the three New Mexico cowboys, Leroy and Don Webb and Johnny Caldwell, pooled their money and came up with a grand total of two dollars. They asked someone for directions to the headquaters. Fortunately, they found that the wagon was "in." The "location of the wagon" in those days indicated which part of the seasonal cattle operation was going on at a specific ranch at that particular time. At the Matadors, the wagon(s) would leave the headquarters in August or September with the cowhand team in place. They would generally stay out in the range, with few trips to town, sleeping under the stars or in line camps and eating out of the wagon until the following June. During those ten months, they would do what was necessary to care for the mother cows and bring the calf crop along, and manage the cattle inventory throughout the ranch's property. Upon returning to the headquarters during the intense heat of June through August, the cowhands would generally break horses, repair fences and windmills, and make sure all the cattle traps were in good condition.

When they arrived at headquarters, only one cowhand position was available; however, the next-door Pitchfork was hiring cowboys. Leroy took the Matadors slot and Johnny and Don headed toward the Pitchfork.

The Comanches left their signatures on the Matador Ranch long before the Scots arrived.

Leroy recalls that Johnny Stevens, the ranch manager at the time, was an outstanding manager, tireless worker, and gentleman. John Stevens was a graduate of Texas A&M (Class of 1937) who had started work at the Alamocitas Division of the Matadors in 1940. He was young and energetic and drove himself relentlessly in setting an example for the men who worked under him. Stevens' day-to-day activities, catalogued from Alamocitas diaries, underscore his "hands on" approach and attention to detail. (Pearce, 1964) When the manager of the Matadors Division died in 1946, John Stevens moved from Channing to the Ballard Springs headquarters to become its fifth and last superintendent. He was there to hire and supervise an eighteen-year-old cowboy named Leroy Webb, who worked under him in 1949 and 1950.[3]

Bill Hemphill was the wagon boss at the Matadors when Leroy signed on. As with John Stevens, Leroy had immediate respect for Hemphill. Hemphill has long since retired and currently lives in Roaring Springs, a small town not far from Matador which has a spring "that does not roar" but provides enough water to fill a public pool. Bill (born in 1926) is very lucid and has fond memories of his time at the Matadors. He remembers Leroy as a "good cowboy," particularly at such a young age. Bill was wagon boss at the Matadors from 1942 until 1953. He then "ran the wagon" at the 6666 Ranch, both at the Texas Panhandle ranch as well as the main ranch at Guthrie. Like many of the wagon bosses at the time, he believed in hard work and total dedication to the task. He told Leroy and the other eighteen to twenty cowhands as the wagon left the Matador headquarters for their ten-month odyssey, "Say *adiós* to town." Bill said all the hands were good, but Leroy seemed more settled and focused than the rest (probably due to a maturing process which followed his New York and Arizona forays). Bill particularly recalls the Red Lake Camp of the Matadors, where he spent a lot of time cowboying. He knew D Burns, who managed the Pitchfork at the time, and had a good relationship with him and the neighboring Pitchfork cowhands.[4] Hemphill confirmed how today's cowboys have such a different lifestyle from those of his and Leroy's days. In the forties and early fifties the Matadors had few trucks or stock trailers, and the cowboys never hauled stock within the ranch. During this period most cowhands slept in the open for months at a time, including the winter months, and going to town was extremely rare.[5]

The 6666 Ranch, approximate to the Pitchfork and Matador, had its beginnings in 1867, when future oil baron Capt. Samuel "Burk" Burnett purchased some cattle, reportedly already having the Four Sixes brand (thus contradicting the "poker game" theory). Burnett settled near Guthrie in about 1900, owning approximately 240,000 acres of rugged grasslands and breaks. The 6666 Ranch is still operational today, and branding is done the old-fashioned way—one "6" brand applied to the calf's hide four times.

*Bill Hemphill—
an oil painting of
Hemphill, Wagon
Boss, and Crew,
Matador Ranch
(1952).*

*Bill Hemphill at
Roaring Springs,
Texas (2001).*

Immediately after the dust settled from the departing old blue Dodge carrying Johnny and Don to their future employment at the Pitchfork, Bill put Leroy to work with his first question: "Have you ever broke any horses?" A quick affirmative and enthusiastic response got the two off to a good start. As part of a trial-run check, Bill took Leroy over to a couple of seasoned Matadors horse breakers, Rosy Deaton and John Andrews. A real tough cowboy, Rosy worked his whole career on the Matadors and stayed there until his body was broken up to the point he couldn't continue. John Andrews was an old Arizona cowhand who had worked on some of the big Arizona ranches, so he and Deaton looked to this eighteen-year-old kid with a high degree of suspicion. The three worked all that afternoon breaking horses. At the end of his first day, as Leroy was watching his first Matador sunset, Hemphill asked Rosy and John to evaluate "this young hand." Rosy's response was as positive as cowhands can make it (seasoned cowboys are not known for using superlative adjectives): "Well, Bill, he'll do to take along." Leroy felt about ten feet tall. He had the job, and an interesting stint awaited him at the world-famous Matador Ranch.

The next two weeks, before the wagon pulled out, was a busy time for all the hands. About 150 head of horses which would accompany the wagon had to be vaccinated. Each had to be roped individually, secured, and given the necessary shots. Leroy remembers one big bay horse that was a bit crazy. When Hemphill finally got a rope on him, the bay forefooted him. With help from the hands, the horse was finally secured and vaccinated. Once this was accomplished, the old wagon boss looked at Leroy and said, "I'm assigning this horse to you!" Welcome to the Matadors.

The wagon left the headquarters with 150 vaccinated horses, a supply of grub, and twenty cowboys, among them an eighteen-year-old New Mexico cowboy. Leroy had never experienced country like this before. He had worked the high country and lush flats in New Mexico, as well as the rugged Davis Mountains on the Long X, but never mesquite country with undulating hills, steep breaks, small canyons, wild cattle, and little water—all accompanied by hot summers and cold winters. Leroy was assigned eleven horses, including the unpredictable bay, and would spend the next ten months sleeping on the ground. He classified the Matadors cowboys as "brush hands" and the horses as "brush horses"—some of the country's best in a very hostile landscape. Leroy thought he could keep up with anyone, and he ended up doing just that. These months were probably his biggest challenge, and he absolutely loved the experience.

The cowboys had their own string of ranch-owned horses and could use whichever set of horses they would need for the day. It was not unusual to go through three or four horses during one day. As the bay horse Hemphill assigned to Leroy was included in his string, and he was stuck with him, Leroy decided to do some homework. It turned out the horse's name was "Greyhound." He was a four-year-old gelding that had been "green broke" (a euphemism for being ridden a couple of weeks in a bronc pen) and was "wild as all get-out."

> I found out about Greyhound. He hadn't been caught in a couple of years except the little he was in the bronc pen. So anyway, I thought, "Well, heck, I might as well get this over with." I just asked the wagon boss to bring me ol' Greyhound as my first horse of the day. He roped him and drug him out to me. He helped me get a hackmore on him and get his foot tied up. We tied up the hind leg on him. Well, then that was it. We were out in the country, and there weren't any pens. We just had a little rope corral to catch these horses. It was big country. Anyway, I got him saddled up, let his foot down, got on him, and away we go! This sucker could buck—man he could buck—but I could ride him all right. He never did buck me off. In fact, he ended up making a sure enough nice horse—about as good a horse as you would want. You could rope anything on him.

One time Leroy was on Greyhound chasing one of the herd bulls down a draw. Leroy threw a rope over him, but the bull (which weighed about twice as much as Greyhound and Leroy combined) took charge. The bull pulled the rider and horse through and around a bunch of mesquites, then down the steep slopes of the draw, and finally gave up before Greyhound did. With the bull in a state of exhaustion, Greyhound "tauted" the rope and declared victory. (Leroy includes this bay in his remembrance list of special horses.)

Another Matadors horse in Leroy's "mount" was a little sorrel horse. Every horse has its own idiosyncracies. This sorrel had a habit of bucking only when a rope was thrown off of him. Leroy was riding the sorrel early one morning while gathering the herd together, and an old mother cow took off, headed for the hills. Leroy took off behind her, hunkered down in the saddle and "spurring" to get a rope around the cow before she made it to cover. He threw the noose, and it encircled her head instead of just the horns. The horse thought it was now time to unpack, and when the cow hit the end of the rope, she flipped right over on her back. Cow, horse, and Leroy went tumbling down a ravine as one unit. Leroy fell about halfway down. At the bottom of the hill, the old cow charged the unmounted horse, still connected by the rope around the saddle horn. The horse took off in a frightful exit, the rope broke, and they headed in opposite directions to points unknown. Nearby cowboys came down and picked up Leroy, who had a hurt leg and wrist (the wrist had just started to heal after an earlier break in a rodeo bronc-riding contest a few months before). They put him in the wagon, writhing in pain. After a few days of soaking his various body parts in Epsom salts, Leroy finally relented to let his partners take him to Matador. The bones in his leg and wrist were cleanly broken. Now Leroy was developing a rather extensive dossier of broken bones—part of the hazard of being a cowhand.

Leroy loved the Matadors experience, especially gathering cattle and branding. "It was a good life—exactly what I wanted to do." He really enjoyed the Matadors hands and especially remembers two "drive" leaders, Wishy Derikson and Rosy Deaton, along with the wagon boss, Bill Hemphill.[6] When the wagon boss would get to a strategic location, one drive leader and crew would head one way and the other team would go the opposite way. They would then circle and converge at a holding area.

The thickets hid quite a few maverick cattle (unbranded and un-

---

Altogether, Leroy had seventeen horses in his mount. He recalls that virtually all of them had "some little nasty habit." There was a big dun horse called "Hot Shot," one that would buck just for the fun of it. Leroy would mount him and let him buck until he got tired, then they would go on about their business. Later on in the day, they would repeat the process. Leroy was developing an interest in doing some rodeo work, his favorites being bareback and saddle bronc riding. Nobody wanted to ride Hot Shot except Leroy, who enthusiastically used him for practice in perfecting his bronc-riding skills. Leroy always asked for horses no one else would use. "I just liked them bad horses."

In reckless spirit the cowboy is born; only in long, hard training is he made.
—J. Evetts Haley
Charles Goodnight: Cowboy and Plainsman

recorded). Leroy couldn't see them, and they couldn't see Leroy; it was a game of hide-and-seek. When they were flushed out of the thicket, it was a wild event. The mavericks would come running right at the horse and rider. The cowhands would dodge the charge, then chase after them. Somewhere along the chase, they would have to change horses and get a fresh mount, then start again. That was just the kind of cowboying that Leroy loved: "chasing and catching those mavericks."

Wishy, Rosy, and Bill Hemphill were all excellent ropers. They would charge the mavericks as a team—rope one, lay him down, and shackle him (using a short rope with a loop on each end, they would tie two of the legs about six inches apart to immobilize the maverick). The cowboys would leave the shackled maverick there and head for the next one. Once the job was done, they would gather all the captives and reintroduce them to the herd. This was tough work, and it took a lot of energy and skill on behalf of the cowhand.

Leroy thought that Wishy, Rosy, a fellow named Stogie Bumpas, and another named Keith Stover were all top cowhands. Even the best had their falls. Old Stogie jumped on Hot Shot one time in the presence of Leroy. The old dun took Stogie into a thicket, and all kinds of ruckus could be heard. After a while, Hot Shot came out—but no Stogie. It took some time for Leroy to find Stogie, lying on his back and all scratched up but ready to go again. The score was Hot Shot–1, Stogie–0.

Leroy once trailed a new young cowhand who was bucked off his horse. Leroy took off in hot pursuit of the riderless horse because he didn't want the kid to have to walk back to camp. In a full run, he threw the rope at the horse, and the noose slipped back over its ears and caught the saddle horn. Off came the saddle, but it didn't slow down the horse.

If being in the brush wasn't action enough, these cowhands would make it into Matador on rare occasions following payday. They would go to a dance and "get pretty wild and raise all kinds of hillbilly hell." Matador's city fathers, the sheriff, and the deputies kept some semblance of control, and jail time was generally overnight only. After all, it was a company town and the cowboys had to get back to work. Once back to the wagon, the rules were strict—no alcohol and no women. One of the cooks, Sam Cates, hid a jug of whiskey in his bedroll. Leroy remembers him as a "mean, sullen, ornery ol' character, who didn't last too long—but what a character."

The sale of Matadors stock about this time resulted in the breakup of its vast range lands, facilitated by the creation of fifteen corporations, dividing up the land, cattle, and other assets. In general, the Alamocitas Division near the Texas Panhandle town of Channing (the North Division) was purchased by a few people (including a well-known Lubbock contractor, R. H. Fulton) while the Matadors Division (the South Division) where Leroy had worked was divided into many small ranches, some of which were broken out and sold to farmers. That the Matadors persisted for seven decades can best be attributed to four features as described by J. Evetts Haley: "a knowledge of good land, a reliance on the best bred cattle, an ample source of reserves, and a sound tradition of business management." (Haley, 1949)

The Matadors experience honed Leroy's cowboy skills. As an eighteen-year-old, he was working with top cowboy hands in an efficiently managed, professional ranch operation. During his stay, they still operated out of a chuck wagon, moving every few days to "work" the various cattle pastures. This generally was a year-round operation except for July and August because of the heat effects on working cattle. Leroy gained much of his proficiency at roping while working on the Matadors. He worked all ages of stock, from young calves ready for branding to four- or five-year-olds that had eluded earlier roundup crews. The latter gave him extensive practice in heading and heeling. (Whitmore, 1970) He was on his way to becoming a big-time cowboy.

The Pitchfork

Following Leroy's employment at the Matadors, Don and Johnny Caldwell drove down Highway 82 to the Pitchfork Ranch, sandwiched in between the Matadors and the 6666 Ranch (reportedly won in a poker game with a hand of four sixes).[7] The Pitchfork Ranch origins followed the same general timeline as did the Matadors, although the history of ownership was quite different. It is unique in that today it has maintained its same corporate structure first established in 1883 by the Williams family of St. Louis. (Murrah, 1973) The Pitchfork is still controlled by the family, and of the major Texas ranches established in the 1880s (such as the XIT, Slaughter, Spur, Matadors, and JA)[8] it is one of the few that exists intact today, having survived drought and dropping cattle prices without the benefit of oil production. The ranch is currently larger than ever and has survived in the difficult profession of raising beef only because of sound management and outstanding leadership.

The first manager was Dan Gardner, who set the standard in his forty-seven years of service. Gates and Eugene Williams of St. Louis controlled the ranch during the 1940s through the 1960s, and were perceptive enough to hire an outstanding manager during that era, Douglas "D" Burns. D Burns was a 1916 graduate of Texas A&M and started cowboying for $25 a month

Cattle are not nearly as hard to work as cowhands.
—Coy Drennan, Pitchfork foreman

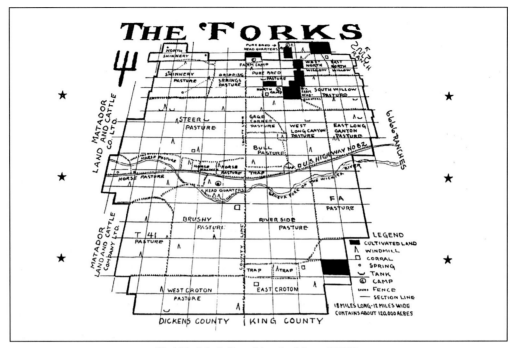

The Pitchfork Ranchlands (circa 1939).

in 1917. He and his wife, Mamie, were a rare combination, and it was their respective talents that enhanced the Pitchfork operations throughout their residence there, beginning in 1942 until D retired in 1965.[9] Mamie Burns recorded this period skillfully in a book published several years after her death in 1982. (Burns, 1986)

Don Webb and Johnny Caldwell enjoyed talking about their experiences as working cowboys at the Pitchfork during the 1950s. As with Leroy next door at the Matadors, this was a great period for perfecting the cowboy skills of the Webb brothers. Although the two ranches had different forms of ownership and management, the cowboy duties were essentially the same.

The Pitchfork was a strict mother-cow operation, with several thousand acres of farmland to raise feedstuff for the horses and cattle. The ranch even operated a feedlot in the late 1950s. It put special emphasis on quarter horses and highly bred Hereford cattle. (Voyt, 1970) Eugene Williams, Gates Williams, and D Burns together forged the Pitchfork into one of the most modern and efficient ranches in the nation. D Burns put special emphasis on good horses, good bulls (highly selected and registered Herefords), good

We have no place on the Pitchfork Ranch for a horse that cannot take our cowboys to the back side of the pasture and return, doing whatever cow work may be necessary coming and going.

—D Burns on horses

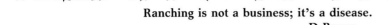

Ranching is not a business; it's a disease.
—D Burns

fences (more than 450 miles of it), good water, good cowboys, and the strict prohibition of alcohol on the premises.

Don Webb currently resides in Raton with a lonesome longhorn steer and a two-year-old, green-broke filly.[10] He is similar to Leroy in several ways, and the two have maintained an amicable relationship throughout their cowboying careers. Don still breaks some horses for Raton friends but is mostly retired from active ranching. He well remembers his days at the Pitchfork and talks about some of its great cowboys, such as long-term foreman Coy Drennan, Veto Austin, Paul Vinson, among others. Don remembers how he was hired on. Leaving Leroy at the Matadors, he and Johnny Caldwell were driving down Highway 82 in his old blue Dodge toward the Pitchfork gate and saw several cowboys repairing the barbed wire fence along the highway. Don got out of his car, went over, and asked for a job. D Burns happened to be there and asked Don for his qualifications. D was unimpressed that Don was a "New Mexico cowboy," thinking they couldn't adapt to the Texas country. But he hired Don nevertheless and later became impressed with his cowboying skills. A good relationship developed. Don loves to tell the story that while he was working cattle one day in a large trap, one or two would break out, and D would yell, "Let them go." As Don loved to chase errant cattle and rope them, he would always pretend not to hear D's command and get in some good roping practice. He described D as a bit cantankerous, set in his ways, but fair and an excellent cowman and manager.

The Pitchfork Ranch was at its apogee when Don and Johnny worked there, with more than 12,000 cattle in residence, and 200,000-plus acres, including a steer ranch in Wyoming and summer pasture in Kansas. It was probably one of the most highly publicized Texas ranches in the 1950s. The "Marlboro cowboys" came primarily from the Pitchfork and the nearby Lambshead ranches. The Roy Rogers movie *McIntosh and T.J.* was filmed there; visitors and dignitaries frequented the ranch; and many interviews and articles were widely published about it. The Pitchfork even purchased 43,000 acres of the next-door "Croton Break" country from the Matadors based on a D Burns-negotiated deal with the Matadors' John Mackenzie about the time Leroy, Don, and Johnny were working on the respective ranches.[11] In a recorded list of cowboys who have a history at the Pitchfork, Don Webb and Johnny Caldwell are proudly included in their ranks. (Murrah, 1983)

Johnny Caldwell, like Don, held many of the Pitchfork cowboys with whom he worked in high regard. These included Coy Drennan, Pistol Martin, "Sucker Rod" Osborne, John Ballard, and Don Blackwell. He remembers D Burns as a competent manager but of short temper. When Don and Johnny decided to leave the Pitchfork and join Leroy across the fence at the competing Matadors, D Burns was so mad when writing out their final paychecks that he smashed his pen on the signature line of the check, splashing ink all over two nervous exiting cowboys.[12]

Leroy, Don, and Johnny had now formed a "New Mexico cowboy tripartite" within the expansive pastures of the Matadors. They would get into minor trouble during weekend forays in the bar at the Matador Hotel, listen to Hank Williams live in the nearby community of Dickens, and dance with any local high school girls that they could round up or throw a rope over. Johnny thought the Matadors was "the best ranch that ever was." Most Matadors cowboys didn't think the cowhands from the Pitchfork, Four Sixes, or King ranches could measure up. (Probably this was a matter of competitive pride rather than reality.)

The last phase of Leroy's stay at the Matadors was his decision to settle down and marry Johnny Caldwell's sister, Nora. It was a huge turning point in his life that would settle him down. One can sense the synergy of this union—a good team. As this book is being written, they're approaching their fiftieth wedding anniversary. They've shared the good times and bad times for half a century and have had an amazing life together.

Since Leroy met Nora, previously married with two small sons, through her brother, Johnny, he was already well acquainted with her family. Nora and Johnny's father, Berlin Caldwell, ad-

Leroy and Nora, Matador Ranch (1951).

mired Leroy for many reasons. Berlin had been the Colfax County sheriff, knew the cattle business, was a good horseman, and sensed Leroy's integrity, energy, and horse skills. Leroy and Nora headed down to Fort Sumner in 1952, borrowing an old Dodge pickup from Joe McLaughlin. They got married as soon as they arrived, and, both being rather poor, they had to scratch around for a motel room that was cheap (an attic room was all they could afford). They then headed back toward the Matadors Ranch. Nora spent most of their first few months of marriage living in a Matador motel while Leroy was out with the wagon.

In the latter part of 1952, Leroy, Nora, Don Webb, and Johnny Caldwell left the "Texas cattle empire" of the Matadors and Pitchfork and headed back to New Mexico.[13] It was a great experience for the three, now in their twenties, to have worked with such professionals as the range cowboys, foremen, and managers of Matadors and the Pitchfork. The work was hard, in rough country, with unpredictable weather and cattle, but these were tough young men.

As Leroy and Nora pulled up stakes and headed back to New Mexico, they most likely would have agreed with J. Frank Dobie, the noted Texas folklorist/historian, who described the "Texas ranching paradise" in the following poem:

> *The devil was given permission one day*
> *To make him a land for his own special sway.*
> *He put thorns on all the bushes and trees*
> *And mixed up the sand with millions of fleas.*
> *He scattered tarantulas along all the roads*
> *Put spines on the cactus and horns on the toads.*
> *He lengthened the horn of the ol' Texas steer*
> *And added a foot to the jackrabbit's ear.*
> *He put three devils in every bronco steed*
> *And poisoned the feet of the centipede.*
> *The rattlesnake bites you, the scorpion stings,*
> *The mosquito torments you buzzing his wings.*
> *The heat of the summer is a hundred and ten,*
> *Too hot for the devil and too hot for men.*
> *And all who remained in that climate soon bore*
> *Cuts, bites, stings, scratches, and blisters galore.*

I lost a hundred thousand dollars yesterday . . . cattle went up a dollar a head and I didn't have a hundred thousand of 'em.

—**An eighty-dollar-a-month cowboy at the Pitchfork**

Johnny Caldwell, Nora Caldwell Webb, and Leroy at The Matadors (1952).

J. Frank Dobie's passion for the American Southwest, its art, and its literature knows no bounds. He grew up on a ranch in South Texas and "belonged to the soil." He was ostracized by his academic colleagues when, as a history professor at the University of Texas, he proposed a course strictly dedicated to the Southwest (in the 1930s within academic circles this was an act of cultural heresy). His response says it all:

> For me, the best talk in the world is made up of anecdotes, pictures of highly individualistic characters, tales with some relish of the saltiness of time in them, about men who "climb for water and dig for food and ride from hell to breakfast before daylight—or sit all day long in the shade of a broken-down chuck wagon and smoke them Meskin cigarillos." Consequently I avoid as much as possible academicians with their eternal shop talk and drawing room ornaments. I have sought the company of goat herders, lawyers with an eye for characters and a zest for hunting, trail drivers and women who know how to cook frijoles in a black iron pot. I belong to the soil myself, and the people of it are my people. I have certainly met many interesting talkers among them—and if they are interesting I don't care what else they are. We hear each other gladly. (Dobie, 1928) (Tinkle, 1978)

Dobie would have enjoyed the company of Leroy Webb and his cowboy friends. It's unfortunate that time and location prevented such a meeting between these "friends of the soil."

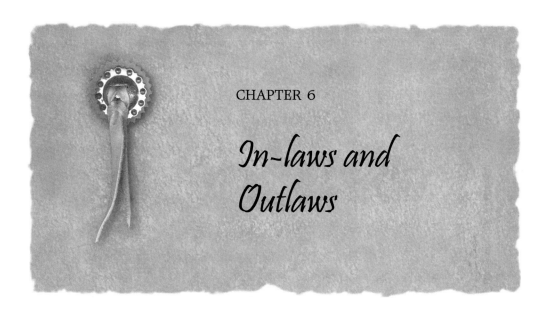

CHAPTER 6

In-laws and Outlaws

*T*he recently wedded Nora Caldwell and Leroy Webb left the Matadors in 1952, Bill Hemphill and Johnny Stevens bidding good-bye with, "You've always got a place here." The newlyweds were anxiously looking forward to returning to their northern New Mexico roots. They didn't know their future and had virtually no money. The big drought of the 1950s was enveloping the Southwest, and the cattle market was heading downward. Like most young married couples at the time, they were probably oblivious to these realities. They were happy chugging along the Texas highways, enthusiastic about the future.

Nora's family roots in many ways parallel those of the Webb clan. The combined histories of this young couple's predecessors provide an amazingly broad insight into nineteenth- and early twentieth-century pioneer life in America. The era was defined by closely knit families, mostly first- or second-generation Americans who emigrated from northern and southern Europe and moved west in covered wagons to seek new opportunities in the country's period of westward expansion. The lure was gold, cattle, farming, and the opportunity for a better life. These settlers came primarily from Georgia, Alabama, Tennessee, and contiguous areas. The creation of an independent Texas following Sam Houston's victory at San Jacinto, the vast new U.S. territory realized by the Treaty of Guadalupe Hidalgo and the

Louisiana Purchase, the exhaustion following the Civil War, and the diminishing role of Indian dominance in the area were all catalysts which drove these settlers, entrepreneurs, and venture capitalists toward the Southwest. The history of the Caldwell family is written on tombstones from the Isle of Wight, to the Scottish Highlands, to the Cherokee Nation, to Georgia, Tennessee, Benton and Washington counties in Arkansas, and ultimately to Ocate, Springer, and Cimarron, New Mexico.

The descendants of the Caldwell (also Colwell, Culwell, or Coldwell) families are traced back to the early 1800s. James Caldwell, a Tennessean,

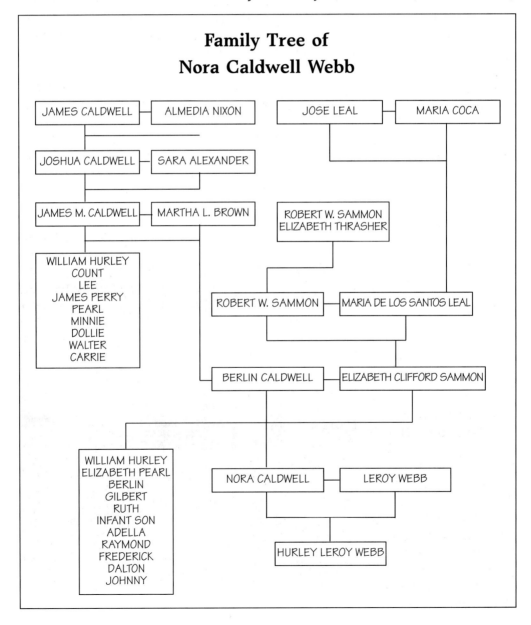

Family Tree of
Nora Caldwell Webb

married Almedia Nixon, who was distantly related to two U.S. presidents, Andrew Jackson and Martin Van Buren. Their son was Joshua Caldwell, who married Sara Alexander. This union produced a son, James Martin Caldwell, Nora's paternal grandfather. James M. Caldwell was only eleven years old when his father, Joshua, was killed in the Civil War. Their home was burned five times during the war, and young James Caldwell knew nothing but hardship during his early days. He was self-educated, reading and learning by the light of campfires. He married Martha Brown in Arkansas in 1877; the two then migrated to New Mexico by covered wagon. After a short stint back in the Cherokee Nation of Oklahoma they returned to New Mexico, again by covered wagon, and camped for a while on the Ponil River south of Cimarron. They later moved their camp into Cimarron Canyon, then progressed to Vanderitas, where they homesteaded several hundred acres. With the help of sons Berlin and Count, they built a house and made a modest living by farming. They then built a house in Springer on Maxwell Avenue, where they spent the rest of their lives.

James M. Caldwell was in the cattle business in Springer, sold cattle, and shared a livery stable with Berlin. They sold cattle to a prominent citizen in Springer, Pat Garrett, who shortly thereafter became sheriff in Lincoln County, New Mexico. It was there that he gained notoriety by killing Billy the Kid.[1] (Garrett, 1954)

On the maternal side of Nora's ancestors was the Sammon family. Robert Sammon, born in 1837, married Elizabeth Thrasher and lived in Georgia. Her family opened the first dry goods store in Atlanta, Johnson and Thrasher. This union produced a son, Robert W. Sammon, Nora's maternal grandfather. Bob Sammon was born in Georgia in 1861, the first year of the Civil War. He eventually migrated to New Mexico at a relatively young age and settled near the small town of Ocate, near Mora. He

James M. and Martha Brown Caldwell (1911).

married a beautiful woman, Maria de Los Santos Leal, of Hispanic and Indian heritage. Bob Sammon was a powerfully built young man and was a successful businessman (he owned a sawmill and ran cattle). Through his marriage to Maria, he had ties to the Mora Land Grant, which was a part of the many land grants awarded from the Mexican territorial governor prior to the Treaty of Guadalupe Hidalgo.

These land grants under subsequent U.S. territorial control were contested and became the primary cause of unrest in the area. Bob Sammon was, therefore, in the center of the disputed areas between the "Grantor interests and the Settlers." Sammon always carried a gun and had been involved in an altercation in Florsheim's store in Springer when a man tried to take his gun from him.[2] Sammon threw him halfway across the store. With his reputation of being a quiet but physically strong and tough individual, he had been active on behalf of the grantor interests in ejecting settlers who had encroached on the Mora Land Grant and were illegally taking timber from within its boundaries. Sammon always said he "would die with his boots on."

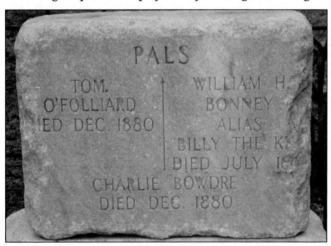

Gravestone of Billy the Kid, Fort Sumner, New Mexico.

In early December of 1910, he had been in the small village of Guadalupita attempting to slow down the rogue

---

Pat Garrett and James M. Caldwell were well acquainted, did business together, and shared many experiences. Garrett later became sheriff of Lincoln County, New Mexico, to the south of Cimarron, and killed Billy the Kid in July of 1881. Garrett and the Kid knew each other well. There is still controversy on how and exactly why Garrett killed the Kid. Garrett, born in 1850, was a cowboy in Texas, buffalo hunter near Fort Griffin, Texas, county commissioner in Uvalde, Texas (a friend being a young city attorney, John Nance Garner, future vice president of the U.S.), former Texas Ranger, and the sheriff of Lincoln County when he killed the Kid.

Frenchy McCormick was a dancehall girl in Tascosa, Texas, during its boom days in the late 1870s and early 1880s. Tascosa was a Wild West town known as the "Cowboy Capital of the Panhandle," and was frequented by Charles Goodnight of Goodnight-Loving Trail fame, by Pat Garrett, who was hired by the big cow outfits to control lawlessness and "mavericking" of unbranded calves by the many cowhands in the area, and by Billy the Kid, drawn to the town with its gambling rooms, saloons, and dancehalls. Frenchy McCormick told many stories about all of these characters to my mother and dad before her death in the early 1930s.

cutting of timber. The settlers had threatened to kill him many times, but he never took them too seriously. About 3:30 in the afternoon he rode off the Guadalupita Mesa with his sixteen-year-old son. As they approached a deep, narrow mountain trail, he and his son dismounted and were leading the horses through the timber down the trail. Three rifle shots rang out, all piercing the back of Bob Sammon. His son pulled out the six-shooter from his father's holster and fired in the direction of the hidden assailants. Bob Sammon then directed his son to go get help. The boy rushed down the trail to a nearby sawmill. When he and a few men arrived back at the scene, they carried his father's mortally wounded body toward the sawmill, where he drew his last breath.

*Robert W. Sammon
(Born November 1861; killed December 1910)*

Bob Sammon was buried at nearby Halls Peak Cemetery next to his wife, Maria, who had died three years earlier. He left a daughter, Elizabeth Clifford Sammon, Nora's mother, who was twelve years old when her father was murdered. Elizabeth later married one of James M. Caldwell's sons, Berlin Caldwell. This union produced twelve children, Nora among them.

Berlin Caldwell was born in 1883, grew up in Springer, and became a lawman and well-respected citizen. He and his brother, Count, had traveled to New Mexico in a covered wagon via the Texas Panhandle, Clayton, New Mexico, and then into the Springer area. The two boys grew up helping their father, James M. Caldwell, in the freight and cattle business. Both boys, still only ten to twelve years old, would drive a team of four or more horses taking freight and supplies up to the Baldy Mountain gold mine (following Ute Creek up through the Atmore Ranch), over to Elizabeth Town ("E" Town) in the Moreno Valley, and other locations in the area. At the time, "E" Town was booming, with a population exceeding 7,000 people, as was the nearby mining town at the foot of Mt. Baldy. Berlin then became a deputy sheriff for Colfax County in his early twenties, eventually becoming sheriff. He was an excellent lawman and was involved in apprehending many of the "bad men" at the time, including rustlers, murderers, and parts of the old Ketchum

74
*The Last
Cowboy*

THE SPRINGER TIMES
A Progressive Weekly Newspaper

Volume 2   SPRINGER, NEW MEXICO, THURSDAY, APRIL 2, 1914   No. 17

DEMOCRATIC CANDIDATES

FLORENCIO TRUJILLO
FOR CLERK

J. M. CALDWELL
FOR TRUSTEE

ANASTACIO HERRERA
FOR TRUSTEE

SIM BROWN
FOR MAYOR

I. C. FLOERSHEIM
FOR TRUSTEE

T. E. VALDEZ.
FOR TRUSTEE.

*Democratic candidates
James M. Caldwell and
I. C. Florsheim,
Springer, New Mexico
(1914).*

*Sheriff Berlin Caldwell at
Springer (circa 1923).*

gang. Knowing that his father-in-law, Bob Sammon, was a victim of the Land Grant-Settlers War, he was cognizant of the dangers that went with the job. Berlin, with his twelve children, was a much respected family man, lawman, and citizen.

Berlin's brother, Count Caldwell, was a marvelous orator who recorded his recollections of Berlin and the Caldwell and Sammon histories shortly before his death in 1977. Count married Bessie Sammon, the sister of Berlin's wife, Elizabeth, producing a number of "double cousins." One of these cousins is Evelyn Marsh, the daughter of Count and Bessie, who currently resides in Austin.[3] As a young man, Count got into an al-

Count Caldwell (1910).

tercation with a local tough who had followed Count outside a dancehall, hitting him on the head with the butt of his pistol. He then pointed his pistol toward Count, who responded by quickly drawing a pistol from his holster, killing the intruder. Self-defense was properly claimed by Count's representative, Fred Lambert, and Count was never accused of any wrongdoing.[4] Berlin was widely known in the communities of Springer and Cimarron, primarily through his law enforcement days followed by cattle raising and philanthropic endeavors.

The old St. James Hotel in Cimarron then and now houses the memories of many of the area's characters during Berlin's time and before. The founder of the hotel, Henri Lambert, was born in Bordeaux, France, in 1838 and immigrated to America in 1858. He then became the chef for U.S. Grant. President Abraham Lincoln, having heard from General Grant about Lambert's flair for fine food, took him out of the field during the Civil War to work in the White House, naming him "head chef."

Following the war, Henri caught "gold fever." He migrated to New Mexico, joining the gold rush in "E" Town. Then in 1870 he trailed over to Cimarron and opened the St. James. He freighted all furniture, decorations, and supplies from St. Joseph, Missouri, by ox-teams. This old building is quite prominently mentioned in the history of New Mexico, and there are records of many killings in the old saloon. It was the "stomping ground" for such noted characters as Lucien Maxwell, Kit Carson, Clay Allison, Davy Crockett (cousin of Davy Crockett of the Alamo fame), Tom Tobin, Tom

Boggs, and many others, both good and bad. Cimarron was a good location for the hotel because it was a stage stop on the old Santa Fe Trail, a trading post for the Utes and Apaches, and an outlet for the cattlemen, freighters, and miners, over into the Taos country and Fort Union, to the southeast.

Fred Lambert, son of Henri and Mary Lambert, was born in the St. James Hotel on January 23, 1887, four years after Berlin Caldwell. The two became lifelong friends. Fred gave a stirring eulogy at Berlin's funeral some seventy-six years later.[5]

Fred Lambert grew up in an era of violence. During his youth, he served as bartender at his father's St. James Hotel—a place where no fewer than twenty-six men died in wild gun battles.

On one bright, sunny day in 1903, sixteen-year-old Fred dashed out to the corral at Cimarron and saddled his horse. Within minutes he had spurred the animal to a gallop out over the rolling prairies southeast of town. Lambert's ride had been prompted by Colfax County Sheriff Marion Littrell. Littrell had phoned the sheriff in Cimarron, and Lambert took the call. Littrell told him two killers had murdered a man in Las Vegas, New Mexico, and were headed toward Cimarron. "I told him the sheriff in Cimarron was sick," Lambert said, "and I asked him if I could go out and intercept them myself. Well, he kind of hesitated for a minute, and then said it would be okay. I rode out of Cimarron. Pretty soon I saw this buckboard wagon bouncing across the prairie about three miles out of town. I circled around until I was behind them, and when they started to cross a creek, I rode up and told them they were under arrest. One of the fellows had a Winchester cradled in his lap. He started to raise it, but the barrel caught on a piece of the wagon framework. I pulled out my old Smokey and got one shot off. It hit him in the arm. They didn't offer any resistance after that, and I took them into town and had them put in jail. When Sheriff Littrell came up to get them later on, he issued me a commission as deputy sheriff of Cimarron."

Thus, Fred Lambert became one of the youngest lawmen in the Southwest. In 1906 he buckled on his pistol for the New Mexico Territorial Mounted Police—first cousin to the Texas Rangers—as one of nine men who began to bring law and order to the bawdy territory. He wore that badge until New Mexico became a state in 1912. Then Lambert was a special deputy for the state, a Cimarron city marshal, a New Mexico game warden, Colfax County constable, a New Mexico cattle and brand inspector, and a U.S. marshal riding for four years through the rugged Sangre de Cristo Mountains in northern New Mexico.

Helluva country—some people came here for their health, others because it wasn't healthy where they were living and found it was a helluva lot less healthy when they got here.

—Old Cimarron cowpuncher

*Left and above: The old Grist Mill.
Cimarron, New Mexico (2001).*

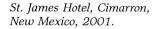

Cimarron, New Mexico, is
very much a historical
treasure of western lore:
center of the Colfax County
War; proximate to old Fort
Union, an anchor outpost
for the old Santa Fe Trail;
home to many historical
figures, such as Lucien
Maxwell, Kit Carson, Davy
Crockett II, Henri and Fred
Lambert, and others; site
of the landmark St. James
Hotel; headquarters for
Philmont Boy Scout camp;
and center of gravity for
many of the old cowboys,
horse traders, and ranching
families. Much of the history is inscribed on the
tombstones of the
Cimarron Cemetery.

*St. James Hotel, Cimarron,
New Mexico, 2001.*

*St. James Hotel, Historical
Guest Book and Registration
area.*

In all those years Lambert never killed a man. "When you're face to face with an outlaw, nine times out of ten, you can just unbuckle your gunbelt and say, 'I'm coming over and talk to you'," he said. "Like as not the fellow you're after has killed someone, and he doesn't want to be hunted down for killing a lawman. I've done a lot of fellows that way." (Lambert, 1948)

The saga of Fred Lambert didn't end when he unpinned his lawman's badge and put away his pearl-handled pistol for the last time. He became a poet, artist, and author. The famous western artist Charles Russell was one of his good friends and

Fred Lambert (1968).

admirers, and University of Texas professor J. Frank Dobie took note of his talents. Lambert authored a book, *Bygone Days of the Old West* (1948), which is a western classic. Dobie introduced the book by stating that the verse inside "deserves to stand up to Pecos Bill and Paul Bunyan"—a wonderful tribute to Lambert's talented recitation of southwestern history.

The two lifelong friends Berlin Caldwell and Fred Lambert, as former lawmen (Colfax County sheriff and U.S. marshal), could spin stories for hours. Berlin and Elizabeth Caldwell named their eleventh child (Nora's brother) after Fred Lambert.[6]

Berlin Caldwell died March 21, 1963. Fred Lambert, then seventy-six years old, had lost a true friend and fellow lawman. His eulogy to Berlin is a reflection of their friendship and the era they shared.

> *BERLIN, didn't think you would be taken out "so soon" but guess the RANGE BOSS over THERE was short-handed and in need of some of the OLD TIMERS he could depend upon.*

BERLIN, if you get a chance to tell the RANGE BOSS to cut us out some good, gentle ponies and fatten-them-up in the REMUDA, so that when we arrive there riding will be a lot easier for us old timers that sorta got a hitch in our get-along and don't move as spry as we used to . . . Let us work around the main headquarters where he will bestow HIS BLESS-INGS on us from DAY-TO-DAY.

The Caldwell and Sammon families endured exceptionally hard times typical in early New Mexico, when it was still a territory. They exemplify the pioneering spirit of the people who had the patience, fortitude, and grit to meet the challenges that faced them. Their descendants have honored them by memorializing the two family histories, which provide an incredible volume of information on both families, spanning over two hundred years. Biography is history, and the documentation of these interesting family stories is attributed to those who took the time to record and perpetuate the events of this era.

Not many years ago it took a pioneer
With his prairie schooner and ox team
A long lonesome half year's journey
To cross this mighty country of ours.
Then a new land, wild, rent, and
Broken up, with a rough track called
The Santa Fe Trail
Ever leading on to the West—
To the Land of the Setting Sun,
A land so strange and new,
Seemingly but half finished
By the Hand of God.
These rugged pioneers blazed
A new country for you
and for me.

—Fred Lambert

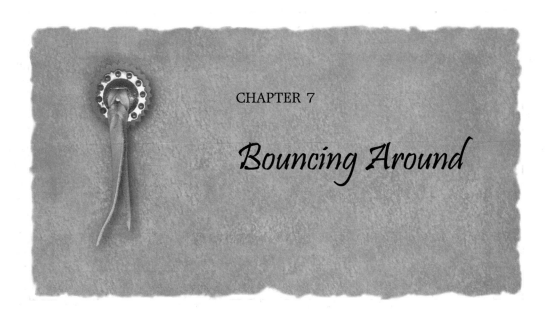

CHAPTER 7

Bouncing Around

Newlyweds Leroy and Nora Caldwell Webb bounced along the New Mexico roadways in a thoroughly used car, this couple rich in family histories but financially dirt poor. Their married life started at the Matadors, and their future centered around ranches and cowboying—somewhere, someplace. By this time, Leroy had developed extraordinary cowboying skills. The old-time cowhands who had mentored him during the past six years at Texas and New Mexico ranches had served him well. Still in his early twenties, he was a skilled horseman, a superb roper, tough, and oblivious to the pain associated with such endeavors. It also was apparent that he was a gifted communicator with horses. He already had successfully broken scores of horses, and with such skills, even though the cowhand profession in the early 1950s was somewhat depressed, he was in demand. The confluence of the couple's background and their respective personalities made a perfect match. It takes an extraordinary woman to move around the country and endure long stretches of separation during calving, branding, gathering, and roundup times.

Leroy's teenage years were typical for young cowhands at that time. They followed the rules while on duty, committing themselves to hard work, dependability, no alcohol or women, and putting in the long hours that the job demanded. Payday and occasional visits to "town" normally meant hell-raising, spending all of their hard-earned money, chasing any available female, drinking and dancing, then returning to the "wagon" to repeat the process. Leroy was no exception. He was a handsome, energetic young cowboy, a respected professional long before his time, and he perfectly fit the western cowboy image so vividly portrayed in western art, western music, and western movies.

Nora—religious, well-grounded, and very attractive—reformed his carousing. Leroy respected and responded to his new "wagon boss." He could not have picked a better partner.

Their early days as a couple were occupied by drifting—seeing new country and following the amateur rodeo circuit. Leroy's reputation as a skilled cowboy was on the rise. He and Nora loved the scene. They were surrounded by new friends, good cowboys, and the excitement of the circuit. Unfortunately, such an endeavor is not one of financial enrichment. Leroy was anxious to get back on a ranch to break horses and work cattle, not make a fortune. He worked at the UU Bar, then the Fort Union Ranch. One weekend in late 1953 he participated in an amateur rodeo at Fort Sumner, New Mexico. Showcasing his skills as a bull rider and roper, he drew the attention of a Texas-born cowboy, Harper McFarland. "Harp" was some twelve years his senior and managed the giant San Cristobal Ranch near Lamy, New Mexico.

Harp McFarland is one of the more interesting old-time cowboys that I have had the pleasure to interview.[1] He was born in Ballinger, Texas, in 1921, followed his cowboy father around various Central Texas ranches, graduated from Mineral Wells High School in 1938, then started cowboying on his own at the Brooks Ranch near Ozona. He was developing into a skilled cowhand, working for the Sawyer Cattle Company, when World War II roped him in. He served in the 45th Division (Armored) throughout the war, moving through southern Europe and eventually into Germany. It should

Newlyweds at Cimarron (1952).

be noted that many cowhands joined Harp in World War II, creating a shortage of available cowhands in the American West during that period.

Following the war, Harp returned to the Sawyer Cattle Company at their Bar S Ranch near San Angelo (Barnhart and Big Lake area). The Sawyer Cattle Company purchased the giant San Cristobal Ranch in 1948, an 81,000-acre spread south of Santa Fe near the small New Mexico

Harp McFarland, Stanley, New Mexico (2002).

towns of Lamy and Galisteo. Harp pulled up stakes in Texas and moved to the San Cristobal, eventually becoming manager.

During a foray to Fort Sumner for a weekend rodeo, he watched Leroy perform. After the event, they discussed the possibility of Leroy hiring on at the San Cristobal. A couple of weeks later, Leroy showed up and started breaking horses. As there were no accommodations for married cowboys, Nora returned to Springer while Leroy lived in the ranch bunkhouse. Harp instinctively knew that he had hired a top-notch cowhand. They began a life-long friendship and one of mutual respect. Leroy remembers:

> I got along real good with Harp. He got to be a good friend of mine—and
> we're good friends to this day, fifty years just about. And I still
> see him regularly. He comes to see me and I go to see him. Through
> the years he stayed at that same ranch through about four different own-
> ers—about fifty years. He retired last year. He's eighty years old and sure
> enough a good man—a good hand.

Leroy recalls his bunkhouse days at the San Cristobal: missing his wife but loving his work, breaking a string of three-year-old horses and colts. He and the other San Cristobal cowhands (Sam Sessions and Glen McFarland, Harp's brother, are two that he prominently mentions) worked hard, broke horses and worked cattle, then participated in amateur rodeos that Nora would occasionally attend. Sessions' wife was a great cook, so Leroy ate well, and he filled seven days per week breaking horses, cowboying, and rodeo performing. He was becoming increasingly accomplished at all three. While breaking colts, he would take the colts out of the corral and, after working them for a while, run them back toward the pen and jump them over the fence instead of opening the gate (much to the chagrin of ranch management, who curtailed such a practice). This was classic Leroy Webb.

When I told Harp McFarland why I selected Leroy as my choice for the figurative "last cowboy," his quick retort was, "You couldn't have picked a greater man!"

In early 1954, Leroy's skill in breaking horses led to his transfer to the Sawyer Bar S Ranch near Barnhart, which had an immediate need for his services. He and Nora, with an adored newborn son, Hurley, settled in at the Sawyer Bar S, which furnished a house for the young family. It was a good life—breaking horses, having Nora and Hurley nearby, and doing what he did best. Shortly after his transfer to Texas, a prominent Texas entrepreneur who eventually controlled Braniff Airlines, William Blakley, purchased the entire Texas and New Mexico holdings of the Sawyer Cattle Company. Blakley, a high-profile businessman and a former U.S. senator, was widely respected for his integrity and philanthropy. Both Leroy and Harp speak highly of him to this day as a wonderful and caring individual who judged people strictly on their ability and integrity, not their net worth.

Blakley instantly connected with his Texas ranch cowhand, Leroy, and was instrumental in getting young Hurley premier medical treatment (the "yearling" son of Leroy and Nora was born partially blind as well as with a partial physical impairment). Hurley's life is such a marvelous and inspirational story that I've dedicated a chapter to him (Chapter 11).

Leroy began breaking Bar S horses full time, and it was a rewarding job.

So we got moved in and I went to headquarters and started breaking these colts—had an old board, round corral. The first bronc I started, he was wild, running around the corral. I had a snubbing post in the middle of

Bill Blakley, owner of the Sawyer Cattle Company, was born in 1889 during a covered wagon trek in Missouri. He became a self-educated accountant and lawyer, eventually gaining control of Braniff Airlines. He grew up hard, working as a farm and ranch hand during the depression. He said he was pleased to be "born into a humble family and live during the depression. It was a blessing because it taught me the value of hard work." Blakley was involved with many industries, including insurance, legal, airline, and ranching. In the 1950s he was appointed to the U.S. Senate by Texas Governor Allan Shivers to replace Senator Price Daniel, who would run for governor.

"Bill Blakley is a close personal friend and will make a fine senator. He's a very modest and unassuming man—but a very effective one."

—*Lyndon Johnson*
Senate Majority Leader

the corral.[2] I got my rope and got in there—roped this ol' horse running around, roped him and tied him to the snubbing post, wrapped him around the post. He pawed, fought, squealed, and choked for a while. When you get up to 'em, get a soft-type rope over his neck and get his hind foot tied up. That's the only way we knew to do it in those days . . . Anyway, I got his foot tied up, sacked him out, got a hackamore on him, wooled him around a little.[3] When he would stand still enough, I'd get a saddle on him and cinch him up—and he threw another little fit and fell down. I was already cinched up. So, I untied the rope off his hind foot, got astraddle of him, bugered him, and he come up while I was in the middle of him and he was a'bucking, and a'pitching and a'squawling around that corral. He ran into the corral fence with the back of his neck—hit it in the boards about the middle of the fence and broke it and went through. The top boards were up against the saddle horn, and that stopped him. I reached over them top boards, over the fence, and slapped him in the face to get him back in the pen. I didn't want that big sucker outside. Anyway, sure enough he come back in—bucked around the corral a little more, then got to loping around, and everything was fine.

Such was the daily routine of breaking horses during this era.[4]

Leroy, Nora, and Hurley were at the Texas Bar S for two years, with Leroy making a premium salary of $200 per month. (Blakley believed breaking horses justified a bonus because of the skill and endurance required of the cowhand.) As at the Sawyer San Cristobal Ranch, Leroy would spend his weekends working local Texas rodeos. Virtually all of the small towns in the area, such as Barnhart, Ozona, Sonora, Junction, and San Angelo, had weekend and holiday rodeos. The rodeo was one of the most popular sources of entertainment, and plenty of area cowboys wanted to participate.

The Bar S had an arena at the headquarters; so, many evenings after work, Leroy would go into the arena with just "ol' ranch horses" and practice roping, further honing his skills. After years of roping cattle in the open range, in canyons, and in brush country, he thought arena roping would be easy. The calves were fence-limited and that, thought Leroy, made it a "slam dunk." He then figured out that it was not that easy, as speed was the requirement for becoming a winner, not necessarily the criteria for open-range roping. Therefore, Leroy practiced intensely on his timing of roping the animal, throwing it to the ground, and tying it. There is no event that requires more horse-rider coordination. Leroy's extraordinary ability to communicate with his roping horses, plus his athletic skill, put him into the select category of the area's most talented ropers.[5] One of the roping horses that he devel-

---

I was eyes to the blind
And feet was I to the lame.
—Book of Job
(One of Bill Blakley's favorite biblical quotations)

oped, "Monkey," was sold to a champion roper, Cotten Lee, who hauled this horse to rodeos all over the country.

In 1956, after a few years at the Bar S, making the big money of $200 monthly, Leroy, Nora, and Hurley bought a new car and headed back to their native New Mexico country. He went to work for the Driggers Land and Cattle Company north of Santa Rosa. Ironically, Buster Driggers owned the Bar Y Ranch, now a Singleton Ranch, which Leroy currently manages. Leroy would head into Santa Rosa for weekend rodeo competitions in steer and calf-roping events. It was there that he met a great old cowboy of Harp McFarland's vintage, Jack Kyle. Kyle is another one of those "great old irreplaceable cowboy characters." He was raised in the Santa Rosa area, fought in World War II on many of the Pacific islands, then returned to cowboying in New Mexico following the war. He was (and is) a top cowboy, horse trainer, breeder, and member of the Cowboy Hall of Fame. Jack and Leroy did some team roping and began a lifelong friendship which flourishes to this day.[6]

We got to roping together at Santa Rosa and beating everyone pretty good. We went around to other places. He had some sure enough good horses. He had an ol' stud horse named Silver Skip—big palomino horse, big stout horse, one of the best-looking horses I've ever seen up to then. A calf horse, a sure enough good calf horse, and he would loan him to me to rope on at these rodeos. That sucker would run and stop—I mean he could stop—and get back. I did pretty good riding him in the calf-roping events. At that time, I never had had a horse of my own. I had to depend on riding somebody else's horse. I was breaking horses for everybody in the world, but I didn't have one of my own.

Leroy also became friends with two other area cowboys, Hugh Cooper and Sonny Burford. As Leroy had no horse or much cash but lots of skill, it was no problem getting sponsors and borrowing someone else's horse to perform.

A couple of years later, working for the Driggers Bar Y and rodeoing part-time, Leroy met a "fella" through Jack Kyle by the name of Shelly Hays. Hays was an old-time cowboy who had a modestly sized ranch near Clines Corner, west of the Bar Y and south of the San Cristobal. He had worked at the old Bell Ranch near Tucumcari at the Los Caros Camp (now the Hampton Ranch) before being able to purchase a piece of land near Palma, New Mexico, in the late 1940s. Leroy had the opportunity to run this ranch by himself, as Hays was moving to nearby Moriarity, New Mexico, in semi-retirement. Leroy, always self-reliant, enjoyed the role as a "loner" cowboy. Jack Kyle and Shelly Hays would help out on occasions, but Leroy ran the show. It was rugged country, lots of breaks and cedars, but a good cow outfit. Leroy was now twenty-five years old with more than eleven years of intense cowhand experience and flirting with rodeos along the way. He put his now totally blind son, Hurley, on a horse, and the two of them plus Nora

Leroy gathering cattle in the rugged New Mexico break country (1958).

enjoyed some good times watching Hurley trying to emulate his cowboy father.[7]

It was on the Hays Ranch that Leroy got "into the horse business." A cowboy who had previously worked there, a fellow by the name of Gary Thompson, left with his mare shortly before Leroy arrived. He told Leroy he had left the mare's colt on the ranch, and Leroy could take possession if he could catch him.

> *Man, this colt was wild as a rabbit. She just ran wild in that cedar country—no other horses, no nothing. And she'd been there a couple of years at least, or longer. So, I went to trying to figure out how to get that buckskin mare, a pretty nice-looking mare. She was wild, and you'd seldom see her. I just watched, and one day I happened to be riding up in some rough creeks and saw her run off. She ran down towards the windmill and the corner of the pasture. I cinched up and took out after her at top speed to try to rope her. She ran up in that corner, and I had her trapped then. She turned around and come back out of that corner over the top of me. As she come by, I roped her, and I mean the wreck was on.*

*I jerked her down—she ran in and out of wherever. I'd jerk her back—
she'd get up and run the other way, and I'd jerk her down. We went all
the way to the house in this manner. I finally got her to camp that way,
on the end of that rope. She would run one way; we'd get a little farther. I
finally got her in the pen. I finally got the rope off. Then I went about
breaking that mare. She was mine—the first one I ever really owned. I
broke her to ride. As always, I'd get her, tie her foot up before she'd get a
way to hurt you, then get her saddled up and let her foot down, get on
her, and away we'd go! She became a real good horse, and I felt good
about owning that mare.*

*The first registered quarter horses I owned, we bought while we were
working for Shelly Hays. Shelly had these two mares of Shoemaker breeding that were bred to a Wiescamp stud that Shelly had bought from Hank.
The stud, Sirlette by Skipper W, was a real nice horse. Shelly offered to
sell me these mares for $1,500. I didn't have $15, much less $1,500, but
I wanted these mares. So, I went to the bank in Santa Rosa for a loan.
They listened to my plan and decided I was way out on a limb and
turned me down. Nora was working for a man, Manuel Medley, who had
a restaurant and a big interest in the bank. We told him our problem; he
gathered his hat and said, "Come with me." We went right back to this
bank. He told them something, and all of a sudden they thought my plan
wasn't so bad after all. They loaned me the $1,500, and I was in the
horse business. That summer the mares had colts. That fall I sold one
mare and colt for $1,750, paid off my note, and had one mare and colt
free and clear plus $200 in my pocket.*

After about a year or two working the Shelly Hays Ranch, Walt Disney
Studios appeared at the ranch to make a movie. The film centered around a
world champion jumper named Natacial. His nickname was "The Horse with
the Flying Tail" because his tail would fly up into the air every time he
jumped. Leroy rode a look-alike horse and did some jumping with him while
they were filming. They shot for several days, using quite a bit of the film in
the movie.

Leroy continued to work the Hays Ranch, taking care of the cattle and
working the horses. There was one "little ol' plain country horse" that Leroy
took a liking to. He trained it to stop, turn around, back up, and a few other
little tricks; so, Shelly suggested that they enter him in some horse shows.
This was a new experience for Leroy, and one that would have a pronounced
effect on his future—even to this day.

*I'd never seen a horse show and never been to a horse show. I didn't
know what they did or tried to do, but ol' Jack Kyle knew about this stuff.
By then he was one of the top showmen in horse shows—roping, all that*

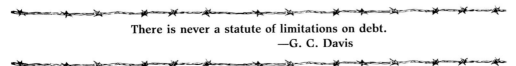

There is never a statute of limitations on debt.
—G. C. Davis

Leroy Webb on the world champion jumping horse in the Walt Disney movie
Horse with the Flying Tail *(1950s).*

*show business stuff. Anyway, I had this little plain ol' horse who I called
"Pete." There was a little ol' town not too far from the ranch named
Palma. So, Shelly named the horse "Palma Pete." We took him on over
to Jack's place in Santa Rosa, and he told me what you were supposed to
do at them horse shows, especially in the reining contest. They had these
patterns you had to run and that kind of stuff . . . It was getting towards
the fall time of the year when the New Mexico State Fair opened in Albuquerque in September. So, Shelly entered ol' Palma Pete and me in the junior ring. (He was just a four-year-old horse and was in the junior class.)
The crowd at the New Mexico State Fair, the horses, and me—none of us
knew what was going on! I was supposed to run down there, stop, slide,
stand, roll back, run the figure eight, stuff like that. Well, it ended up that
we almost won the whole deal. We came in second at the New Mexico
State Fair and had a really good time! I figured that might be something
I wanted to do.*

The year was 1959, and one of the top breeders in the country was at that fair. His name was Hank Wiescamp from Alamosa, Colorado, and he had a national reputation for breeding, raising, and training some of the best quarter horse stallions in the world. Hank's son, Ron Wiescamp, happened to watch Leroy and Palma Pete perform and mentioned to his father that this young cowboy and "plain ol' country horse" had put on quite a show. Moreover, Jack Kyle and Hank Wiescamp were well acquainted. So, Leroy's name began to emerge in the Wiescamp "talking circles." Hank offered Leroy a job in Alamosa to help him train about a hundred of his show horses. Leroy and Nora talked it over, but Leroy loved working at the Shelly Hays Ranch. He ran the show, had lots of freedom, a house, his own mare, and a wife and son close by—and all the money he needed at $200 a month. He therefore turned down the offer, loaded up Palma Pete, drove out of the State Fair gates, and headed back to Clines Corner and the lonely Hays Ranch headquarters, where there were no phones or any means of communication.

When Hank Wiescamp returned to his headquarters in Alamosa, he found that he had a good-looking palomino stud that his guys had been trying to break for some time without success. Hank called his friend, Jack Kyle, and asked him to drive over to Alamosa from Santa Rosa to advise him on what could be done with this stud. Both admired the conformation and physical quality of the palomino, but he was mean and no one could ride him. Jack told Hank Wiescamp that there was a "feller down in New Mexico who could ride him." Well, Hank never sent horses out, particularly stallions; so, he kicked the dirt, looked up at the sky, rubbed his belly, and pondered for a while, finally consenting to let Jack Kyle take the horse down to New Mexico to see if this "young feller," Leroy Webb, could do anything to salvage him.

> *Well, sure enough, Jack brought this palomino stud out to Shelly's place. I went to riding this horse and working with him and in a couple of months, I had him going real good. He was riding good and a real good-looking horse. When the horse was ready to go back, Jack came and picked up me and the horse, and we headed for Colorado. That was the first time I had met Hank personally. We unloaded him out of the trailer, saddled him up, and I rode him around for Hank. He thought we looked pretty good, especially when they couldn't even get close to him when he left there. Anyway, Hank wanted Jack and me both to stay there and train horses for him.*

When Leroy returned to his Hays headquarters in late fall of 1959, one

---

Leroy and Nora lived life very simply, as did most range cowboy families of the day. Living every day to the maximum was their lifestyle, not necessarily the accumulation of wealth.

---

of the worst snowstorms in history hit central and northern New Mexico. Leroy couldn't get around. He could get to the barn to milk the cows, but couldn't get out to the herd because of the deep snow. Leroy decided to use the good-looking two-year-old filly he had bought from Jack Kyle (a registered and expensive horse). He and the filly tried to move out into the pastures with no success. The horse would push through the snow for a while—then just "give out." They were isolated for a week or so. Leroy was finally able to coax the unruly filly into being a "pack horse," then put feed and salt on the pack saddle and led her through the snow to the drifting cattle.

Meanwhile, Shelly Hays hired a man with a Caterpillar to try to get into the ranch. It took the Cat driver and Shelly almost ten days to get into the ranch and make contact with Leroy. He then joined them on the Caterpillar in making the rounds to try to save the cattle. It turns out that the cattle had sought refuge under the cedars to weather out the storm. They "had eaten the bark off every cedar they could reach." At any rate, they started feeding the cattle off the Caterpillar. This process continued for several days until the snow started to melt; then they had to contend with deep mud. They got Shelly's four-wheel power wagon with a front winch to make it through the mud, having to winch from tree to tree in order to get to the cattle and feed them. In the end they did save the cattle, but it took a toll on the horses and cowboys.

So, here was Leroy in the spring of 1960: twenty-seven years old, a wife, a seven-year-old son, a talent for horses and cattle, a real love for the rodeo circuit, and an offer of a promising new career in Colorado. It was time to decide which fork in the road to take.

CHAPTER 8

Rodeos

*R*odeo participation was an important part of young Leroy's professional and personal evolution, beginning when he was just eleven years old and lasting through his mid-forties. The history of the American rodeo is reflective of the cowboy's evolution in demonstrating his competitive skills, starting with the working "range" cowboy, who competed in local ranch events, to a participant in amateur "purse" rodeos, then a semi-professional "weekend" rodeo performer, and ultimately to a full-time rodeo professional (very seldom skilled in working ranch cattle).

American rodeo dates back to the 1860s and 1870s, when tired range cowboys would "play" at the end of a long trail drive or at a railhead once the cattle were safely on their way to market. *Rodeo*, a Spanish-derived word meaning "to surround," provided a forum to display competitive skills between range cowboys. These contests, which led to American rodeo tradition, is reflective of ancient history. In Homer's *Iliad* there were games "for the speed of foot of horsemen" and "the fast running horses who were the pride of those raced in this country," and "the biggest prizes had been left for the horse race." (Lattimore, 1961) The Olympics model likely had its origins from these ancient stories.[1] This is an indication of athletic competition enduring throughout history in spite of wars and disruptions. The American rodeo perpetuates this tradition.

The 1880s and 1890s were the decades when the open range and big ranch operatives prospered. The "Wild West" then became highly publicized in literature, photographs, and song. Reality was embellished with excessive hyperbole and became the subject of many a movie in the following century. In other words, there was a commercialized byproduct of the American West extracurricular to the raising of beef. The American rodeo fits this definition. The cowboy's "play" during this period perfectly fit the attraction of show-casing the skills of the trade.

The skills of successfully breeding, fattening, and moving beef ultimately to the consumer's table were being universally recognized at the end of the nineteenth century. These were the professional tools Leroy so adroitly developed a half-century later—the combination of horse and rider to manipulate and control the less intelligent bovine. There was a huge, uninformed, but curious population willing to pay a price to see the display of such talents. Nobody recognized this better than "Buffalo Bill" Cody, whose "Wild West Show" made its debut in North Platte, Nebraska, in 1882. (Fredriksson, 1985) Admission was now being charged to watch these cowboys and their horses play in competitive games. Amateur or "purse" rodeos gained popularity up to World War II, before many of the rodeo cowboys marched off to war, and continued after the war ended.

In 1929 the Rodeo Association of America (RAA) was formed at Salinas, California. It was primarily a recordkeeping organization, but not all rodeo performers were members. The "Turtle Association" was formed in 1936, when a group of cowboys staged a walkout at a Boston Garden rodeo. It seems this protest resulted from the rodeo promoter's refusal to add the cowboys' entrance fee to the prize money. The unique name was proposed and accepted because "we rodeo performers are so slow in getting ourselves organized and not afraid to stick our necks out." The Turtle Association became the Rodeo Cowboy Association (RCA) in 1945, when organizational structures and rules were formalized. This organization became known as the Professional Rodeo Cowboys Association (PRCA) in 1975.[2]

About that time, only a hundred or so annual rodeos were held in the United States, primarily in the American West. (Fredriksson, 1985) The mix of rodeo performers then began to change. While working cowhands had many of the rodeo skills, they simply couldn't hold two jobs. Many of the early professional cowboys came directly off ranch jobs, but this percentage has decreased in the past few decades. Professional "rodeo schools" appeared on the scene in the 1960s. Today there are two categories of rodeos. The first is *professional*, guided by PRCA and the International Professional Rodeo Association (IPRA) rules with certain requirements for being "permitted."[3] The second is *amateur*, where virtually anyone can enter by paying an entrance fee, signing a liability waiver, and hoping to win a modest purse. As Larry McMurtry points out, "Small-town amateur competition is the kind to watch—the level of skill will be lower, but the fun quotient much higher." (McMurtry, 1999, p. 139)

Leroy Webb was both an outstanding amateur and professional rodeo performer.

> *Back when I was younger, the real cowboys—the working cowboys— they'd just go to rodeos on special occasions and show their skills, on the Fourth of July, Labor Day, their local state fairs ... Where I grew up, the main rodeo, like around the Fourth of July, was at Cimarron, New Mexico.*[4] *All the ranch cowboys from miles and miles around would all be there, competing against each other. They weren't professional rodeo hands; they were just real working cowboys.*
>
> *The very first rodeo I competed in I must have been ten or eleven years old, in 1944 or 1945. All the cowboys where Dad was working were getting ready to go to the Fourth of July Rodeo in Cimarron. At that time at rodeos they had all kinds of events: wild cow milking, wild horse races, plus the calf roping and bronc riding and lots of races. They'd have about twenty races—relay races. There was a racetrack around the rodeo grounds, all them ol' rodeos, fairs had a racetrack around outside the arena. They also had a kids' race for kids fifteen and younger.*
>
> *Well, all the older kids were pestering my brother, Don, and me that we couldn't keep up with them. Don and I had a pair of high-strung horses; so, we entered the race and we came in first and second. We really impressed my dad and all the ranch cowboys that worked with him. That was my first rodeo competition.*

The Atmore brothers (2001).

The Cimarron Rodeo where Leroy made his first appearance in 1944 is the longest continuously running open rodeo in the Southwest and is still a spectacular July Fourth event today.[5] The "Maverick Club" was formed in 1923 and incorporated in 1929 for the primary purpose of sponsoring the rodeo at Cimarron. Signators to the articles of incorporation included such family names as E.T. Springer and Waite Phillips.[6] It was a perfect niche—located in the center of giant ranching country and in a town that is rich in history and tradition.

Early participants in the famous Cimarron Rodeo included Don Webb, Frank Atmore, and Johnny Atmore, as well as Leroy, who made his debut at ten years old. Following some ranching experience at the Phillips Ranch and others in his early teens, Leroy was ready for bronc riding.[7] He selected saddle bronc riding as his favorite, and at the age of sixteen he entered the bronco contest at Cimarron. He was joined by the Atmore brothers and a few other rodeo novices who had no fear.

Bronc riding was special to Leroy. Even before his teenage years, he idolized his grandfather, Juan Cordova, who was widely known as the best bronc rider in the northern New Mexico-southern Colorado area. As a boy, Leroy would mount old barrels turned horizontal and would go through imaginary rides. He then tried young colts and, in his early ranching years as a

Fifty-year reunion of some original participants of the Maverick Club.

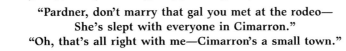

"Pardner, don't marry that gal you met at the rodeo—
She's slept with everyone in Cimarron."
"Oh, that's all right with me—Cimarron's a small town."
—Local rodeo cowboy

fourteen- and fifteen-year-old, spent his spare time riding the wildest outlaw horses in the remuda.

I was about sixteen before I entered a rodeo in bronc riding. That was my first event. Saddle bronc riding was always my favorite event, and I was bareback riding, bull riding. All this time at the ranch we'd be practicing our stuff, getting ready for later on. We'd be riding the milk pen calves, riding every outlaw horse we could get.

Like I said, bronc riding was always my thing. My first thought was I wanted to be a bronc rider. My granddad on my mother's side (Juan Cordova) was an old-time bronc rider. He rode in rodeos quite a bit and broke horses all his life. He was well-known as a rash bronc rider in them ol' time rodeos. He was my hero, and I really looked up to him.

So, when I was fifteen or sixteen I was riding broncs in these rodeos. The first bronc riding I won was in 1953, in the bull riding and saddle riding—I won the all-round cowboy several times.[8] Before that, we'd played all those local rodeos—just riding broncs.

Frank Atmore recalls the early Cimarron rodeo days participating with Leroy. Leroy would come over to the Atmore ranch, and he and Frank would rope milk cows or anything else that moved. Frank recalls an early participation at the rodeo when he, Leroy, and John Atmore all entered the bronc-riding event. As was the custom, the participants would "shoot the bull" around the chutes to get the scuttlebutt about the various horses to be ridden:

We all entered the bronc riding, and all the talk around the chutes from guys that were there was about a palomino called Leo the Lion, a saddle bronc that had never been ridden. There was also a black horse, bareback horse, that either hadn't been ridden or had only been ridden once. Anyway, when we drew up our horses, Leroy drew Leo the Lion and my brother, John, drew Midnight. I don't recall what I drew. But anyway, by golly, Leroy rode Leo the Lion the first time ever. He didn't win it because of a technicality, but he should have. I remember John coming out on his bareback, and he and I both bucked off. I remember when John got bucked off, he was spinning like a helicopter blade, flat. I bucked off, too, and was caught by a photographer in the air heading vertically toward the dirt.

Leroy progressed from the Cimarron to rodeos all over the Southwest, an avocation which would carry into the 1980s and beyond. He won an in-

*Frank Atmore and bareback bronc have a difference of opinion,
Cimarron Maverick Rodeo (1949).*

credible number of saddles, boots, belt buckles, and trophies as an amateur performer. Leroy cited many memorable experiences to me during our interviews.

> *I remember one time when Harp McFarland and his brother, Glen, Sam Sessions and I went to a rodeo in the northern part of the state up around Chama. They entered the calf-roping contest and I was in the bronc riding. They also had a wild horse race at that rodeo. So, we got into that event.*

Leroy beats the clock rodeo calf roping (1960s).

Harper and Sam did the mugging, and I done the riding. We won the wild horse race. Then these ropers come up and had a mule that nobody had even been able to ride, so they asked me if I wanted to ride that mule. I said that I would ride anything that they would lead up there or try to. They took up a hat collection, put this mule in the chute, and adjusted loose rope—no bareback—like I was riding bulls. Anyway, I rode that mule, and I probably got a grand total of three or four dollars out of that hat collection. They didn't know it, but I would have given them that much or more just to have rode that mule.

Leroy's talents as a rodeo performer became obvious early in his career. With neither horses nor cash, he was working his way into the circuit. His rodeo skills brought plenty of bystanders and admirers who knew this young cowboy had a rodeo future. The decision to move from amateur to professional rodeo participation was easy for Leroy. His experience with horses,

Leroy and partner rodeo team roping (1970s).

Ready to compete—Leroy Webb at the Wyoming State Fair (1970).

and the fact that he had steadily moved into professional horse training, gave him the opportunity to use horses that he personally had trained. Thus, the synergy of horse/rider coordination so necessary in professional rodeo competition could now be realized.

He was riding such a horse—Streaks Bracket—when he first got his RCA rodeo card.[9] The next step was to get his RCA permit, which at that time required winning a minimum of $1,000 in prize money at a professional rodeo.

The first rodeo we entered was Prescott, Arizona, on the Fourth of July. My partner who I was roping with (team roping) was a young fella from Colorado named Doug Kaess. He was a real good roper and good hand. We entered, and just before we were to go, ol' Doug broke his foot. Man, we didn't know what to do! He got a cast on it, but he couldn't put it in the stirrup or nothing. Well, we decided to rope anyway so we went on to Prescott—him on crutches and his foot in a cast. It turned out we placed in the first round. We made the short round. Anyway, we had to stay a *couple of days for the short round finals. His foot was hurting pretty good—like I say, he couldn't put it in a stirrup. Well, we ended up placing in the short round and won third overall. We made $900 something each—just lacking a few dollars filling our permit at the first professional rodeo we went to. We went to two more rodeos, finished our $1,000, and got us our PRCA cards.*

Leroy was now a permitted rodeo professional. He went on to win many trophies and a fair amount of prize money.[10] I tried to tabulate his rodeo achievements by counting the numerous citations in his trophy room. It was an overwhelming task that I could not accomplish. He participated in many different rodeo events, including one of his favorites, team roping.[11] World champion performers all praise the rodeo skills of Leroy Webb as being equal

Leroy receiving another trophy, Albuquerque, New Mexico (1977).

with anyone in the profession. A professional rodeo performer's life, though, is a tough one. The transient life and demands were at variance with Leroy's dedication to his family, his love for the open range, and his later affinity for breeding, training, and showing quarter horses. Nevertheless, he and his old-time rodeo friends still find time to hold reunions and get into the arena after-hours and compete with each other.

The boy who started his rodeo career in a lonely, dusty pen eventually won amateur contests as a teenager and grew into a first-class professional performer as a young and middle-aged man. His reputation throughout the rodeo circuit of the day, the stories still circulating, and his extensive trophy room are a few ways of measuring his accomplishments.

The professional rodeo in 2002 is quite different from the one Leroy Webb experienced with his friends. The rodeo now is big business. More than 170,000 fans attend the National Finals Rodeo in Las Vegas, and about thirteen million viewers tune into ESPN to watch these finals. Professional rodeo is the only major sport in America that evolved from a working lifestyle.[12] Large arenas such as Las Vegas are accompanied by a circuit system composed of twelve geographic circuits. Most professional rodeo cowboys today "follow the circuit" by loading up their horses and equipment to compete at the nearest PRCA rodeo. Points accumulated at the circuit events lead to a cowboy's standings as a national performer.

This evolution of the rodeo—from the roots of the *Iliad*, to the 1800s of range cowboy competition, to the Leroy era, to the PRCA era of professionalism and organization—is another element that defines the transformation of the American cowboy.

There's nothing better
for the inside of a man
than the outside
of a horse.
—Ronald Reagan

A few of the rodeo trophies—Leroy and Nora (1960s).

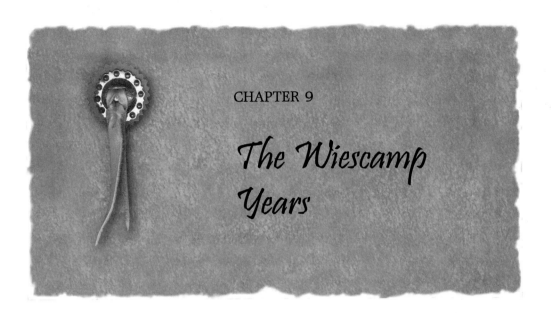

CHAPTER 9

The Wiescamp Years

*I*t was a landmark year for Leroy Webb. He had come to a fork in the road. In 1960 he was twenty-seven years old, a seasoned cowboy, and now a family man. He had a job offer from Hank Wiescamp, a legendary Colorado horseman, who had built a multimillion-dollar land and livestock empire in the San Luis Valley of southern Colorado. Leroy accepted the job through the encouragement of Jack Kyle, loaded up his wife, son, and a few belongings, and headed for Alamosa. He would spend the next ten years training and breeding horses for Wiescamp and would develop a new set of skills which would carry him into a new era of his life.

Henry J. "Hank" Wiescamp was born in 1906 in a small Nebraska farming community near Lincoln. His paternal grandparents had emigrated from Holland with their six children some eighteen years before his birth. His father, Christiaan, married Catherine Schneider, this marriage producing

---

One man can make a fortune selling shoes on a street corner, and another can go broke selling the same shoes on the corner across the street. It's not the shoes or the corner that are responsible for either result. It's the man who's doing the selling.[1]

—Hank Wiescamp

---

fourteen children. Hank was the fifth born and was raised on the small family farm. Hank's early loves were horses, trading, and auctioneering. As their 200-acre farm in Nebraska was too small for the family and additional land was hard to come by, the family moved to the Colorado San Luis Valley in 1922. Hank left school in the eighth grade, and, using the work ethic he had learned practically from birth, took on jobs related to farming and railroading. In 1926 it was time for twenty-year-old Hank to choose a permanent career. He narrowed it down to becoming a minister or an auctioneer. (Holmes, 1996) Hank had developed unique communication and storytelling skills, was a people person, and possessed insatiable energy. His love for horses led him to an auctioneering school in Indiana.

Hank Wiescamp was an entrepreneur and trader. He began his career in auctioneering and eventually purchased a sale barn. After he married Freda Flint and had five children, his whole family became involved with horses. Throughout the 1950s and 1960s, the Wiescamp horse program prospered. His Alamosa sale barn became the best known in the valley, and he concurrently built up a registered quarter horse breeding and training program. His reputation was nationwide as a quarter horse auctioneer and promoter when Leroy came to work for him in 1960.

There was a natural link between Hank and Leroy: their mutual love for horses. Wiescamp had the financial resources, reputation, and experience in developing quarter horse stallions, while Jack Kyle and Leroy Webb assisted his program as energetic and skilled horsemen. It was an extraordinary learning experience for Leroy in combining a new set of horse breeding and training skills along with his previous knowledge of range horses and the performance criteria.

The quarter horse was Wiescamp's focus in the breeding, development, showing, and racing business, although in the later 1950s he decided to expand into an appaloosa breeding program and registered paint horses. He raised some top-quality stallions and mares, winning many awards throughout the region. His top stallion, Red Plaudit, was the foundation stallion for

Several breeds of horses made their appearance on working cattle ranches, such as thoroughbreds, Arabians, appaloosas, paints, and just plain range horses. However, virtually all the ranch managers and working cowhands prefer the American quarter horse as the breed of preference. The stocky, powerfully built quarter horse traces its origins back to English colonial ancestors on one side and the steeds left by the Spanish conquistadors on the other.[2] The quarter horse is America's oldest and only native breed. The American Quarter Horse Association (AQHA) was formed in 1940 to collect, record, and preserve the pedigrees of American quarter horses.[3] The headquarters for this organization, with almost four million registered horses worldwide and more than 320,000 members from twenty countries, is located in Amarillo, Texas. The American Quarter Horse Heritage Center and Museum is located there.

Hank's well-known line of Plaudit appaloosas. (Holmes, 1996) Wiescamp
grew interested in paints in the early 1940s after buying Philmont and Ghost
Ranch mares.[4] This was twenty years prior to the origin of the paint registry.
Quarter horses with high stockings or other spots make them ineligible for
AQHA registration but can be registered as paints. Wiescamp knew that ei-
ther kind of horse would sell:

> *I've always had paints. I've tried to breed 'em up over the years. I've
> tried to make 'em look just like my quarter horses with a little extra color.
> The only thing that loud color on a horse does is make 'em more saleable.
> It always has and always will!*

When Leroy and Nora arrived at the Wiescamp spread in Alamosa in
May of 1960, they were following a dream, but one tainted with a degree of
uncertainty. Wiescamp doubled Leroy's Shelly Hays salary of $200 per
month and provided an expense account. Leroy, Nora, and Hurley moved
into a small house in Alamosa and began their new career.

> *When we went to work for Hank, we didn't have nothing—just a pickup
> and a few personal items. He financed us to buy a small house, and I
> went to work training and showing horses for Hank. He was a great
> man ... really a smart man. He liked me, and we got along. He was a
> hardheaded Dutchman and a tough ol' man in business ... just like Waite
> Phillips. Hank was really smart—had an eighth-grade education, didn't
> go to school, but learned the hard way.*

At the time Leroy went to work for him, Wiescamp had not shown that
much, even though he had been in the horse business "forever." Hank
wanted to accelerate showing horses, primarily as a method of exposure and
advertising. He did not breed outside mares—only his own. If people wanted
one of his premium horses, they had to buy from Wiescamp. As Leroy explains,

> *Wiescamp is one of the few people that really made money strictly in the
> horse business. He didn't have any oil wells or major outside income. It's
> a tough business. Most people can't make it at all. Those big-time breeders
> you hear about, they got their money from somewhere else.*

Wiescamp's main thrust was in the stallion business. He figured one
stud could produce twenty to thirty colts per year, whereas you would spend
the same amount of time on one mare and just get one colt. Leroy made special mention of another famous name in the quarter horse industry: Warren
Shoemaker. Shoemaker was an early breeder of quarter horses, even prior to
Wiescamp. In the early years of his breeding program, Wiescamp was adroit
enough to purchase a palomino stallion, "Nick Shoemaker," from Shoe-

maker's stock to match with some of his best broodmares bought off of the Philmont (Waite Phillips) and Ghost Ranch.

Warren Shoemaker was born in 1902, and his Bar O horses out of his ranch at Watrous, New Mexico, played an important role in the development of the American quarter horse.[5] One of Shoemaker's best horses came out of a trade with an "ol' trading friend" named Jim Leftwich. Shoemaker got his first palomino in the trade, as he had always wanted a palomino. Leftwich sensed he had the upper hand in the trade and wanted "some boot." Warren said he had no money but would give Leftwich his pocket knife to "make it even." The trade was consummated, and as soon as Shoemaker saddled his new palomino, "he knew he had been suckered." The palomino unleashed with Shoemaker and was virtually unrideable. The horse was spoiled and dangerous and totally undisciplined. Leftwich laughed at his old friend for months, but Shoemaker had the last laugh. Following a period of "Shoemaker reconstruction," the palomino, which he named "Chief," went on to win numerous shows and became a real money horse. There was a lot of synergy between Shoemaker and Wiescamp. They were old pros in the business, knew their horses, and were skilled traders with reputations of honesty and integrity.

Wiescamp had a more difficult time purchasing his first real "producer" stallion from Shoemaker in 1942. The horse, Nick Shoemaker, was selling for $1,500—big money that Wiescamp didn't have:

> *That was a lot of money. I still owed $1,500 on my sale barn and paying it off at $100 per month. In 1942 you could buy cows and calves for $15 to $20 a pair. You could buy a brand new Buick for $1,500 or a Model T for $900.*

Wiescamp really wanted Nick Shoemaker, the producer stallion he had been looking for to get his breeding program into high gear. He judged Nick Shoemaker to have everything he wanted: "a beautiful head with a big eye and little fox ears, long slender neck, short back, long underline, long hip, deep-forked chest with a well defined forearm, and a lot of stifle and hind leg." (Holmes, 1996) All Wiescamp lacked was $1,500; so, no deal. A few months later, Shoemaker called Hank and told him if he'd be at his place the next morning with a trailer, he could have Nick for $500. Hank wrote him a check for $500 but only had $30 in his account. As it took a week or so for a check to clear in those days, Hank figured he had time to make up the deficit. With some old silver dollars he had stored from horse sales and a personal loan from his banker, he was able to cover the check.

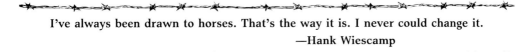

I've always been drawn to horses. That's the way it is. I never could change it.

—Hank Wiescamp

By the time Nick Shoemaker had sired many colts a few years later, Wiescamp had realized a return of more than fifty times his original investment. Moreover, Nick Shoemaker had sired fourteen foals in 1945, one of which was Skipper W, a sorrel stallion (from Hired Girl, a member of Nick Shoemaker's broodmare band). Skipper W became an AQHA legend. He reached maturity at about fifteen hands in height and weighed a very well-distributed 1,300 pounds. Although he was not exhibited at many shows, he was the grand champion at every one he entered. Skipper W sired 123 registered foals, fifty-eight of which were halter point winners and twenty-seven of which were performance point winners (1,392 points in halter and over 586 points in performance). Thirteen of Skipper W's offspring earned AQHA championships, seven became Superior Halter Horses, and one earned a Superior in Performance Registers of Merit, and four earned the same honor in racing. Skipper W's most lasting legacy as a breeding stallion, however, was the fact that he consistently sired both sons and daughters better than he was, and those went on to become top sires and producers themselves. Wiescamp said:

> *Skipper W flat outproduced himself. I don't know any other way to put it. When I bred him to a mare, he consistently sired a foal who was better than both he and the mare!*

Skipperette, foaled in 1950, was a good example of a broodmare sired by Skipper W. She raised four sons who were retained by Wiescamp as breeding stallions, which is a rarity. Wiescamp notes:

> *Some of my greatest show mares were never able to reproduce themselves. On the other hand, some of my mares who never saw a show ring or racetrack just kept on producing champions for me, year after year. Skipperette, however, was an exception. She did it all!*

This is the kind of breeding program success that Hank Wiescamp had achieved by the 1960s. The quarter horse show scene had grown exponentially, and that had prompted Hank to hire Jack Kyle and Leroy Webb to train his horses for the show circuit.

The decade of the 1960s was a memorable one for Leroy. Unlike cowboying on the open range and moving around, he had a house, a knowledgeable boss, and a fixed home base for Nora and Hurley. He loved his job and adapted quickly to the training and showing of top-quality horses. Jack Kyle left Wiescamp in 1961, returning to Santa Rosa to run the family ranch,

The stallion provides the strength but the mare gives the stamina.
—Winston Churchill

which left Leroy in a key position as Wiescamp's most skilled trainer and horseman.

Leroy had been moving around all of his life—first with his father and brother, and then as a drifting cowboy who loved different ranch countries and challenges. He was uncertain about establishing a taproot anywhere, but the ten years he spent with Wiescamp were a significant transformation in his life. Undoubtedly, his family responsibilities, his opportunity to work with some of the finest horses in the world, and his respect for Wiescamp all converged into this newly discovered "era of permanence."

> *So I went to working horses—just to show. I was breaking colts and start-*
> *ing them, all this training to show. Hank had a forty-foot semi, just an ol'*
> *straight bed stock truck. In 1960 we started out hauling nine studs, three*
> *mares, and one gelding. Now, Hank didn't believe in geldings—he wanted*
> *something that reproduced. The only reason the gelding was with us is*
> *that Hank had sold him as a stud. He turned out to be sterile; so, Hank*
> *bought him back and gelded him. He turned out to be a good performing*
> *sucker. Anyway, we put all these horses into that truck and down the*
> *road we'd go, squealing and rattling like a bunch of tin cans. We showed*
> *these horses all over Colorado and Wyoming—state fairs and such.*

It was Leroy's first major foray into the quarter horse show circuit. He was a quick study and was good at what he did, and Wiescamp liked what he saw. The following winter Leroy started breaking a lot of colts, about sev-

Leroy Webb, in signature red boots, with two Wiescamp show horses,
Stillwater, Oklahoma (1964).

enty to a hundred each winter. He broke those yearlings and two-year-olds all by himself, ten to fifteen each day. He would catch them, saddle them up, run them around the corral, and settle them down to channel their energy into disciplined and responsive show horses. Although he had never worked with such high-bred horses before, there was an instant understanding between colt and trainer.

Over the next few years, Leroy and Wiescamp showed and competed horses in New Mexico, Colorado, Arizona, Wyoming, Chicago, Texas, and cities such as Salt Lake, San Francisco, and Louisville. Leroy was a major player in breaking, training, hauling, and showing them. He was responsible for more than twenty-five state champions.

> *The first AQHA Champion to my credit was Skipper's Smoke in 1962. Then came Skip's Princess, Skippette, Skip's Ink, Skip's Trauma, Skip's Tres Bar, Skip Six Bar, Skip's Three Bar, Silver Son, and Pawnee Eagle. During this time I was awarded the Rocky Mountain Quarter Horse Association All Around Year End Award five times and awarded the Golden Spread All Around the only year I tried for it.*

Although one has to drag these credentials out of Leroy, as his nature is unassuming, quiet, and self-effacing, the awards gave him broad recognition in the quarter horse business as early as the mid-1960s, and his reputation led to a series of articles about him in trade and association journals. He was on the road constantly, appearing at rodeos (still riding broncs and roping) and horse shows. The Wiescamp organization and reputation provided the exposure, and Leroy was up to the task.

> *As far as training and picking out the horses for showing, Hank gave me complete control. He never told me what to do. He gave me his checkbook, his credit cards, and cash. He never put a limit on what I could spend for expenses. He'd always ask me if I needed more money, and he'd give it to me in a minute. I had two compartments in my billfold—one for his money and one for mine. He believed in me—trusted me—and I believed in him. I never cheated him out of a nickel, and he knew it. He was smart and knew how I spent it. I took care of his money exactly the way I took care of mine. I always stayed in cheap motel rooms and ordered from the cheap side of the menu. I didn't stay in Holiday Inns or eat steak on his money. I just didn't believe in that.*

This is pure Leroy Webb. His character is written on his face and is consistent with all of the old-time cowboys I've interviewed. They obviously were "not without sin," but honesty and integrity were paramount during that era and with that breed of men. As a young summer cowhand working in Deaf Smith County for my dad, I was around a lot of old cowboys and farm hands. I also saw my dad and granddad cut cattle and land deals with no notes taken or lawyers present. Your word was your bond—a deal was a deal. As I left the 1950s world of agriculture and entered the world of business, I had to adjust to the more structured and formal way of conducting business transactions. All of the old-timers stressed positive virtues. In my conversations with them, I never heard a profane word (although I'm sure profanity was widespread during their earlier cowboy days). Maybe the "last cowboy" is a metaphoric expression as to the integrity and simplicity which were so typical of that era.

Hank Wiescamp rarely went to the shows where Leroy took his "best" horses, ones he had broken and trained. Hank would hang around in the background, watch prospective buyers, make contact with them, calculate what the horse was worth, then set his price. As Leroy said,

He'd always be right on the money. He was smart and really knew people. He handled the sale of horses all by himself. He knew every mare. If he had 300 mares, I guarantee you, he could look at any one in the bunch and tell you all about her. He was a big heavy man, and you wouldn't think he could move around, but he could walk up and down those alleys all day long. On breeding, he would turn out pasture studs with a bunch of mares, but most of them were controlled. He'd bring the mares into a

Horse trainer Leroy Webb and Wiescamp quarter horse stallion.

pen with the stud. He had rows of studs, over twenty of them. He'd use
"teaser studs" to determine when the mares went into heat.

During the mid to late 1960s, Leroy, with Hank's blessing, was getting some of his own horses together. He had saved his money and now had a colt out of a mare he bought from Jack Kyle. He named this colt "Pawnee Eagle," the first of a long string that Leroy would own, train, and ride in his subsequent years. He then bought two mares from Shelly Hays, which had lineage from Wiescamp's Skipper W.

Leroy was working long hours, fulfilling his responsibility to Wiescamp and initiating his own string of horses. In the late 1960s he and Nora bought an eighty-acre farm near Monte Vista, Colorado, in the San Luis Valley. He had spent almost ten years with Wiescamp and was thinking about making it on his own. Leroy was well known, had a sterling reputation, had a few good horses, and for the first time in his life, had a little money. In the spring of 1969, Leroy left the Wiescamp organization and entered the new world of ownership.

Hank Wiescamp drastically cut back on his horse show development by the mid-1980s. During the latter part of that decade, he focused on survival, as the recession was particularly hard on the horse business. In the late 1980s and early 1990s, he continued to breed quarter horses with the same intensity as always, ballooning his horse numbers to over 1,000. (Holmes, 1998) During the 1990s, he remained "hands on" with respect to decision-making. Wiescamp horses were found in Canada, Panama, Germany, Poland, Argentina, and Uruguay. Volker Laves, owner of the Circle L Ranch in Wenden, Germany, had imported more than fifty Wiescamp horses to Europe.

At the age of ninety-one, Wiescamp died on August 10, 1997. It truly was the end of an era. His involvement in the horse industry had spanned over seventy years. He bred some of the best quarter horses in the world. Moreover, he had a major impact on all four of the major western horse registries: quarter horse, appaloosa, palomino, and paint. The Wiescamp honor roll included fifty-eight AQHA champions, thirty-six Superior Halter Horses, and eleven Superior Performance Horses.[6] His impact on Leroy Webb was profound.

> *He helped me in many ways—introduced me to a lot of people while*
> *working and showing for him. A lot of people thought Hank was a great*
> *man, and he really was. He was good to me.*

Leroy was fortunate enough to have known or be exposed to three of the icons of the American quarter horse: Coke Roberds, Warren Shoemaker, and Hank Wiescamp. One of his fondest memories is the recollection of Albert Mitchell, Warren Shoemaker, Coke Roberds, Hank Wiescamp, and others holding court at the New Mexico State Fair in the 1950s. They were sitting on bales of hay back in the barn area discussing the future of quarter horses.

Leroy just hung back like a mouse in the corner, happy to be on the fringe of such great horsemen.

The Wiescamp Dispersal Sale was held in Alamosa the year following Wiescamp's death. More than 3,000 people attended, including Jack Kyle and Leroy Webb. The dispersal sale included 264 Wiescamp stallions and mares along with two geldings. The sales totaled over $3 million, marking a glorious end to the Wiescamp legendary breeding program.[7]

A Tribute to the Breeder

A field of mares between the glistening peaks
Gets a piercing stare through wind-burned cheeks
That well trained eye studies every mare
Not a flaw slips by that awesome stare
He knows his stock like a horseman should
And the worst one there is still mighty good
There's an ornery grin on that knowing face
That dares someone to try and take his place
But the time has come for him to part
And leave what's been dear to this heart
He'll go and walk now with his Lord
And receive what is his great reward
Either his days of breeding mares are through
Or God's stock has some improving to do.

—A tribute to Hank Wiescamp
By Ray Shoop, grandson-in-law

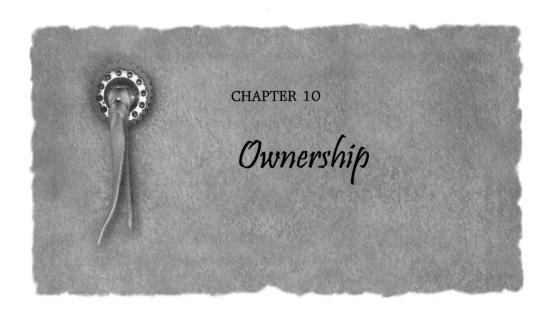

CHAPTER 10

Ownership

$\mathcal{I}$n the latter years with Wiescamp, Leroy was in transition. He had accumulated a few horses and purchased eighty acres of irrigated land. He was working around the clock finishing up with Hank while getting his own business started.

> *I was sure enough doing overtime work. I was showing everybody's horses, breaking everybody's horses, riding and training horses for everybody, then showing my own. We raised feed for the horses. We tried to do it all ourselves—water the oats and alfalfa, cut it, bale it, and haul it in by hand. Then we got to adding to the farm. I bought a neighboring place of eighty acres, then in a few years bought another eighty acres, and soon I had a total of 400 acres, about seventy head of mares and six to eight studs. I was showing, breaking, shoeing, training, and farming. It was some busy years that was . . . and many friends helped us out.*

Two individuals provided invaluable help during the early ownership years. Warren Shoemaker assisted Leroy in financing his Monte Vista prop-

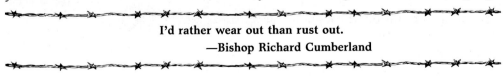

I'd rather wear out than rust out.
—Bishop Richard Cumberland

The Webb Ranch, Monte Vista, Colorado (1970s).

Leroy and Nora at Monte Vista.

erty, and Dr. Ben Konishi, a veterinarian, provided much of the original and necessary veterinary care for Leroy's livestock. Dr. Konishi rarely accepted pay from the struggling young couple. At that time, Hurley was adjusting to his blindness both in his schooling and cowboying activities, and Dr. Ben, rather than taking pay for his veterinary assistance, would say, "Give my fee to Hurley." Leroy and Nora will remember always those acts of kindness. Dr. Konishi told me he has been repaid many times over just having the Webb family as friends.

Leroy now had an ever-expanding reputation throughout the American Southwest as an all-around cowboy, horse trainer and breeder, and horse show performer. With his Monte Vista

*Streak's Bracket—World Champion Heeling Horse.
Leo Camarillo, Leroy Webb, and actor Ben Johnson (1979).*

ranch as a base, the following eight to nine years were expansive and exciting. Just a year or two out on his own, a major newspaper in the area noted "with an enviable reputation as a horse trainer, he was one of the best!"[1] He was also described as a "handsome cowboy with deceiving gray hair" and "always willing to give youngsters a hand in learning the arts of the cowboy."

Leroy was raising cattle feed, breaking, training, and breeding his own horses as well as those owned by others, traveling about 20,000 miles each show season, calf and steer roping in rodeos (as well as some bronc riding), riding in parades, helping youngster cowboys along the way, and freely giving his time to his sight-impaired son, Hurley, and his wife, Nora, both of whom he adored. It was a busy time, and it bore fruit. Even now, as he approaches seventy, Leroy has amazing energy, work ethic, and ability to get by on four hours of sleep a night without impairing his quiet grace and constant good humor.

As the peripatetic Leroy moved from state to state in his travels, his talents attracted a variety of clients. He was retained by Bing Crosby's son, Lindsay, to train his personal horses, and was befriended by the Oklahoma

Pawnee Eagle—Grand Champion All Around.

cowboy and later Academy Award winner Ben Johnson. Johnson was a unique actor, particularly suited for his roles with John Wayne in John Ford's classic *She Wore a Yellow Ribbon* (Trooper Tyree), with Alan Ladd and Jack Palance in *Shane*, and most notably for his Academy Award Best Supporting Actor role in Larry McMurtry's *The Last Picture Show* (Sam the Lion).[2] Leroy still recalls the time he had the opportunity to ride the Ben Johnson-owned horse that allowed Johnson to escape pursuing Indians in *She Wore a Yellow Ribbon* by jumping a deep crevice in the Monument Valley area of Arizona.

The centerpiece of Leroy and Nora's professional life at their Monte Vista ranch was developing their quarter horse breeding program and performing in the quarter horse show circuit. Leroy had developed the necessary skills and knowledge during his tutelage under Wiescamp, knew the prerequisite importance of the right bloodlines, and became immediately successful. Pawnee Eagle was his first stallion, and he was a great one. Grandson of Skipper King, the horse Wiescamp considered to be the top son of Skipper W,

*Pawnee Hawk—
World Class Stallion.*

Pawnee Eagle had both the Skipper W bloodline as well as those of the dam, Santa Mia, from the lineage of a Shoemaker mare.

Leroy had trained and shown some of the world's best quarter horses during his tenure with Wiescamp, and now his homegrown stallion was setting all kinds of records and receiving numerous awards. Leroy stated that "I have had the pleasure of riding some exceptionally great horses, but the most outstanding was Pawnee Eagle. His character, size, and ability left nothing to be desired. As a sire, he passed on all these characteristics to his offspring."

Pawnee Eagle accumulated more than 1,100 AQHA Adult Working Points (AQHA awarded points in various events) and was in demand as a sire. The horse had it all, including an amazing speed, being clocked at over forty miles per hour by Leroy driving parallel to his dashing stallion. This AQHA champion's many credits included All Around Champion designation by the Rocky Mountain Quarter Horse Association and Grand Champion All Around in the Phoenix, Arizona, competition. Pawnee Eagle sired many great horses in Leroy's breeding program, including Webb's most famous horse, Pawnee Hawk. Leroy eventually sold Pawnee Eagle to a Houston syndicate. (He got an excellent price for Pawnee Eagle but really didn't want to sell him.)

Pawnee Hawk was now Leroy's top stallion, and his earlier prognosis that Pawnee Eagle could "pass on all his good characteristics to his offspring" proved to be accurate. Pawnee Hawk was the leading junior horse in the nation in heading, heeling, and calf roping (AQHA Junior Class consists of five-year-olds or younger). Pawnee Hawk was one of the ten in the nation to qualify for the prestigious World Champion Quarter Horse Show in Louisville, Kentucky. When the show was over, Pawnee Hawk placed third out of

Clockwise from top left: One of the many rodeo parades (1970s).

Always willing to help out a future cowboy.

World Class Gelding, The Untouchable.

The Webb Ranch, Monte Vista, Colorado (1970s).

America's top 800 quarter horse stallions, an unbelievable accomplishment for Leroy, who was short on financial backing and resources but long on talent and tenacity.[3]

> *Pawnee Eagle was working really good and made a great reputation for himself. Anyway, I got a real chunk of money for him, and I thought we couldn't afford to keep him, so we let him go. His son, Pawnee Hawk, was a great horse and kind of took his place. He was a crowd-pleasing horse— the right size (15-2 hands and 1,250 pounds), a lot of bone, and the agility of a cat. He was cheered in every arena in the West.*

The Webb horse success was not limited to Pawnee Eagle and Pawnee Hawk. Sirlette was another stallion who sired a three-time world champion steer-roping horse, Leyba Chester, AQHA champion Sir Teddy, and AQHA champion Sir Leyban. Pawnee Watrous, full brother to Pawnee Hawk, was a world champion heeling horse in 1978. Racing horses were also included in the Webb inventory. Chipper's Susy, winner of many futurities, ran against some of Wiescamp's horses.

Throughout the 1970s, Leroy Webb was recognized as one of the most talented horsemen in the country and was in constant demand as a trainer and show performer. It was hard work. He was on the road, with very few days off, and he and Nora were doing all the work themselves. By this time, Hurley was a teenager and a real horse lover. Now totally blind, he attended the Colorado School for the Deaf and Blind in Colorado Springs. Hurley spent all of his summers and vacations with Nora and Leroy at their Monte Vista ranch and tried in every way to emulate his cowboy father. He could saddle, ride, gather, and even tried roping. He was an extraordinary young man and the absolute pride of his parents. During the school year, Nora and Leroy took time to visit him in Colorado Springs.

The Webb quarter horse business was a great success, but after about ten years, it was wearing the Webbs down.

> *Both of us were getting tired. We couldn't get good help—just doing it all ourselves. We were just working ourselves to death: all those horses, all the farm work, and all the traveling and hauling. So, in 1978 we had a horse sale. The market was good and so were our horses.*

The dispersal sale, held at the Webb ranch in Monte Vista on July 22, 1978, was a large success. The Wiescamp pedigrees that Leroy had helped develop and then incorporate into his own program, along with his name recognition for skill and integrity, were key to this success. He and Nora kept only six mares and two young studs of his ninety-plus inventory of stallions, mares, and yearling colts. His personal invitation to friends, colleagues, and serious horse buyers throughout the nation is typical of the man and his wife:

Welcome Friends:

We are pleased and happy to welcome you to our ranch for this sale. We extend a special welcome to our friends, the Caspers. We appreciate their joining us for this sale. Our breeding programs, our use of the horses, our pedigrees, and even our locations parallel each other very closely.

We have loved our horses very much. We have enjoyed the "Good Life" they have provided for us. We have especially appreciated the great "heart" our horses have given whenever we've asked them to perform. This is what has made it possible for us to achieve the honors they have brought us.

They are honest, hard working horses, like we are people. Yet they are capable of World Championship conformation when given the chance. We would like not to have to sell them but we've found we can't do everything alone, nor have we been able to hire any help. So something has to go.

Please feel welcome while you're here. Even if you don't buy a horse, we appreciate your being interested. However, if you find a horse you like well enough to buy, we'll appreciate you even more. A little bit of "us" will go with each one.

Sincerely,
Leroy and Nora

Following the dispersal sale, Leroy and Nora had their Monte Vista ranch, a few horses, and for the first time in their lives, some savings. They continued their horse breaking, training, and show performance activities at a reduced scale for the next several years, then decided it was time to "return home" to New Mexico. They sold the ranch, loaded up their remaining horses, tack, saddles, trophies, furniture, and other belongings, and headed back to their native state. They drove into Springer, New Mexico, where Nora had grown up and where Leroy had spent many of his early cowboy days, and found a place they liked on the Cimarron River. It belonged to cowboy artist Keith Avery, who was wanting to move. This was a perfect setting for them. Leroy was returning to his cowboy roots—roping cattle, entering rodeos, and entering into a ranch leasing phase in order to raise beef.

I was roping a lot by then. About all I wanted to do was rope. I fixed up a really good arena—had a bunch of steers, and we put on a lot of roping exhibitions and contests in New Mexico and Colorado. I liked to work them rope horses. I'd get up early in the morning and saddle up six or eight horses at once—tie 'em to the fence, get all the steers (I kept about thirty head of roping steers) and just go to roping. Then I'd go to lots of rodeos and enter all the roping events. I did that for about six years— nothing but rodeos and roping and training, working rope horses. I had a couple of studs. I'd breed some mares, but mostly it was just riding horses.

Long about 1987 I was still rodeoing a little. I was breaking horses. I

Clockwise from top: Heading up to the UU Bar high country.

In transit.

A long day at the office.

The UU Bar high country. The cattle belong to Leroy; the elk belong to Nature.

Home in the high country.

got a bunch of horses to break for the UU Bar Ranch, a big ranch up by Cimarron that my dad had worked for and I'd worked for over the years. Anyway, I was breaking horses for this ranch. One year I broke all their colts. Next year they wanted me to break 'em. They had a camp open, and I made a deal with the UU Bar that I just go over to that camp in the high country and stay in that camp and break these colts right there on their place. That's what I did—camped up there in the high country by my-self, breaking these colts.[4]

The UU Bar Ranch is a magnificent property—several hundred thousand acres of both prairie land and high country beauty, full of timber, game, water, and rich grass for summer grazing. At one time, the UU Bar and Philmont were all one ranch owned by Waite Phillips.[5] He sold off the part called the UU Bar to the McDaniels brothers out of Arizona and gave the rest to the Boy Scouts. Leroy recalls his personal history with the UU Bar:

Dad worked for Phillips when it was all one big outfit. I came along later and worked for McDaniels when I was single and then again after I was married and Hurley was a baby. It was there that we lived in a line shack with no water, no electricity—just nothing, making $125 a month.

In the mid-1980s, when Leroy worked there, the UU Bar was owned by the Faudree family of Midland, Texas. He knew the ranch well and had fond memories of his previous stint at the UU Bar with Nora and young Hurley. Then the owners decided to lease some of their country out.[6] Leroy, who had great credibility with the owners, jumped at the chance. He leased the high country, where he had been working, planning to take some yearling steers up there in the summer. Yearlings do well in that country during the summer and early fall. The temperature is moderate and the grass is high in protein, insuring a daily pound or two gain which can be quite profitable. Leroy then added more of the UU Bar land to his lease agreement and started building

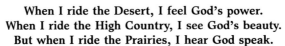

When I ride the Desert, I feel God's power.
When I ride the High Country, I see God's beauty.
But when I ride the Prairies, I hear God speak.

up his cow herd. He had a year-round lease now of greater than 85,000 acres. At this point he cut back on rodeos and roping and went back to his cowboy ways. Everything Leroy would make on yearlings, he would throw back into buying more cattle.

> *I went back to where I really belonged—punching cows . . . what cowboys really do. Over the next two to three years I put together a good herd of cows. I had accumulated about 500 head of mother cows and was running over 3,000 head of yearlings in the low country and high country. I trailed them back and forth between the two, just like it had been in the old cattle trail drive days. About the first of May I'd start moving the cattle to the high country. Trail them to one camp in the foothills, let 'em rest. Then to the next camp higher up, let 'em rest. Then to the high country camp for the summer graze, and back down again in the fall.*

These UU Bar days of leasing land and working cattle were some of Leroy and Nora's happiest. They were living at the UU Bar "Riata" headquarters near Cimarron, the cattle business was good, and Leroy was loving every minute of his life, breaking a few horses along the way, roping an occasional bear, elk, deer, or coyote to test his roping skills and have some fun, and enjoying his family.

Then a tragedy intervened. Leroy and Nora's only beloved son, Hurley, who had overcome so many handicaps, died of a stroke at the age of thirty-five.

Rodeo calf-roping competition—
Leroy at his best.

CHAPTER 11

Hurley

*L*eroy and Nora's only child, Hurley, was born in 1953 and was an immediate source of joy to the young couple. Leroy was cowboying at the Bar S Ranch near San Angelo, Texas, at the time. Hurley was a beautiful child with big brown eyes.

When he was just over a year old, Nora took him in for a routine checkup. His fingers were slightly closed, but everything seemed normal. The doctor wanted to have his eyes checked and called for a specialist. The prognosis was that he would go blind. It was quite a shock, as Nora would look into his "beautiful brown eyes" and not sense anything was wrong. As Nora and Hurley drove the ninety miles back to the ranch, she tried to cope with the fact that her son would be robbed of ever seeing his parents or the world around him. Bill Blakley, owner of the Bar S, and a man with virtually no available time, took a special interest in Hurley and hired some of the best specialists in the state to see what could be done. To this day, Leroy and Nora treasure the generosity shown by this individual. Despite the special treatment he received, when Hurley reached the age of three he was totally blind.[1]

Leroy and Nora were temporarily devastated that this beautiful and otherwise normal child would be blind for the remainder of his life. Then, as parents must do, they adjusted and accepted the reality.

Leroy raised Hurley as a cowboy—he was a little cowhand. During his youth, Hurley became an excellent roper and rider. As Nora recalls:

Daddy's little cowboy, Leroy and Hurley (1954).

*He could really ride. We put him on horses when he was just two or three
and sometimes just turn him loose. We had this gentle rope horse that a
man from Colorado Springs had given him; we would put Hurley on the
horse and just let him ride around in the corral. Sometimes when we
couldn't find him in the house, we'd go down to the pens and there he'd
be, trying to mount by climbing up this gentle horse's leg. He loved horses
and would ride all day long.*[2]

Incredible as it sounds, Hurley became an excellent roper at a very early
age. Leroy would set up a roping dummy and tap it so that Hurley could direct his loop. Then father and son would team rope. In team tying, the
header would have to dismount and run down after the steer was heeled and
tie a square knot around the steer's hind legs. Hurley practiced that exercise
with Leroy's guidance until he developed an incredible skill. Leroy could rope
the calf and tie its legs in a few seconds, but Hurley learned to match or even
beat his father's time. The two spent days and months together—riding, roping, and practicing other cowboy skills. The bond between father and son
was extraordinary.

A happy family—Nora, Leroy and Hurley (1957).

Hurley first attended the New Mexico School for the Blind, then finished grade school and high school at the Colorado Springs School for the Blind. He subsequently went to college at New Mexico Highlands University in Las Vegas. It is well known that when one loses one of his senses, the others seem to compensate. This was certainly true with Hurley. He developed uncanny compensating skills in roping, riding, and gathering horses and cattle. Some people who visited the Webbs at their Monte Vista ranch didn't even know he was blind. When told that he was, they didn't believe it. Hurley sat tall in the saddle, could maneuver his horse normally, walked erect and straight, and didn't use a cane. Nora recalls:

He would ride going full blast. We probably had fifty to sixty mares, and we'd move them from pasture to pasture, and he could gather those mares. When we would exercise them in the ring, we'd put bells around

*their necks, and Hurley could tell exactly what to do based on the sounds
of those bells.*

When attending rodeos, Hurley could tell which of the cowboys was his
father simply from the sounds of Leroy's jingling spurs. When Nora and
Hurley were sitting in the rodeo grandstands, Hurley would say, "There goes
Dad," and he was always right. Nora was amazed because she could tell absolutely no difference in all the background sounds.

While in Colorado, Hurley would sometimes saddle his horse and ride
by himself all around the country contiguous to the ranch. Nora recalls one
time he was out gathering mares, all heading full speed toward the corrals.
There was an irrigation ditch in front of them, and Nora watched in awe as
Hurley's mare pointed her ears toward the ditch as she approached it and
jumped the ditch at full stride. Hurley could sense this from the mare and
made the jump as well as any experienced rider would. On several occasions
when Hurley was a teenager, Leroy and Nora would have to make an out-of-
town rodeo or horse show and leave Hurley at the ranch. He would cook his
own meals and totally take care of himself. One time (and against his
mother's instructions), he walked from the ranch to Alamosa—some fifteen

Hurley saddling up, Webb Monte Vista Ranch (1971).

miles away. There were many irrigation ditches and roads to traverse. When Nora returned and learned of this venture, she chastised him.

"Hurley, why in the world did you do that? You could have been run over, fell in the ditch and drowned or just anything." He didn't swim. We never taught him that. He said, "Well, I didn't think there would be too many cars. It was twelve o'clock at night when I left." I asked him how he knew what time it was, but we had a clock that you could feel the hands, and he felt them. (He had braille talking watches after that.) He said that when he got to town, it was still night. He walked to downtown Alamosa to the Alamosa National Bank where we banked. He knew that's where he was and could tell someone was there even though it was nighttime. He asked the man at the bank, "Would you tell me what time it is?" This man said, "Well, can't you see? There's a clock up there." He said, "No, sir, I can't see. I'm blind, and I'd like to know what time it is." It was about three in the morning, and he said that he was really tired. He didn't know why he walked to town—he just wanted to go somewhere and not just stay at home by himself. He knew where Hank Wiescamp's show barn was because that's where Leroy worked, training the horses. That was probably a mile or two from the bank. Hurley then walked over there, went into the office, lay down on the couch and went to sleep—and that's where Hank's son found him the next morning and brought him back to our house.

Hurley's capacity to overcome his handicap with his extraordinary perceptions continued to amaze his parents and all who knew him. When Nora would drive from Monte Vista to Colorado Springs to visit Hurley, she would invariably get lost. She'd call him on the phone from some transitory location, and Hurley would give her precise instructions on how to get to designated points. The same was true when he was at his parents' ranch and would receive calls from visitors to get directions to the place. He could tell them precisely how to come, regardless of their distant location. Moreover, Hurley had an incredible memory. He memorized all the addresses and phone numbers of his parents' friends, clients, and visitors who frequented the ranch.

Aside from his blindness, Hurley subsequently developed other physical disabilities. The prognosis was difficult to define, but he had to go through a series of exploratory and very painful operations. Johnny Caldwell, Nora's brother, said of Hurley:

He was one of the happiest persons you would ever meet. He would always laugh and tell jokes and make everyone around him feel better. It's hard to explain because he was always in pain—and always happy. He was really something—quite a person. Later in his life, and after many of these operations, he had more difficulty in walking. He then had to use a walker. Then one time, some guy working with Leroy left a gate partially opened, and Hurley's horse went through the opening. Hurley caught his

*foot in the gate as the horse brushed by and broke his ankle. Just one
thing after another.*

Hurley loved everyone around him. When he was going to school in
Colorado Springs, he had countless friends. He kept mentioning a special
friend to his mother, a young man named Jimmy. Hurley told Nora that
Jimmy was a wonderful person and wanted her to meet him on her next trip
to Colorado Springs. The next time she was at Hurley's school, and was introduced to Jimmy, she was somewhat shocked by his appearance. He had
bulging eyes and somewhat deformed arms and legs. Jimmy offered to carry
Hurley's bags from the car, but Nora was a little uneasy being around Jimmy,
being careful not to show any discomfort. When Hurley and Nora were alone,
he sensed his mother's reaction. "You didn't like Jimmy, did you?" Nora's response was diplomatic, stating that she did like him but was a little surprised
by his appearance. Nora comes close to tears when recalling Hurley's response:

> *Mom, you looked at him through your eyes. I looked at him through my
> heart.*

In 1988 Hurley died at the age of thirty-five, suffering a stroke resulting from a long series of physical pains and major operations. It devastated
Leroy and Nora as well as the many people who had gotten to know Hurley
through the years.[3]

Our [son] was a loving one
Our [son] was forgiving
And though today his hands are dust
The things he touched are living.

—**Robert Lee Brothers**[4]

Hurley Leroy Webb was buried in the Cimarron Cemetery next to the
plot reserved for his father. Today Nora can talk about their son, but Leroy
cannot. He has asked himself the age-old theological questions: Why do bad
things happen to good people? Why did God let this happen? But life moves
on, and Leroy and Nora are very spiritual people. Their pain endures, but so
does their faith.

> Don't grieve for me, for now I'm free,
> Walking the path God laid for me.
> I took his hand when I heard Him call,
> I turned my back and left it all.
> I could not stay another day,
> To laugh, to love, to work, to play.
> Tasks left undone must stay that way,

I found His peace at close of day.
If my parting has left a void,
Then fill it with remembered joys.
A friendship shared, a laugh, a kiss,
Oh yes, these things I too will miss.
Be not burdened with times of sorrow,
I wish you joy for your tomorrow.
My life's been full, I savored much,
Good friends, good times, a loved one's touch.
Perhaps my time seemed all too brief,
Don't lengthen it with undue grief.
Lift up your hearts, and peace to thee,
God wants me now, and now I can see.

—Author Unknown

"Life has many tollgates, where we pay our way with tears" (1988).

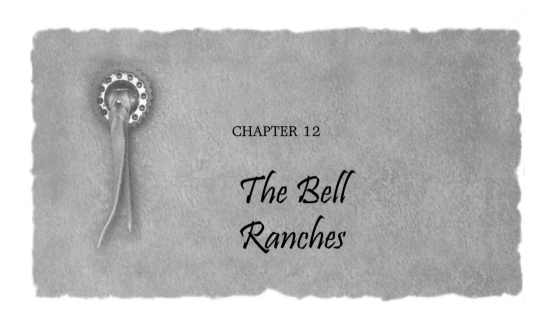

CHAPTER 12

The Bell
Ranches

*L*eroy was enjoying his ownership years and began leasing all or parts of large ranches for grazing rights. Before the UU Bar sold, he had developed a sizable herd of mother cows and yearlings. It was 1995, and he was looking for new country to lease.

I had gotten to know Leroy well by this time and knew enough about his reputation and cattle operations possibly to assist. I had moved in and out of partnership, buying and selling stocker and feeder cattle, teaming up with two men who had leased and actually purchased a portion of our family's land in western Deaf Smith County near the New Mexico state line. Ted Eicke and Jim McGowan were sound farmers, good cattle people, and excellent partners. As I have been immersed in the environmental engineering business over four decades, I depend on such people to advise me on issues concerning the lease of grassland and mother cow operations. After conferring with Eicke and McGowan on possible lease opportunities suitable for Leroy, I began the search for a large ranch that Leroy could lease.

A good starting place were the ranches that at one time were a part of the famous Bell Ranch, north of Tucumcari, New Mexico. Leroy would lease or contract cattle operations on four such ranches, namely, the Hampton and Fort Bascom Ranch, while working at the Chappell Spade Ranch, the Clabber Hill Ranch, and the Trigg Ranch.

130

Origins of the Bell Ranch can be traced back almost two centuries, when a captain in the Army of the King of Spain, Don Pablo Montoya, left the military and became a Comanchero, trading with the Indians east of Santa Fe.[1] He had been the *alcalde* of Santa Fe, was well known in the area, and had good political connections with the Spanish rulers and the Mexican surrogates. Just three years after Mexico gained its independence from Spanish dominion, Montoya petitioned for land east of Santa Fe and away from the "crowded conditions." This grant was awarded to him twelve days later (November 20, 1824), giving him rights to more than 650,000 acres ideal for raising cattle. As one can imagine, reckless generosity was an element of the granting process, and a portion of this land was simultaneously granted to and overlapped another applicant, Don Luis Cabeza de Baca. Their conflict was ultimately resolved by separating out a portion of the Montoya Grant, designating it as Baca Location No. 2. (Ellis, 1973)

Montoya was immediately confronted by Comanches and Kiowas, who had occupied the area for centuries. He managed to keep control of the disputed land, however, leaving the property to his seven sons following his death in 1841. Subsequent to the annexation of this land by the United States in 1848, when New Mexico became a U.S. territory, title disputes obviously followed. The Montoya brothers retained a Santa Fe attorney, John Watts, to secure confirmation of title, half of the land to be awarded to Watts if confirmation was successful. (Attorney contingency fee arrangements evidently were as common then as they are today.) Over time, Watts was able to gain total control over both the Montoya Grant and Baca Location No. 2.

Another character entered the scene shortly thereafter. Wilson Waddingham was a Canadian-born entrepreneur who had followed the masses westward toward Colorado during the gold rush days of the mid-1850s.[2] Through a series of complex financial option deals, and with the help of U.S. Senator Jerome B. Chaffee and aid from English sources, he was able to exercise the options and gain control of the Maxwell and Montoya land grants. Even though the Treaty of Guadalupe Hidalgo protected the original land grant titles, the complexity of subsequent title transfers, U.S. political influence, and aggressive attorneys were able to resolve the title conflicts in favor of the English and American investors helped by foreign capital, nefarious transactions, and tenacity.

It was Waddingham who can be credited with creating the Bell Ranch during the 1870s and 1880s and with giving the Bell Ranch its name during its reorganization in 1889. (Ellis, 1973) Waddingham ranching activities at the Bell were very successful during the 1880s, with the cattle inventory approaching 17,000 head. Hundreds of cowboys were hired to control this

One always has time enough if one applies it well.
—Goethe

ranch of over 1,000 square miles. A hiree's past history was never questioned. Tom (Blackjack) Ketchum and his brother, Sam, did early cowboying at the Bell and were "good cowhands" according to some accounts. The Ketchum brothers, who worked on the same lands that Leroy would subsequently work some sixty years later, met their demise following their outlaw days at the hands of Leroy's in-laws.

The 1890s were not good to the cattle business, and Waddingham lost control of the ranch. After he died in June of 1899, Ezekiel Stoddard and his Red River Valley Company were able to pick up the remnants of the ranch in 1899 and to control the property until they divided and sold it in 1946 and 1947. The 1899-to-1947 era was a period of stability in terms of management. Ezekiel Stoddard, Julius Day, Charles O'Donel, and Louis Stoddard in the early years were the primary individuals to provide good successor management and sound operation of the Bell. New water sources were developed; new fencing, canals (built at government expense), and windmills were built; and other improvements were implemented. When the Rock Island Railroad (Dawson Branch) reached Tucumcari in 1901, the transfer of Bell-raised livestock to markets, as well as coal from area mines, was smoothly facilitated.

In 1917 the Bell management sold about 30 percent of the ranchland to the Trigg brothers, bringing the remaining Bell land to less than 500,000 acres. In 1934 Albert K. Mitchell succeeded Charles O'Donel as ranch manager. The World War II years had been good for the Bell Ranch, but in 1947 the management decided it was time to sell. The ranch was divided into six segments. Mrs. Harriet Ellwood Keeney of Connecticut and her son, William Keeney of Lubbock, Texas (through gifts of shares), bought 130,000 acres surrounding the Bell headquarters; Frank Chappell of the Chappell Spade

Branding time, Hampton Ranch Spring (1995).

Ranches bought a large segment, as did Sam Arnett, Sr., and his son, Dr. S. C. Arnett, Jr., of Lubbock, carrying forward the name of one of their other ranches, the Clabber Hill. A short time later, Howard Hampton of Lubbock bought the old Fort Bascom segment of the ranch from John Hill (an old-time Bell cowboy), later known as the Hampton Ranch. Albert K. Mitchell also was involved, as he owned the nearby Tequesquite Ranch. Dr. and Clara Cone Hoover also purchased a large portion of the Bells (the Mesa Rica).

It was the Lubbock investors (Arnett, Chappell, and Hampton) who were able to purchase the most significant portion of the Bell. The three investors knew each other, had diverse reasons for buying, but shared the resources, connections, and backgrounds to make such an investment.[3] Leroy Webb would lease land or help other cowboys on each of these ranches.

The obvious choice of these former Bell ranches for Leroy to lease was the Hampton Ranch. This ranch was purchased by Howard Hampton, who happened to live next door to another Bell Ranch purchaser, Frank Chappell, Jr. (Howard and Val Hampton were good friends of my parents in Lubbock, living only a few blocks away.) Howard was born in 1898, attended Texas A&M, then served in World War I. Following the war, he worked for the Four Sixes Ranch near Guthrie, Texas, then purchased a small ranch in East Texas, hiring a young cowboy along the way named William Hall. Hampton then moved to Lubbock, purchasing the nearby Clark Woods Ranch in 1945. It was at this time that I got to know the Hamptons well, taking care of their yard and selling them anything they would buy from a ten-year-old. In 1950 Hampton purchased the Fort Bascom Ranch located near Logan, New Mexico. His original purchase included approximately one hundred sections (square miles) or 64,000 acres. It included a stretch of the Canadian River as well as an abandoned army outpost, Fort Bascom, within its boundaries.[4] The Hamptons had allowed my friends and me to hunt the ranch, so I got to

know the country rather well. It had a good combination of rugged mesas, canyons, foothills, and rolling prairie land. Such topography, combined with sufficient quantities of gramma, sideoats, buffalo and bluestem grasses, made it an excellent mother cow ranch. Howard Hampton died in the ranch bunkhouse in 1967. Following his death, Val, his widow, ran the ranch with Howard's hired cowhand of many years, William Hall.

Leroy shows 'em how.

Leroy at work in his office (1996).

By 1995, Val was slowing down, having run the ranch since her husband's death in 1967. Moreover, William Hall, a great cowboy who had done all the "hands on" work at the ranch, was nearing retirement. I asked Leroy to drive down to Lubbock and meet Mrs. Hampton to try to consummate a lease arrangement. She was immediately impressed with Leroy, and they readily consummated the lease. Leroy moved his cattle to the ranch, immediately cleaned up the headquarters, barns, and tack room, and rebuilt portions of the fences. Although this is normally a landlord's responsibility, Leroy did all of this with his own labor and funds—typical of the man and his integrity. It was during this time that I realized Leroy Webb truly represented the virtues of the old-time cowboys.

Leroy would spend the next year or so at the Hampton Ranch, running it all by himself, occasionally calling in his friends to help out during roundup and branding times. I made several trips to the ranch during his tenure and marveled at the amount of country he could cover each day in caring for his livestock. I'll never forget helping him out one day as I was passing through. After serving me some warmed over son-of-a-gun stew for lunch at the old Hampton headquarters, we had to put cake out for his cattle in some twenty troughs spread out over 30,000 acres. He had the sacks of cake in the back of his pickup, and off we went. With the idle turned up pretty fast, he'd jump out of the pickup, unload a couple of sacks of cake, pull the strings, and dump them in the trough. Meanwhile, that empty pickup would be fifty yards down the way, so we'd have to run to catch up with it. Then we'd repeat the process at the next trough. The pickup never stopped all day. Neither did we.

As Val Hampton was near death, the ranch was put up for sale by the trust department of a Fort Worth bank. Leroy and I tried to sell it to several friends or acquaintances in order to perpetuate his lease, including Henry Singleton (who had bought up many ranches in the area, including the Bar Y, where Leroy would eventually work). However, we were unable to negotiate a sale to a preferred buyer. The trust department finally found a purchaser, who did not renew the lease; so, we searched for other country. Fortunately, Leroy was able to lease a good portion of the nearby Albert K.

Howard and Val Hampton were great people and good citizens. Howard was active in ranching circles, serving as president of the West Texas Museum associated with Texas Tech University, and he contributed countless cowboy and Indian artifacts and memorabilia to both the Tech museum and the Panhandle-Plains Museum in Canyon, Texas (West Texas A&M University). In 1957 he put together an exhibition entitled "Cattle, Cowboys, and Cowpokes," a stunning collection of artwork and a showing implemented by displays of western gear and regalia reflecting life of the great ranches in the brush country of South Texas, the Plains of West Texas, and the high country in New Mexico.[5] Moreover, he was instrumental, along with Frank Chappell, Jr. and others, in creating the National Ranching Heritage Center at Texas Tech.[6]

Mitchell Ranch near Roy, New Mexico, avoiding any major disruptions of his own cattle operations. For the next few years, he operated at the Mitchell Ranch as well as at some of the other former Bell ranches, such as the Arnett Clabber Hill Ranch and the Trigg Ranch.

The Chappell Spade Ranch in New Mexico, where Leroy spent some time the past few years, evolved from a long and complex ranching empire. It takes a book to describe fully the origins of the Spade Ranch in Texas from which the New Mexico Bell purchase originated. Steve Kelton wrote such a book, now out of print, which chronologically describes the history of the Spades as well as the individuals who were a part of this history.[7] (Kelton, 1989) The 130-year history began with a U.S. cavalry officer named Joseph Rendlebrock, a member of the Fourth Cavalry stationed at Fort Concho, Texas. On one of his patrols in 1872 they moved north of what is now San Angelo into the Colorado River (Texas) watershed, finding "several fine springs." After a brief skirmish with Kiowas in the area, they trailed the elusive Indians, finding another larger spring. (Flowing springs have considerable significance in this part of semi-arid Texas.) A few years after Captain Rendlebrock had recorded the location of these springs, a man by the name of Isaac Ellwood entered the picture. He was an adventurous entrepreneur, transplanted from New York to Illinois, had worked as a teamster on the Erie Canal, and gone to California during the gold rush. Settled back in Illinois, he became acquainted with a local farmer named Joseph Farwell Glidden, the inventor of barbed wire. In 1872 they formed a partnership called the "Barb Fence Company." It was to become a very successful and lucrative venture.[8]

While Isaac Ellwood was pursuing his successful business in Illinois, the Snyder brothers (Dudley and John), a couple of Mississippi natives, were putting together a ranch at the springs discovered by Captain Rendlebrock (named Renderbrook by this time). The Kiowas and Comanches were under control; the cattle business was starting to thrive in Texas; and prior to the invention of the windmill, any country that had "living water" was attractive. By 1882, the Snyder brothers had firmed up title to thousands of acres in the vicinity of Renderbrook Springs. Their foreman was a cowboy and former Texas Ranger by the name of David Nathan (D.N.) Arnett, whose descendants also would later become players in the Bell Ranch purchases.

A drought in the late 1880s prompted the Snyders to look for a buyer. Isaac Ellwood, who had become wealthy from his barbed-wire venture, arrived on the scene. Ellwood purchased the ranch and inherited Arnett as his foreman. Isaac Ellwood eventually turned the ranch over to his son, W. L. Ellwood, who, along with his very talented foreman, D. N. "Uncle Dick" Arnett, significantly expanded what became known as the "Spade" ranches throughout the area. The Spade ranches, and later farms, covered an expanse which now encompasses cities such as Colorado City, Lubbock, Sweetwater, and Snyder. Like the other ranch histories, the Spades went through the transformation of range cattle operations before the turn of the century—

One cowboy working 40,000 acres,
Hampton Ranch (1995).

from open range to more controlled cattle management with barbed-wire fenced pastures and strategically located windmills. This was further enhanced when the Texas Pacific Railroad reached Colorado City (1881) and the Santa Fe Railroad reached Lubbock (1913), opening up more efficient access to markets. During the first fifty years, the Spades successfully survived droughts, the dust bowl, fluctuating cattle markets, and the screwworm ordeal.

Throughout the early part of the twentieth century, W. L. Ellwood and Uncle Dick Arnett created a vast ranching empire. They were astute enough to know that with underground water available, farming would increase the value of much of their property. Their breaking out (plowing) a good portion of grassland for cultivation was the beginning of the vast agricultural development in the North Plains near Lubbock (Lamb, Hockley, and Hale counties), which is so productive today.

At the time of his death in 1934, W. L. Ellwood had two married daughters—Jean (Jessie) and Elise (Harriet). Harriet Ellwood Keeney and Jean Ellwood Chappell were the primary heirs to the Spade ranches and farms. It was Harriet Ellwood Keeney who purchased the Bell Ranch headquarters area in 1948 and Jean Ellwood who purchased another portion of the Bell at approximately the same time. Jean's son, Frank Chappell, Jr., has provided continuity in this acquisition. Frank, Jr. was born in 1920, served in World War II, moved to Lubbock shortly thereafter, and was active in the management of the Spade properties, including the New Mexico Chappell Spade Ranch.[9] The Chappell Spade Ranch is still in the family, although the Keeney family sold their interest in the Bell Ranch in 1970 to William N. Lane II of Chicago, chairman and CEO of General Binding Corporation.[10]

The Arnett Clabber Hill Ranch, where Leroy spent some time, particularly with a Clabber Hill cowboy named Carlos Ortiz, had a history similar to the Spades. Uncle Dick Arnett, who was employed by Isaac Ellwood, had developed into an Ellwood business partner with both Isaac and his son, W.L. Uncle Dick's oldest of his ten children, Sam Arnett, also grew close to the Ellwoods, and they partnered on many cattle, ranch, and farming deals throughout the early 1900s. (Kelton, 1989) W. L. and Sam first bought the Nunn Ranch, then partnered with a man named Rube Clayton and purchased the Clabber Hill Ranch, which was located in Andrews County just south of Midland. Sam Arnett eventually bought out Clayton and Ellwood, then sold the Clabber Hill Ranch but kept the name (which carried over to the subsequent Bell Ranch purchase by Sam Arnett's son, Sam Arnett, Jr.). Sam Arnett, Sr. and his wife moved to Lubbock in 1918 from the old Nunn Ranch near Meadow, Texas. He and his wife lived in the now restored "Arnett House" until 1956.[11]

Sam Arnett, Jr. was born in 1908, and broke from the family tradition of ranching to become a physician. He attended Texas Tech College the first two years the school was open (1925-1926)[12] and then transferred to the

Leroy's last calf has been branded—Leroy and friends, Mitchell Ranch (1998).

University of Texas, receiving his M.D. in 1932. After interning in Brooklyn, New York, where he met his future wife, Olga, he returned to Lubbock in 1935 and became enormously successful as a physician, businessman, and philanthropist. He and his father purchased part of the Bell Ranch when it became available, along with the Keeneys, Chappells, and Hamptons, who purchased other Bell tracts. (The Hoovers were interim owners of the ranch that Howard Hampton purchased.) Sam, Jr. carried the Clabber Hill name to this ranch, and it is family-owned to this day.

In my research I contacted Sam, Jr.'s son, Sam Arnett III, who told me some great stories about his great-grandfather, "Uncle Dick" Arnett, as well as his grandfather, Sam, and father, Sam, Jr.[13] Most interesting was a story about Uncle Dick which was not in the material I researched. This great-grandfather of Sam III drove a large herd of cattle to California in the 1870s to satisfy the beef demand created by the gold rush. On Uncle Dick's return, he was on a train near Fort Worth carrying his cattle-sale money in a large trunk. The notorious train robber Sam Bass robbed him and made his getaway. The Texas Rangers later killed Sam Bass in Round Rock, Texas (just north of Austin), but Uncle Dick never retrieved his money, and it temporarily broke him. According to Sam III, the trunk was later recovered as well as a gun holster and a few other items which now are in the University of Texas archives.

Sam III recalls some other interesting stories. One involved his grandfather, Sam, Sr., and W. L. Ellwood during the stock market crash in 1929.

My grandfather (Sam, Sr.) was on the Board of the Citizens National Bank (Lubbock) in 1929 when the crash occurred. All the directors had co-signed a note to the First National Bank in Fort Worth for money this bank had loaned to Citizens. Mr. Ellwood (W. L.) and my grandfather (Sam, Sr.) were feeding 6,000 head of cattle on some of this borrowed money. My granddad called up Mr. Ellwood and told him that all of the directors of the Citizens National Bank had declared bankruptcy; there would be a run on the bank, and they were going to lose everything, including all the cattle. Mr. Ellwood told my granddad, "If you will go and run that bank (Citizens), I'll send you all the money you need down on the train, and you can keep that bank open." He did, and I have a picture somewhere of my grandfather spreading all that money over the counter of the bank. That saved the bank which Mr. Ellwood and my grandfather owned. They sold it in 1949.

There's a long history between the Ellwood family and the Arnett family. So, that was one reason my grandfather went to the Ellwood Estate to get them to buy part of the Bell Ranch (1947-1948). He thought a lot of that country up there. Howard Hampton was a close friend of my granddad, and he bought part of it. With a few exceptions, it was all Lubbock people who ended up with it.

Carlos Ortiz is a cowboy of long association with Leroy, a relationship marked by great mutual respect. Carlos now lives on his own ranch near Tucumcari but spent many of his cowboy years working for the former Bell Chappell Spade and Clabber Hill ranches, both located between Tucumcari and Conchos Lake. His father died when he was six. Carlos grew up hard, and actually started cowboying about the time he reached the seventh grade. The Clabber Hill was leased out at that time to the Matador Ranch successors, and Carlos started his young cowboy career branding calves. For the next eighteen years he worked off and on at the Clabber Hill for the various lessors who had cattle at the ranch. He recalls the ranch was 86,000 acres, with one pasture comprising over 45,000 acres.

He first met Leroy in the early 1980s at a team-roping contest. Carlos

It's uphill, you know, but if you love it, you love it. It's worth it all, and I'd never do anything else but punch cows.

—Carlos Ortiz

asked Leroy if he wanted to team up with him and got no response (not re-
alizing Leroy was partially deaf). He was disappointed in Leroy's lack of response, figuring Leroy was not interested in teaming with such a relatively
young cowboy. Once he figured out the communication problem, he asked
again, and Leroy readily agreed. That was the beginning of a long-term personal and professional relationship that still remains. Carlos commented on
Leroy as a friend and as a skilled cowboy:

> *Leroy never did anything halfway—it was always one hundred and ten
> percent. He always had a rope in his hand—loved to rope—but a lot of
> time he doesn't need it. I've seen him tie his rope to his saddle when
> working cattle and leave it there. When he gets around a mother cow and
> its calf, he can tell you what they're saying to each other. He has an un-
> canny sense with livestock—with both cattle and horses. He can make
> horses do things they don't want to do—always gentle and smooth. I ad-
> mire him a lot. He's kind of a god to me. He's the reason I went out on
> my own. I'd still be working for wages if it wasn't for Leroy. He'd tell me
> stories about starting out as a ten-year-old, always working for wages.
> Then later went on his own, starting up his own mother cow operation
> and leasing ranches. That's when I started doing the same thing. One
> time when Leroy lost one of his leases, he sold me a bunch of his cows
> and gave me a real good deal. Of course, it's hard—you've got to fight the
> market and you've got to fight the drought. It's uphill, you know, but if
> you love it, you love it. It's worth it all, and I'd never do anything else but
> punch cows.*

Both Leroy and Carlos tell the same story, which goes back to the mid-
1990s when Leroy was leasing the Hampton Ranch and Carlos was running
the Clabber Hill Ranch. There were about 3,800 yearlings spread out over
one pasture of 45,000 acres plus a lot more at the Clabber Hill that had to
be gathered and shipped out. When Carlos and his crew finished gathering,
the count showed 100 head still missing. The owner told Carlos that he
would pay him $30 a head for finding and bringing in these lost yearlings.
Carlos called his good friend Leroy to help him out, contracted with the
owner on the deal, and told Leroy he would split the money with him for
helping him find these calves. Leroy agreed, and off they went.

Only people from that part of the country can perceive the difficulty in
finding 100 yearlings located somewhere within an area of over seventy
square miles of rough county. The Canadian River, which split the main pasture, was wide and boggy, with lots of salt cedars and brush. Moreover, there
were many mesas, rugged canyons, and rocky hillsides—good places for
calves to hide. There was no way to get a pickup in the main pasture, as it
was impossible to cross the Canadian River with a vehicle. Therefore, Leroy
and Carlos had to unload the horses and gear at an old hunting cabin and
then took off on horseback cross-country, carrying what gear they needed to
gather the calves. Carlos knew the country. They would ride all day, gather

what they could, secure them, spend the night on the ground, and start again the next day. Leroy recalls:

> One day we found twenty head—that's $600 or $300 each. Man, we'd never have to work again! We were going to get rich and were having a lot of fun. The next day we were in the saddle twenty hours and rode down four horses—and found one calf. Fifteen dollars apiece for twenty hours in the saddle wasn't very good wages! Anyway, we did this for ten days, and I mean we rode hard. We rode all our horses down, borrowed horses, used every horse we could find. Slept on the ground, cooked all our meals over a campfire, and kept our horses shod. There's no telling how many miles we rode those two weeks. We had to cross the Canadian with our gathered calves as most of the country was on the north side of the river and the pens were on the south side. On one crossing Carlos was riding a horse named Blackie that I didn't think much of ... He was a runaway sucker. I mean this horse would take off and you couldn't turn him or stop him. You just had to hold on. Well, this heifer jumped out of the salt cedars near the river, and Carlos and ol' Blackie took off after her. I mean, the race was on, trying to get close enough to that heifer to rope her. Then we lost her in the brush. She just bedded down, and we couldn't find her. Well, we finally saw her just lying down in the brush, and she wouldn't move. Then she'd get up, run a hundred or so yards, then lie down again. She hung in the brush, and there was no way to get a rope on her. Anyway, she finally broke out of the river bed, and I was able to catch up and rope her. This black horse was still running in circles with ol' Carlos, and when Carlos saw I had the calf and finally slowed down his horse, he came over to me just as mad as I've ever seen him. Although he was disgusted with the horse, he'd lost his hat in the chase. He said, "It was a hell of a note to lose a $150 hat chasing a $30 heifer."
>
> Ol' Carlos is a hand. If you give him an even break on anything, he'll beat you. You would never learn to rope following ol' Carlos around waiting for a second loop. He never missed.

Carlos and Leroy gathered ninety-nine calves during those weeks. They thought they'd made good money—almost $1,500 each. Then, as Carlos related to me, they started figuring out how much they'd made per hour in the saddle, or per mile ridden, or per acre covered, and realized it just wasn't that much. Still, Carlos said those were the best two weeks of his life: up in the morning, Leroy cooking breakfast while he wrangled the horses, and off to work. Of the eighteen years Carlos had worked on the Clabber Hill he never had more fun than that. Leroy concluded that if you want to gather a bunch of wild cattle, "you won't find a better cowboy than Carlos Ortiz."

Leroy had now leased the Hampton Ranch, then contracted work at the Chappell Spade, the Arnett Clabber Hill, and the Trigg ranches, all during the period of 1995 to 1997. He was doing what he loved to do, and he left his mark on each of those four old Bell ranches. Next he was able to lease a portion of the nearby Mitchell Ranch.

The Mitchell Ranch was organized by Thomas Edward Mitchell, who had moved from Colorado in 1881 to the Tequesquite Valley just east of Mosquero, New Mexico. He managed the Bar T Ranch and was able to purchase adjoining acreage over the years. He established New Mexico's first herd of registered Hereford cattle in the early 1900s and later served in the New Mexico State Senate, introducing the bill that created Harding County, where his ranch was located. (This was shortly after New Mexico had established statehood in 1912.) He named his ranch the Tequesquite Ranch, building up a sizeable tract of land. After Mitchell died in 1934, his son, Albert K. Mitchell, took over, while working a "day job" as general manager of the nearby Bell Ranch. When the Bell sold, Albert K. was able to expand his own holdings at the Tequesquite, at one point comprising 180,000 acres. Like his father, Albert K. served in the New Mexico Senate.

Albert K. Mitchell died in 1980 at the age of eighty-six. His daughter, Linda Mitchell, married Frank Springer's grandson, J. Leslie Davis, ultimately managing the CS Ranch. Albert K. Mitchell's only son, Albert J., was killed when the plane in which he was flying over the ranch crashed. When Leroy obtained his lease at the Mitchell Ranch, it was being run by Albert J.'s four children. Leroy recalls some of his memories at the Mitchell Ranch:

> About 1997, I leased part of the ol' Albert K. Mitchell Ranch. I was running about 500 cows. The last year I was there, I believe that was 1998, I had this bunch of calves to brand, and I called my friends together to help. I called ol' Jack Kyle to come down, ol' Charlie Duran, the sheriff from Cimarron, people from all over and all the neighbors—the McCarty Ranch, the Craig Ranch, and others. We ended up with thirty cowboys, most of them really good hands, and had these cattle in five different bunches—had them up pretty close to the branding pen. So, they all come over there one morning, about four o'clock. We had breakfast and started out. We had one bunch right at the pen, put them in and started branding. Half of us started branding these calves and the other half set out to bring another bunch in. Sure enough, we just had this one bunch branded, and they come with another bunch. They'd pick up this branded herd and start back with them, and start another bunch in while branding this bunch they just brought in. Anyway, by eleven o'clock in the morning, we had this 500 head of calves branded.

Leroy and his guests took a little lunch break after branding 500 calves that morning, then decided to have some fun before dinner. There were about sixty to seventy head of wild burros up on the mesas of the Mitchell Ranch that had been running wild up there for about forty years. Leroy and those who had any "post-branding" energy remaining decided to go up on the mesa to try to rope some of the burros. They chased the burros through cactus and mesquite, uphill and downhill, and were able to rope fifteen of them. They tied them down, brought up stock trailers, and loaded them up—just like cattle. Anyone who wanted a burro could then get one to take home. After the burros were all secured with their new owners, they cooked steaks over the campfire, told old cowboy stories into the night—and went home. This was a typical Leroy Webb day on the range—4:00 A.M. gathering and branding calves, then lunch after all 500 had been branded, then chasing and roping wild burros until dark, then dinner and tall tales into the night. Leroy's summary of it all: "We had lots of fun and got lots of work done. I had a lot of good friends and good neighbors. With this crew we were able to brand about 120 to 125 calves per hour. That's hard to do."

In 1998 Leroy Webb was brought to the attention of a man by the name of Henry Singleton, a Texan who had made billions of dollars in the electronics business in California (Teledyne) and had been buying up ranches all over the state of New Mexico. He asked Leroy to run his Bar Y Ranch north of Santa Rosa, and Leroy agreed. The Bar Y phase brings Leroy's life full circle. In 2002 the Bar Y headquarters, some seventeen miles north of Santa Rosa, is where Leroy and Nora call home.

Leroy and friends—lunchtime at the Hampton Ranch.

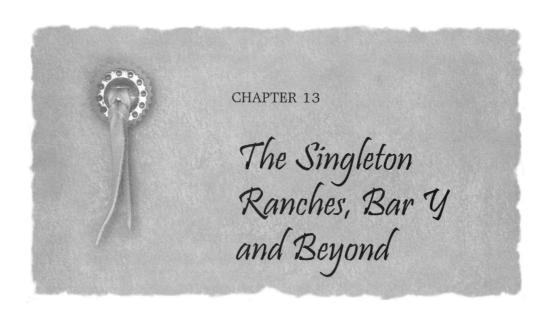

CHAPTER 13

The Singleton Ranches, Bar Y and Beyond

*L*eroy and Nora established their home at the headquarters complex of the Singleton Bar Y Ranch north of Santa Rosa in 1999 at the request of Henry Singleton. The famous business executive, founder of the corporate conglomerate Teledyne, Inc., had heard of Leroy's reputation as a man of integrity and as an excellent cowboy and manager. The two became friends in the early 1990s through Harp McFarland. Singleton had approached Leroy to manage his Bar Y Ranch on several occasions, and once his lease had expired at the Mitchell Ranch, Leroy decided to accept the offer.

Henry Singleton, starting to divest his interests in Teledyne, felt there was no better investment than to place some of the proceeds into good ranch properties. He developed an affinity for land and ranching as a youth, having been raised in North Texas. In the mid-1980s he contacted selected ranch realtors in New Mexico and was first led to the San Cristobal Ranch located on U.S. Highway 285 just south of Santa Fe. This ranch, like the others that Leroy had worked, served as home to many peoples and cultures over the last several millennia, and all left some traces. (Mednick, 1996) Singleton selected ranches to purchase, not on the quality of improvements but on the quality of the land.[1]

The San Cristobal, previously owned by the Sawyer Cattle Company,

*Above: A Singleton stallion on the
Bar Y Ranch (2001).*

*Right: Nora and Leroy at the Bar Y
Ranch Headquarters (2001).*

(Photographs by Gray Hawn)

then Bill Blakley of Braniff Airlines, consists of 81,000 acres of rolling grasslands, low mesas with scrubby forests of piñon pine and juniper, and dissecting canyons and arroyos. The ranch lies within the great expanses of the Galisteo Basin, surrounded by the Sangre de Cristo Range, the Sandia Mountains, the Rio Grande, and the High Plains. Its history is complex, but generally follows the patterns of the other large New Mexico ranches. Santa Fe's Governor Armijo, the Treaty of Guadalupe Hidalgo, and a partnership between a grantee (Nicolas Pinto) and an Anglo

Leroy sorting mamas from calves, Bar Y, 2002.

Enjoying a Leroy-cooked breakfast before gathering, separating, roping, dragging, flanking, branding, castrating, and vaccinating unweaned calves, 2002.

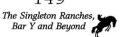
(Thomas Catron) were factors in the genesis of the San Cristobal during the nineteenth century.

Subsequent transactions during the late nineteenth and twentieth centuries were filled with land and treaty disputes, various owners, politics, and court battles. Thomas Catron, a Civil War veteran from Missouri, arrived in New Mexico as a young man, and between 1869 and 1917 served as state attorney general, state legislator, district attorney, and finally one of New Mexico's first two U.S. senators. Catron obtained a piece of the San Cristobal Ranch in legal fees. Saron Laughlin eventually bought out Catron's share and became sole owner of the San Cristobal. Then Benjamin Pankey, a farmer from Illinois, bought the San Cristobal from profits he made in the early telephone business. (Mednick, 1996) The Sawyer Cattle Company out of Texas bought the controlling interest of the San Cristobal in 1948. In 1955, Bill Blakley, then a U.S. senator from Texas, purchased the ranch. Later he transferred the land to the Blakley-Braniff Foundation, a charitable corporation run by Blakley.

Dr. Singleton and his wife, Carolyn, purchased the ranch from an interim owner in 1986.[2] Following this purchase, Singleton acquisitions included the Bigbee Ranch (now Lobo Ranch), Bojax Ranch, Canon de Agua Ranch, Conchas Ranch, Dan Trigg Ranch, Dunlap Ranch, Hollywood River Ranch, Latigo Ranch, Marley Ranch I, Marley Ranch II, Moon Ranch, 9-Bar Ranch, Payne Ranch, Pino Springs Ranch, C A Ranch, Shepherd Ranch, V. K. Jones Estate Ranch, Worley Ranch, Agua Verde Ranch, and the Bar Y Ranch, where Singleton hired Leroy as manager.[3] The total Singleton holdings today in New Mexico total 1.2 million acres (about 1.5 percent of the total New Mexico area) located in the counties of Chaves, DeBaca, Guadalupe, Lincoln, Quay, San Miguel, Santa Fe, and Torrence. (Crosswind, 1997)[4]

The San Cristobal Ranch was one of Henry Singleton's favorite places, and he spent much of his later years there. According to his manager, Harp McFarland, he could relax there, ride the ranch and look after his cattle, and generally unwind from the frantic pace of his Teledyne and Los Angeles life. Singleton said:

> *My greatest reward is just being out in the country, the association with the land, animals, and people. I like the feeling of participation—of taking care of the land. It's a nice feeling. I like to do it under a normal constraint: Take care of the land, and in turn, take care of the people who work on it.*

In 1987 he asked his daughter, Christina Singleton Mednick, to put together a pictorial history of the San Cristobal. With support from her husband, Murray, her siblings, John, Will, Jim, Diana, and Pamela, as well as others, she created an extraordinary book on the San Cristobal Ranch. (Mednick, 1996). This book, rich in history and photography, is a real tribute to her family and predecessors.

Today, the Singleton ranches in New Mexico are run by an overall manager located in Santa Fe, who is responsible for the individual operating units (divisions). Leroy manages the unit headquartered at the Bar Y Ranch north of Santa Rosa. His good friend, Harp McFarland, has retired and lives just south of the San Cristobal, where he still occasionally "helps out." Leroy recalls how some of these Singleton ranches came together:

> *Well, Henry [Singleton] started buying up these ranches. I think the San Cristobal was one of the first. Then ol' Ronnie Meyers, a real estate guy out of Roswell, sold him a bunch of ranches. He bought the Lobo Ranch [formerly the Bigbee Ranch] near Vaughn, the Bojac Ranch on the Pecos River near Fort Sumner and over 200,000 acres, the Conchas Ranch which is next to the Bar Y, and the Trigg Ranch plus some others. The Trigg brothers bought about 218,000 acres from the Bell many years ago, then sold some to the Waggoners and split up the rest. Singleton then bought out one of Trigg's. He then bought the Agua Verde Ranch, about 100,000 acres, which joins the Shelly Hays Ranch where I used to work. Then he bought the Worley Ranch which was a part of the Hampton Ranch (where Davis Ford got me the lease).[5] I tried to get Henry to buy the Hampton Ranch as it was up for sale while I was leasing it in 1996. I showed the ranch to Henry, and he told me if he bought it, he would go against his practice of not leasing any of his ranches and let me continue leasing it. That made me feel good, and I appreciated that. Mrs. Hampton's trustees wanted $87.50 per acre, and Henry offered slightly less. Well, someone come along and offered the asking price. So, it was sold out from under Henry, and I lost my lease. Henry later told me and Harp that he wished he would have bought the Hamptons.[6] Earlier, Singleton bought the Bar Y and Jones Ranches. I had worked on the Bar Y in 1957, when it was owned by Driggers. Driggers had leased the Jones Ranch for many years, and a lot of people thought the two was just one ranch. Well, Henry bought the Jones Ranch first, then patiently waited until he could buy the Bar Y. He was a good businessman, had good timing, and was awful good to me. I had gotten to know him good through Harp McFarland, and when he offered me the chance to manage his Bar Y division in 1998, I took it. So, after first working at the Bar Y in 1957, here I was again, and I'm still here today.*
>
> *Singleton was just one of the best guys in the world . . . a very humble man. He didn't put his name on gates or fences or nothing. Got along with the cowboys who worked for him—just a good man.*

Leroy and Nora have resided at the Bar Y throughout the process of compiling the materials for this book. I made several trips there to interview

If you can talk with crowds and keep your virtue
Or walk with kings yet keep the common touch
Then the world is yours and all that's in it . . .
—Rudyard Kipling

them and to get a personal feel for the daunting and challenging task Leroy has in managing such a large ranching unit (more than 100,000 acres with some individual pastures of over 18,000 acres). He runs this ranch with virtually no help, spending seven full days a week caring for cattle, branding, and shipping while maintaining fences and other improvements. Moreover, he is frequently called on by other Singleton managers to assist them on adjoining ranches. The energy and efficiency of the man is remarkable. Many of my large corporate clients over the years have prided themselves on their complex "time and motion" studies designed to maximize manufacturing efficiency. I would suggest that none have attained the efficiency level that I've observed from this seventy-year-old isolated cowboy operating at the Bar Y Ranch near Santa Rosa, New Mexico.

The Bar Y has it all: excellent and relatively undergrazed prairieland for fattening yearlings, ample water from the Pecos River, which meanders some forty miles through the center of the ranch, and rugged country that provides good protection from the elements for mother cows and their young calves. Leroy describes the Bar Y and his work there:

*Faces of today's cowboys, young and old—
Bar Y Ranch, May 2002.*

I like it—man, I like this business! This is a good ranch and a good job. Sometimes I feel like I ought to be payin' them to have this job! I still got lots of energy—can't do some of the things I used to do, but I put in a lot of twelve-hour days sittin' on a horse, feedin' cattle, and checkin' on things. I don't need much more than four hours of sleep a night. But it's not that hard. Every once in a while we've got to get with it. Last Saturday I went to another division, and we branded 350 calves. I had to get up at 3:00 to get my horses saddled and loaded. I got to the pens about 5:30 (I like to be early), and we branded until 3:00 that afternoon, then had lunch. I don't rope as much as I used to. Anyways, it's a good job. I have lots of freedom on running the division. Of course, the owners keep track of things, but I'm pretty well on my own. They very seldom come out here, so I make most of the day-to-day decisions.

What lies beyond the Bar Y? Leroy plans to continue managing it for another year or so and eventually play out his career at a modest farm/ranch property he recently purchased near Tucumcari at the base of the famous landmark, Tucumcari Mountain. That will give him more time to "run a few cows and raise, break, and train his continuing line of good, quality horses." I've encouraged him to slow it down a bit and "smell the roses." But based on my recent observations of his seventy- and eighty-year-old cowboy friends I've interviewed, I doubt that he will ever do this. His energy level is too high and his love for what he does is too intense. As D Burns of the Pitchfork Ranch said, "Ranching is not a business—it's a disease." These "last cowboys," such as Leroy and his friends, seem to display all the symptoms of this disease and will likely carry it with them all the way to the end of the trail.

CHAPTER 14

Cowboys
I've Known

Throughout my time with Leroy over the past several years, he's mentioned many of his cowboy friends. I interviewed all those I could locate and have cited a few in this book. My regret is not being able to find some of them or missing the opportunity to have interviewed others prior to their death. The opportunity to get to know these cowboys and their family members has been one of the most satisfying experiences in my flirtation with cowboy history. I have reserved this chapter to record, to the greatest extent possible, a brief commentary on each of these cowboys whom Leroy so fondly remembers as true "cowboys" or "cowhands." He sets the stage with the following commentary:

Well, to start with, there's all different kinds of cowboys. The ol' original cowboy was just a ranch hand—worked on ranches, took care of the cows and drove them to market, just generally took care of them cows. He slept on the ground most of the time and seldom went to town at night. That was the real cowboy. Then there was the rodeo cowboys that evolved from the ol' ranch cowboys. Then came along the feedlot cowboys, and they are different. Now, today, there are a whole lot of "wanna-be" cowboys. So, I'll start out with telling about some sure enough cowboys. You seldom see the early cowboys. Back then there wasn't that many rodeos to start with. Then those ol' time cowboys started getting together, putting on a contest

Leroy with Hugh Bennett.

once in a while—once a year or a couple of times a year. Then rodeos just evolved from that and got to be a real big thing, and most of the top rodeo cowboys during my time got their start on ranches. I've just had the opportunity in my life to be around some of the best—real cow-boys—who are good people, good friends.

Leroy and I got to-gether at a remote booth in Santa Rosa's Denny's Restaurant one wintry af-ternoon in early January 2002 to conduct our last interview, devoted strictly to cowboys and horses. For almost three hours we talked on these two subjects. The discussion could easily have lasted through the night. The fraternal bonds among these cowboys as well as the horses they've ridden are beyond description, and Leroy reveres such associations. I learned that he frequently uses the descriptors "top hand" or "good cow-boy," reserved strictly for the top one percent of his profession. If I spent a week helping him at the Bar Y, the best I probably could get is "Well, he's got a way to go" or "Pretty good ol' boy, but he oughta stick with engineer-ing." At any rate, he recited comprehensive descriptions of a few cowboys he remembers during his last sixty years as a cowhand. Using these tapes as a guide, I compiled his thoughts on cowboys he has known.

We started off with John Stevens, manager of the Matador Division when Leroy was a teenage cowhand there. Bill Hemphill, wagon boss at the time, and Leroy both hold the man in high esteem both as a manager and as a good working cowboy. Bill recalls that many times Stevens would exit his manager's role and help the old cowhands with the hot and dirty work of the day. Leroy was impressed that Stevens knew all the cowhands' names at the Matador, and was a "hands-on" kind of manager. John Stevens is alive today and was present (although confined to a wheelchair) at the last Matador re-union. John Holleyman started off on a ranch and was a "top calf roper—one of the best." Holleyman has his own ranch and is now in his eighties. Leroy would see Holleyman at rodeos quite frequently, and they would do a lot of roping together, especially team roping. James Kenny is an old-time cowboy

*Above: Leroy Webb and Jack Kyle checking
out the country.*

Right: Jack Kyle—Yukon, Oklahoma (2001).

who currently has a book out about his cowboy life. He was a bronc rider and roper. Kenny is in his nineties and has a ranch near Carlsbad, New Mexico. Hugh Bennett was an Arizona cowboy. He started rodeoing in the "Turtle Association," precursor to the Rodeo Cowboy Association (RCA). Bennett helped start the RCA, and was a world champion bulldogger in 1938 and a world champion steer roper in 1942. Being an older cowboy than Leroy, he had Leroy break horses for him. Leroy told me a story about his good friend Hugh, "a good man and a good cowboy":

> In the early days, back in the '40s, he was trying to put a ranch together up around Falcon, Colorado. Times were tough. He

Leroy and Ben Johnson.

was rodeoing to make payments and pay expenses. He would have a fellow at the ranch taking care of things. When Hugh would come through, he would go to town to pick up supplies for the hand and to buy necessities. He would shop for the least expensive stuff. One day, his hand (Keith) had a visitor, and he was complaining about some stuff and told his visitor that Hugh had brought him some cheap toilet paper that wasn't any better than the Montgomery Ward catalog. "Why, that toilet paper is just like my boss." His friend asked him how can that be. Keith replied, "It is rough, tough, and won't take no crap off nobody." I don't know about the paper, but that sure fit my friend Hugh.

Dick Yates was a great cowboy. He started out riding bareback, then started rop-

Four cowboys—Billy Rey, Jack Kyle, Carlos Ortiz, and Leroy Webb.

ing. Probably in his late sixties, he lives in Pueblo, Colorado. His son, J. D. Yates, is "as good a roper there is." Leroy remembers him "with a rope in his hand about the time he learned to walk." At the age of fifteen he was the youngest man to ever qualify professionally for team roping. George Cowden recalls seeing J. D. Yates interviewed on television following the National Finals Rodeo (NFR), in which

*Bud Webb and Uncle John Cordova with Leroy—
"Sure 'nuff good cowboys."*

he and his father won the heading and heeling event. When the interviewer asked J. D. why his father made him the heeler, his reply was, "Daddy can't heel, so he made me do it." Jud Knight was just an "old-time cowpuncher" who worked with Leroy's dad, Bud Webb, as early as 1928. He ran the WS Ranch for a while and worked at the UU Bar. When Leroy was fourteen years old, he went to work for Jud Knight.

Juan Cordova, Leroy's grandfather and early mentor, was a Trinidad, Colorado, cowboy. Juan started out breaking horses, then did a lot of early rodeo work in southern Colorado. He was a great bronc rider, good cowboy, and "top hand." Don Webb, Leroy's older brother, has had a long and close relationship with Leroy. I've gotten to know Don through several interviews at his home in Raton and elsewhere. In his early seventies, he still breaks horses and has a great sense of humor. He and Leroy have cowboyed together since their childhood and have an obvious mutual respect. Don spent a good portion of his career training race horses while Leroy focused on training roping and show horses. Like Leroy, he fits the perfect profile of an authentic old-time cowhand.

Lefty Wilkins was an old-timer who came off a ranch and got into rodeos as a roper. He later became one of the top "pickup" men in the country.[1] I asked Leroy if rodeo performers got paid much as pickup men. His response was, "No, but it was far better wages than they would have got as a ranch hand back in those days." Jim Payne has been friends with Leroy a long time.

*Good shipping crew on the Fort Union Ranch (includes shipping boss,
Chester Norman, and cowboy, Leroy Webb).*

He lives in Logan, New Mexico, and has helped Leroy out when working the
old Bell Ranches (he took some of the photographs in this book when gathering and branding cattle on the Hampton Ranch). James Rinestine, an old
cowpuncher, also lives near Logan, and has his own ranch now.

Keith Slover was a Matador cowboy who broke a lot of horses with
Leroy in the early days. The two left a lot of hard-earned ranch money in Fort
Worth on a few weekends during their youth. Keith now lives in Paducah,
Texas. John Andrews is an Arizona cowboy and somewhat older than Leroy.
He was breaking horses with Rosie Deaton at the Matador when Leroy first
showed up looking for a job. He's back in Arizona still doing some cowboy
work. The Kyle brothers, Dub, Joe, Red, and Jack, came off a Fort Sumner
ranch, and all four stayed with the profession. Jack got into training and
showing horses while the other three brothers settled in for "just old hard
ranch work." Two of the brothers, Red and Jack, are still living. Red has retired in Fort Sumner, and Jack is in his seventies and still drags and brands
calves as well as anybody. Leroy calls Jack a "high-class gentleman." Jack
Kyle, whom I interviewed at his ranch in Yukon, Oklahoma, is a tough and

Clockwise from top:

Checking out some horses
(Wanda Ridley, Leroy, and
Dennis McKinley).

Leroy and friends at sunset—
"The perfect fusion of the
human soul with sun and
sky and land."

Dennis McKinley—cowboy,
roper, and evangelist.

remarkable man, still working long hours training and selling quarter horses. It was Jack who got the job for Leroy with Wiescamp and helped Leroy get started in the quarter horse training and breeding business. Leroy says, "Ol' Jack Kyle can do more with a two-year-old colt than anyone I ever knew." The two have been best friends for more than forty-five years and have done "a lot of roping together."

Ben Johnson, the cowboy and movie actor, started out in Oklahoma working cattle and roping in rodeos. He then took a string of horses to California for director John Ford and actor John Wayne and became a full-time character actor in the movies. Ben took a year off from his acting career and did some full-time rodeoing, becoming a world champion team roper. Leroy and his cowboy friend Bill Hemphill "never saw Ben Johnson on a bad horse." Leroy added, "All top hands have good horses because they make 'em that way." Another friend of Leroy, Oscar Crigler, helped train horses for the actor. Ben Johnson maintained a lasting friendship with these cowboys, his western roots firmly established before he hit the Hollywood scene and maintained long thereafter.

Bill Hemphill was another Matador cowboy friend of Leroy's, now in his eighties. Bill is still working mother cows and calves at his ranch near Roaring Springs, Texas. He is a well-respected gentleman, having spent most of his life as a wagon boss on both the Matadors and Four Sixes. He started with the Matadors when he was sixteen and became the youngest wagon boss ever for

Leroy's list of "cowboys I've known" goes on and on. It's difficult to include them all in this book. During our fifteen years of association, Leroy has mentioned countless other cowboys he's known and admired. Many of them are now gone, and he's nostalgic about the memories he has of those cowboys. The following is an incomplete list of those, both living and dead, "who have spent years on the range tending to livestock."

Jack Kyle	John Andrews	Troy Fort	Dennis McKinley
Bud Webb	Hugh Bennett	Sonny Davis	Charles Good
Juan Cordova	Ben Johnson	Mozaun McKibben	King Merrit
Jud Knight	Bill Hemphill	Bill Smith	John Cordova
Joe McLaughlin	Albert Lopez	Chester Norman	Chuck Wolf
Rosie Deaton	Oscar Crigler	Colin Lane	Carlos Ortiz
Donn Davies	Stogie Bumpas	Craig Gudsell	Ken James
Toke Harp	Tom Morehouse	Keith James	Matlock Rose
Wishy Derikson	Lewis Kincaid	Warren Shoemaker	Shoat Webster
Harper McFarland	Keith Slover	Ralph Tixier	Monte Rook
Waldo Haythorn	Buster Welch	Paul Tierney	Freddie Martinez
Jim Payne	Don Dodge	Levi Garcia	Mark Voss
Don Webb	Sam Sessions	Magin Martinez	Leo Camarillo
James Kenny	Dub Kyle	Billy Allen	Charlie Duran
Lefty Wilkens	Joe Kyle	Bobby Lewis	Dick Yates
John D. Hollyman	Red Kyle	James Rinestine	

Leroy, Shoat Webster, and Ward at old-timers reunion, Cimarron, New Mexico.

the Matador Ranch. He was then and is now a "quiet, unassuming cowboy who works well with men and is very competent in what he does." Charles Good, a New Mexico cowboy raised around Fort Sumner, was one of the top steer ropers in the country. Billy Allen and Bobby Lewis were both about Leroy's age, good friends, and outstanding horsemen. Albert Lopez is a South Dakota cowboy and a relative of Leroy on his mother's side of the family. He is a "great breeder of horses and an excellent horseman."

Bud Webb, Leroy's dad, was a "sure 'nuff good cowboy," teaching Leroy his first cowboying skills. Leroy said he got his "itchy feet" from his father, who just took off with his horse and a pack horse and worked from one ranch to another. "I just followed him around and learned how to be a cowboy. He never had to discipline Don and me very much, but he would when he had to."

Carlos Ortiz is a New Mexico cowboy who lives west of Tucumcari. Carlos lost his father early and had to do a lot of things on his own at an early age. "I went to the Clabber Hill Ranch when I was in the seventh grade and got my first real job," he said. The Matadors had the ranch lease then, and there was a lot of branding to do. The teenager got started with branding. Frank Chappell later leased the Clabber Hill Ranch for five years, and Carlos got to know him. (I talked to both Carlos and Frank on this subject.) Carlos remembers that "Frank wouldn't come to the ranch much, but when he did, he'd make it a point to go around to all the line camps and talk to all of the wives. He'd remember everybody's name. He is really a nice man." Carlos'

Harp McFarland—
San Cristobal Ranch (2002).

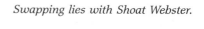

Swapping lies with Shoat Webster.

Leroy, Jean Hancock, Shoat Webster, and Nora.

son-in-law currently works at the Pitchfork Ranch and "loves ranching like I do . . . My son is an electrician and helps me out on the ranch, but doesn't really like it that much. My son-in-law is like me—get in the saddle and go, while my son wants to go wire a house. He makes a good living at that, but that's not what I want to do. I want to punch cows." Carlos thinks the reason western clothes have become so expensive is that "everybody wants to wear a hat and boots . . . Now, I was looking down at a bunch of wanna-be cowboys the other day, and I started thinking, 'What would they think of me if I went into their office and tried to punch a computer?' But, I don't want to do that." Carlos is still a relatively young man but a very skilled cowboy. Like all the others, "I wouldn't change being a cowboy for anything. I love what I do."

Charlie Duran is a Colfax County sheriff. He loves ranching and is a good cowboy but he really enjoys being a lawman. Charlie helps Leroy out in his spare time. Leroy stated that Charlie "likes people . . . is good with people, and a good lawman. He even stopped me for speeding one time in one of those speed traps." Buster Welch is a cutting horse man—a good cowboy and top professional rodeo man. Everybody around Nebraska knows Waldo Haythorn. He owns a large horse operation, and "everyone knows about Haythorn horses in Nebraska. I got to know him on the show circuit, and he got to liking me because he thought I also was a good cowboy. He judged a lot of contests—still lives up there."

Chester Norman was a New Mexico cowboy Leroy met at the Fort Union Ranch when Norman was manager. "We got to working together, helping each other out, and later I neighbored with him. He was a good horseman, good cattleman, good roper." Dennis McKinley, Leroy's stepson, started roping at the Shelly Hays Ranch under Leroy's watchful eye when just a little fellow and became a "sure 'nuff good roper." McKinley won a bunch of roping contests in the United States; then, as a mature cowboy, he moved to Australia, where he became a champion calf roper. Both Nora and Leroy think the world of Dennis, who now is an evangelist living near Fort Worth. He is described as a "first class fellow."

Chuck Wolf, a Nevada cowboy, met Leroy in Colorado when Leroy was breeding and training horses. They shared a lot of stories about good horses. Colin Lane was a Texas cowboy who worked with Leroy on several ranches. Lane rodeoed quite a bit, team roping primarily, but Leroy said he "was a cowboy first." He grew up on a ranch, and that's where he belonged. Virtually all the cowboys recalled by Leroy were raised on ranches, developing their skills there. Some later migrated into rodeos or horse training and showing. Greg Gudsell was a New Mexico cowboy whom Leroy recalls being "a big stout fellow." He and Leroy and a few others were in rough country trying to load a calf into a horse trailer on the Trigg Ranch a few years back. Leroy recalls, "We had this calf roped . . . drug him up to the trailer . . . and couldn't pull him no more 'cause we were afraid we'd break his legs. Well, a couple of guys tried to lift him up to the trailer and couldn't. So, ol' Greg got off his horse, grabbed the calf by the ears, and pulled him straight up into that trailer. Man, he was stout! I sat there on my horse and told ol' Greg, 'Man, if I were as stout as you, I would not even need to own a horse!'"

Troy Fort was a champion calf and steer roper who befriended Leroy in the rodeo circuit. Leroy visited him many times after their rodeo years and "now ol' Troy is no longer with us." Ken and Keith James were brothers who were raised on a ranch. Their dad was a cowboy, and both of his sons never wanted to do anything else. Leroy first met them at rodeos (Leroy was roping, and they were riding saddle broncs). They were amateur rodeo contestants but spent their careers as "range cowboys." Leo Camarillo of California was a top professional rodeo performer—a world champion roper and "all around cowboy." Leroy never worked cattle with him and didn't know about his skills out on the range, but "boy, could he rope . . . In his day I think he was the top roper in the world." Levi Garcia is a good friend, now retired near Roy, New Mexico. Leroy says he "still ropes and works cattle even though he's in his seventies." Magin Martinez was a real "ol' time cowboy" who worked on the Bell Ranch for many years before it split up.

Freddie Martinez grew up with Leroy and started cowboying on the Cimarron-area ranches about the same time Leroy began. Freddie was a ranch hand all his life and is now retired in Cimarron. Leroy recalls that when they were young cowboys, they roped a coyote one time, tied him up, and loaded him behind Freddie, who was mounted on a horse named Josephine. The coyote was docile at first, but minutes into the ride, the coyote decided "he wanted to get off," and Josephine was more than willing to accommodate him. The coyote and Josephine parted company while Freddie Martinez hung on to Josephine for dear life. Once the coyote and Josephine separated, Leroy and Freddie roped the terrified coyote again, but then turned him loose and let him disappear "into the west." Leroy often uses the phrase "good hand," and Freddie was one of those. Mark Voss was a younger cowboy who was "a good hand." Leroy recalls that Mark was one of the younger cowboys he knew who fit into his "good hand" category.

Matlock Rose specialized in cutting horses and "really knew the horse business." Leroy said he "could train cutting horses better than anyone I knew." Don Dodge was a California cowboy whom Leroy recalls as another "excellent horseman." Monte Rook was a "good all-around hand." Leroy met him in the Colorado San Luis Valley while they were working on separate ranches. He had "great horses and a great family." Sonny Davis was raised on a ranch near Fort Sumner and followed the footsteps of his dad. He was a good ranch cowboy and became an outstanding rodeo performer, particularly as a calf and steer roper. Oscar Crigler was an excellent horseman who trained a lot of Ben Johnson's horses. As Oscar and Leroy were good friends and good horse people, they would spend a lot of time with Ben Johnson as well as his horses. Paul Tierney was a world champion cowboy and an all-around good hand.

Joe McLaughlin, now gone, was the manager of the CS Ranch when Leroy first went to work there. (It was on this ranch, working for McLaughlin, that Leroy and Freddie Martinez did their coyote roping act.) Leroy recalls that the CS at that time, during World War II, had "some real bad horses." Most of the cowboys were in the service overseas, so there was no one around to train and discipline the horses. Leroy still recalls some of those bad horses: Streak, Joker, Pud, and Josephine (of coyote fame). Leroy remembers Joe McLaughlin well: "Anyone who wanted to work at the CS, ol' Joe would put 'em on one of them bad horses—to see what kind of hand you was. As soon as you put your foot

*Warren Shoemaker—
cowboy, breeder, mentor to Leroy.*

in the stirrup, they'd wheel and run. If you could hang on, you got the job." On the Fourth of July, Joe would herd the horses to the Cimarron Rodeo and let them use them for bucking horses, then drive them back to the CS. He finally sold them to a rodeo stock outfit for bucking horses. As Leroy said, "They was sure qualified to do that!"

Harp McFarland is one of those wonderful people who worked at the San Cristobal for fifty years under many different owners (now the Singleton estate). Leroy told me often what a good man he is. I had the opportunity to interview him twice at his home in the lonely town of Stanley, New Mexico (south of Galisteo and near his former place of employment, the San Cristobal Ranch). It was Harp who told Leroy some forty years ago to "git in this pickup right here" following a job inquiry, and got him a job at the Bar S (then the Sawyer Cattle Company, which owned the Texas ranch near Barnhart and the San Cristobal Ranch). That was the beginning of a long and fruitful friendship that lasts to this day. Harp's wife, Elsie, is a very capable and interesting person. She has taught school, Sunday school, painted, and worked porcelain as well as help Harp raise three successful sons. Two of their sons became civil engineers after spending their youth as cowhands on the San Cristobal.

Ralph Tixier came from a long line of cowboys and was raised on a ranch. He and Leroy were good friends for many years. Rosie Deaton was a Matador cowboy whom Leroy first met when he started to work there in the early 1950s. Rosie worked for the Matadors all his professional life—forty years or more. Rosie specialized in breaking horses and was a drive leader when the wagon was out (the drive leader answers directly to the wagon boss). Leroy thought Rosie could do it all—just "punched cows for one outfit all his life." He was one of those "real old-timers" who recently died. Sam Sessions was another great cowboy who also was at the San Cristobal when Leroy was hired, as was Harp's brother Glen McFarland. Both were good cowboys and good ropers. Leroy still appreciates the good cooking skills of Sessions' wife, who kept him fed while "baching" at the San Cristobal.

Bill Smith (four-time world champion bronc rider) with Leroy at the UU Bar La Grulla Camp.

Another of Leroy's good, long-time friends is a four-time world champion roper, Shoat Webster. Shoat, now retired, lives in Lenapah, Oklahoma. The mutual admiration that Shoat and Leroy share is obvious. Shoat tells a story about the time Leroy and he were in a roping competition together at the Astrodome in Houston. Shoat was sure he could beat Leroy's roping time, but Leroy beat Shoat, the world champion. Shoat said he accused Leroy of "paying off the judge." (I reminded Shoat that Leroy was too tight to do that, and he agreed.) Shoat and Leroy still meet and exchange lies at old-time rodeo reunions.

Stogie Bumpas was another Matador cowboy whom Leroy admired. Stogie had worked for the Upper Matadors Division (near Channing, Texas) and had transferred down to the Lower Matadors, where he met the young cowboy Leroy Webb. Stogie was killed rather early in his career, when he was bucked off his horse while doing some "range cowboying." Many forget that this can be a somewhat dangerous profession. My own father, Frank Ford, Sr., died prematurely at the age of seventy-one from complications after being bucked off a horse.

Toke Harp, who was of Native American ancestry, ran the WS Ranch when Leroy started working there as a teenager. Both Leroy and his father, Bud, worked for Toke. Tom Morehouse was a Texas cowboy who worked for the Matadors with Leroy. Both Leroy and Bill Hemphill remember Tom

Morehouse as an outstanding cowboy and ranch hand. Morehouse is now retired and lives near Roaring Springs. Warren Shoemaker was one of the key individuals in initiating and perpetuating the American quarter horse breed. He started out working as a cowboy in the area of Watrous-Wagon Mound, New Mexico, and then raised some of the world's best horses, starting in the 1930s and 1940s. He and Hank Wiescamp did a lot of horse breeding and trading up through the 1960s. Warren was a great help to the younger horseman, Leroy, helping him trade mares and studs, co-signing some of Leroy's notes, and helping him further his career. Leroy thinks Warren Shoemaker was one of the great men he had the privilege of knowing.

> *In the early 1970s Warren Shoemaker backed me by signing my note for $100,000 to buy a piece of land in the San Luis Valley. I was scared to death owing that much money. I did not want to do it, but he told me it was a good deal and to go ahead. That was the case, and I got it all paid off. That is the kind of man Warren Shoemaker was. A great friend and human being. He also helped me a lot with my horse business, loaning me mares and studs. One of the best pieces of advice I ever had came from Warren. When I had a lot of money offered for Pawnee Eagle, I didn't know what to do. I called Warren, told him my problem, and he told me to just remember "that whatever I turn down, I had just given that much for him." I have used that philosophy in all my business transactions ever since.*

Wishy Derikson was one of Leroy's heroes when they cowboyed at the Matadors. "He was a wild sucker, and a lot of fun—a good cowboy." Their boss, Bill Hemphill, told me those two would get into some "off-hour" trouble from time to time. Leroy said that "ol' Wishy knew every bootlegger in that part of the country" (dry at the time). As they'd roam around the small Texas towns of Dickens, Matador, Guthrie, or Crosbyton, "Wishy could pick up a little bootleg alcohol in a short period of time." Wishy died young and tragically after being gored by a steer while working at the Matadors. Lewis Kincaid is a New Mexico cowboy, about Leroy's age, and worked on ranches in the Tucumcari area, then did some rodeo work—a good cowboy and a good roper. Mozaun McKibben and D. King Merrit are two other good cowboys Leroy remembers.

Donn Davies lives in El Prado, north of Taos. Donn is a member of the Cowboy Hall of Fame (the top honor for a cowboy or an occasional writer or producer) and is probably one of the top "rawhide" men in the country.[2] In his studio, he has a rawhide inventory of quirts, saddles, and other paraphernalia that is an outstanding display of this art form. Donn was born in 1916 on an Indian reservation in Montana. (He is still unsure of his tribal ethnicity.) At the age of four, he was adopted by an Anglo family, the father being a chemist for the Great Northern and Canadian Pacific railroad companies. He went to Culver Military Academy, then to the University of Arizona, majoring in agriculture (and collegiate rodeos). His father later bought him a ranch in Montana, sold it, sent Donn the money, and Donn has been on his own ever since. He first went to full time "rodeoing." Donn then went to work at the CS and Philmont ranches as a range cowboy in the 1930s and 1940s, taking a brief stint in the military at Fort Bliss (1935-1937) with the Seventh Cavalry (which then used horses while slowly phasing into tanks). He remembers that when the military made the decision to quit using horses, he participated in a ceremony which ended the 150-year tradition of the "horse-mounted cavalry." All the mounted cavalrymen and officers formed a single line and dropped their sabers for the first time in their illustrious history into one pile. It was a very emotional time for Donn and his compatriots. He spent a good portion of his late life training thoroughbreds as polo horses, and comments that quarter horses (the old "steel dusts"), heavily muscled short-distance horses, are the best breed for cow work.

Donn first met Leroy during the Wiescamp years in the 1960s. He liked the way Leroy worked with horses and worked together with him on many ranches. Their mutual love of horses is obvious. I asked Donn, who worked with the gauchos in Argentina, how Argentine cowboys compared with American cowboys. "Gauchos have been oversold. They loop and catch a steer around their bellies—they don't care for the finesse of roping. Leroy could outperform any Argentine cowboy I've ever been around." After more than thirty years of friendship, Donn calls Leroy "a perfect gentleman. He doesn't have a big ego, doesn't use profanity, and I've never seen him lose his temper. He's never tried to be a ladies' man or big-time cowboy—he's just a true gentleman."

This recount of some of Leroy's "top hands" is far from complete. As I finished our discussion about many of his cowboy friends, I asked him for some final comments:

> What I mean by a top hand, good cowboy is this: a top hand is a cowboy who can do it all—break and train his own horse, shoe him, gather any kind of livestock that needs gathering, by himself. If it needs to be roped, he can get it on him right quick without running him out of the country. He takes care of his horse first before himself. He looks like he is always riding a good horse. The horse may be good or it may just look good because he has a real hand on him. A good hand can make a sorry horse look good, and if he rides him long enough, he will be good. He must be able to ride a horse if he bucks, but keep him from bucking if he can. He can handle horses and cattle as easy and gentle as possible for we are their caretakers and they are our bread-and-butter. I have made this list of some top hands that I have known; it is not complete as my memory is not too sharp. I wish I could recall all of you, but it might take another book. I know all of you are proud to be top hands, and I am proud to have known you. For my part, I would dedicate this book to all the cowboys that have been out on the open range tending to the livestock and who are the real top hands—good cowboys, good people.

*Donn Davies, Cowboy Hall of Famer
and rawhide craftsman,
at his Taos office (2002).*

*Donn Davies as a young man
honoring his Indian heritage.*

*Leroy and Jack Kyle receiving the award from AQHA Executive Director Bill Brewer—
Winners, Old Timers Match Roping Contest, Amarillo, Texas (1998).*

CHAPTER 15

Horses I've Known

*H*orses are unique in many ways, each with a distinct personality. They are intelligent but generally concentrate on one thing at a time. They tend to take on the personality of their owner and/or rider and have a unique sense of knowing how much their rider in the saddle knows or doesn't know about them.

I read with great interest *The Man Who Listens To Horses* (Roberts, 1957) describing the ability to communicate with horses through common body language.[1] The story is convincing. And I've seen it happen with Leroy Webb. As Johnny Caldwell, Leroy's brother-in-law, told me in an interview:

> *Leroy is a cowboy, but maybe one can call him a "horseboy." He's got a uniqueness with horses that I believe is unusual. He just seems to have that quality about him that the horse always understands him and he always understands the horse.*

I've witnessed this during my visits to the Bar Y Ranch, observing Leroy corral, saddle, mount, ride, dismount, and load many different horses. There is an obvious respectful level of communication between the two. Many of his friends have also noted this. Any horse being ridden by Leroy just seems to want to please the man. Leroy told me:

170

*It just seems like they're not many bad horses anymore. The way we
break and train them now is much more gentle than it used to be.
Gentle . . . Gentle. I think the breeding program has got something to do
with that. They just pay more attention to breeding up and culling out the
dumb ones. They're just a lot better these days. I've had a few bad horses
over my life, but a bunch of really good horses, some of them just old
ranch horses and some of them resulting from good breeding programs.
I've just had a bunch of really good horses—top rodeo and show horses
and top range horses.*

Leroy has broken, trained, and ridden thousands of horses over the past
sixty years. I calculated that he's spent more one-on-one time with horses over
his lifetime than he has with people. (In engineering parlance, his horse-days
far exceed his people-days.) As he is gregarious and has more friends than virtually anyone I've ever met, one can understand the significance of his time
with horses. As Leroy has said many times, "The rider makes the horse and
the horse makes the rider." He further comments that in breaking and training horses, timing is important: "You have to know when to do something and
when not to do anything." All horses can sense immediately whether the rider
is scared or not. "That's the reason I got along with horses when I was a
youngster, 'cause I just didn't know what scared was," Leroy said.

Today's horses, having a much higher level of breeding and training, are
much more disciplined than they were during Leroy's young cowboy days.
He recalls that in 1950 the Matadors brought in fifty untrained horses that
hadn't been touched, "and they had only two weeks to get them cowboy
ready." Leroy remembers a lot of "bad horses" then (young and old)—a rarity today. Horses learn by repetition and that takes time, but Leroy notes that
every horse is different and is to be handled as such.

On the subject of breeding top horses, Leroy says that good foals are
probably the product of "60% dam and 40% sire." Good horses generally
produce good foals. The sire quality can be rather quickly determined as they
produce well over a hundred offspring each year. However, it is more difficult to determine the quality of the mare as she only produces one foal each
year. There are also some unknowns which are difficult to quantify. It's a
complex business, and successful breeders such as Wiescamp, Shoemaker,
Kyle, and Webb, have to be knowledgeable to succeed in a difficult and
market-sensitive profession.

In my last interview with Leroy, I asked him to highlight some of the
horses he remembers. He prefers quarter horse geldings, normally registered.[2]

They talk about men having "horse sense." The problem with that is that horses
seem to have a corner on the market.

—Will Rogers

Leroy started off with Happy Hooligan, which was just a good gentle ranch horse that would carry both Leroy and Don bareback to school in their early years. Ol' Hooligan would take the boys from their line camp home to the ranch headquarters where the bus would pick them up, wait patiently for their return, then head on back to camp. Banjo was a long-time working horse for Leroy. Leroy raised him, worked him, and papered him. Leroy just retired the quarter horse (normally, the horses are retired at around ten to fifteen years old). Badger was another good quarter horse that Leroy used for a long period of time—good disposition, good working horse.

Blackie was different. He was bad and "wanted to hurt you." I asked Leroy if that was genetics or the way he was broken. "It's hard to tell. I broke him right, and his full brothers were good horses. Sometimes that just happens. He was a good looking sucker and hung around good horses. His brothers, including Chappo, were good horses. But, he just stayed bad all his life! He got me into trouble a few times working cattle." Greyhound was a good Matadors horse, although he'd buck you off if he could. Leroy didn't mind a bucking horse if he'd straighten out. He was able to teach Greyhound some good manners, and the horse turned out to be a "real good working horse." Hot Shot was "born to buck." Hot Shot was a Matadors horse, had had little training, and "just bucked all the time" that Leroy was there. Joker was a CS horse, just like Josephine. Both were pretty unruly horses. Leroy commented that during his early tenure at the CS, "They just didn't have good horses around—maybe Ol' Joe McLaughlin preferred it that way." Monkey

Still have to keep the horses shod.

Above: Leroy Webb and Pawnee Eagle.

Left: Pawnee Hawk—World Class Stallion.

Below: Leroy and Pawnee Hawk, another first place.

*Pawnee Watrous—
World Champion Heeler.*

was a good Bar S Ranch horse. Leroy broke him, and he turned into a "good cow horse."

Pawnee Eagle was Leroy's first high-bred quality show horse. The stallion had Wiescamp bloodlines (Silver Skip) owned by Jack Kyle, who then sold him to Leroy. Leroy described Pawnee Eagle as "the most outstanding horse I've put a saddle on. His disposition, size, character, and ability left nothing to be desired." Eagle won AQHA points in nine events, fifteen All Around awards, and four saddles in a six-month period. He was named All Around Horse of the Rocky Mountain Quarter Horse Association in 1971. Pawnee Eagle sired Pawnee Hawk out of Dial Seven Seven. This stallion, 15-2 hands and 1,280 pounds, placed third in the world championship competition and won many other honors. Pawnee Watrous was a full brother to Pawnee Hawk and was a world champion heeling horse. Untouchable was another full brother and outstanding horse. He had too high a white stocking on one leg, however, and at the time couldn't be registered. (Today he could be registered.) Therefore, Leroy sold him to Tommy Manion of Springfield, Illinois, as a registered gelding which subsequently won many honors.

Other notable show and race horses owned by Leroy included Chipper's Susy and Spanish Bar Lad. Leroy also raised and trained some of the top Wiescamp horses, such as Silver Son, Skip Princess, Skipette, Skipper Moon, and Skipper Smoke, all finding their way to the winner's circle.

Leroy owned many other horses when he went back to leasing ranches and raising cattle, along with occasional rodeoing. Some of these include Streak, Streak's Bracket, Tumbleweed, Bullit, Silver Skip, and Smokey.[3] I had the good fortune to purchase one of Leroy's horses, which had just retired. My daughter, Katy, named him Leroy Buck, and I took him to Middle Creek Ranch, where he is the most popular horse in the remuda. I've owned quite a few horses over the years. I've had quarter horses, a Tennessee Walker, and an appaloosa, but ol' Leroy Buck is by far the best—a reflection of his long-term training from the world's best rider, Leroy Webb.

CHAPTER 16

Sunset

*L*eroy and Nora Webb, at the time of this writing, are not in their "sunset" years, maybe not even in the twilight phase. Leroy today is working as hard as he was at the beginning of his career some sixty years ago. He is, however, seeing an attrition of the old cowboys he has admired and teamed with most of his professional life. Many have gone on their "last roundup." Most of those remaining have retired. Certainly one has a more profound sense of mortality at this stage and becomes more reflective of where one is in life and what lies ahead in the chapters that remain. Maybe "sunset" is the proper metaphor to describe this stage of life. I tried metaphorically to use this sunset description some years ago through verse:

> The cyclic communion of sun and land
> So oft' ignored by men
> Is a picture that only God can make
> And only by His hand.
>
> It brings together our inner thoughts
> Which the manmade cannot do
> And though available to everyone
> It's savored only by the privileged few.

Sunsets reflect that tranquil peace
And only from His hand
The perfect fusion of the human soul
With sun, and sky, and land.

I believe that the old-time cowboys, who have witnessed more sunsets than most of us, do possess a special appreciation for that fusion. Land, seasons, loneliness, tranquility, sunsets, stars, horses, and livestock are all words that commonly permeate the conversations I've had with Leroy and his friends. The lyrics of many of the great old western songs attempt the same. I have yet to hear any of the old-timers I've interviewed say that they would have done anything else with their lives. They say they never made much money, always worked hard, seldom realized equity, but all savored the memories of the trails they have ridden. Leroy has articulated this much better than I could ever do because he actually lived it—a necessary prerequisite for credible expression. He summarizes his life as follows:

When I was young, there was no way I could see any further ahead than pay day. When pay day rolled around and I got my hundred dollars or whatever, it was a brand new world—a new lease on life—and I thought I'd never see another poor day. I was free as the wind to go where I

One more ride.

wanted, to do what I wanted, and not a worry. I always knew I could get a job on another ranch punching cows. It may just be for my room and board, but what the heck, that's really all you had to have. You could just ride the grub line for a while— ranch to ranch, camp to camp 'til you found a steady job. Oh, for the good ol' days! I went to work for room and board and what I wanted to do. You work hard, make a hand, and they'll pay you something. I am a firm believer in hard work, no matter if you are getting paid or not. Too many people now days would starve before working for what they think is too little pay. I have no time for those kind of people. I have heard my dad say a hundred times: "Hard work never hurt nobody." I had that hammered into me from day one.

I feel like I'm about the luckiest man alive. Lookin' back on all my life, as far as I can remember, I've done just what I wanted to do. Now,

Painting by Veryl Goodnight, Santa Fe, New Mexico (2002).

Above: Coffee starts the day.
Left: An ol' cowboy who knows where he's been and where he's goin'.

Just another working day.

Never too old to flank.

Solitude and relaxation.

Leaving Leroy footprints on the Bar Y.

Photograph by Gray Hawn

Leroy, his rope, and Singleton broodmares.

Photograph by Gray Hawn

The end of a long branding day.

Photograph by Gray Hawn

177

mind you, I didn't do everything just right. If I wanted to leave an outfit, I left. If I wanted a certain job, I'd get it. Whatever I wanted to do, that's what I did, and I'd do the same thing over again. When I wanted to punch cows, I did. When I wanted to break and train horses, I did. When I wanted to go roping, I did. When I wanted to compete in rodeos, I did. When I wanted to quit working for wages and get my own cattle and lease some ranches, I did. One thing I didn't do was to actually buy my own ranch. I would loved to have done that, but I never really figured I'd be able to afford one. So, maybe it was not really such a disappointment. I just feel so fortunate on what I was able to do. I did have my own cattle and raised a lot of good horses. I've still got some of the best cows and horses in the business.

And, I'm not through yet. I'm going to start back raising some more good horses, and I've still got some good cattle. I'm just going to keep on truckin'.

I wouldn't give anything for the friends I've made. I know a lot of

Leroy and Nora today.

people all over the place, and I'm real fortunate! Perry Johns from Fort Worth is a great man, and he's helping me get back into the horse business. Manuel Medley co-signed a note to help me get my first mare back in 1958, and I'll never forget that. Warren Shoemaker helped me out a lot when I needed it. Jack Kyle was always there along the way to give me support. Harp McFarland has been a great hand. All I want to do is to try to return some of those favors. I believe that's the way it works. I can never help all the people who've helped me along the way. Many are dead and already gone, but you're supposed to help somebody else, then they're supposed to pass that on to someone else. That's the way it's supposed to work.

My wife, Nora—nobody has helped me more than her. I wouldn't be where I am today without my wife! She's helped me and stood by me all these years, in good times and bad. There's no way to say how much she has helped me or how much I appreciate her.

Our one son, Hurley, died at an early age—beautiful child. Hurts too much to talk about him. I loved him dearly—a special person. Bless his heart. Then I was blessed with two stepsons—two fine men, Dalton and Dennis. Dalton was killed a few years back in a truck wreck. So, all we are left with now is one son, Dennis. He lives in Amarillo—a man of the Lord and best preacher I know. A good cowboy and a good hand. He's a good roper—roped professionally and still does some. Just a fine young man. I just can't tell you how much I appreciate all these people.

Leroy is effusive and sincere when he talks about his wife, his sons, and his friends. It's obvious he has found personal strength in all these associations. I've observed firsthand the depth of these ties. When Leroy needs help, the word gets out, and there are always more friends who show up than anyone would expect. They'll work long hours helping Leroy gather, brand, or whatever without any compensation. It's just their expression of respect for the man. These "lend-a-hand" traits are not uncommon with range cowboys. I've seen it many times with my granddad, dad, or Deaf Smith County partners, but I've never seen it at the level Leroy receives.

I don't have enough adjectives to describe the loyalty, dedication, and sacrifices Nora has made in their almost five decades of marriage. She has been the ideal partner, moving from ranch to ranch, on the road to rodeos and shows, raising the children, and enduring many days of loneliness as a working cowboy's wife. I've been in their homes at the several ranches Leroy has worked during our acquaintance. The headquarters where they are housed, always owned by others, is meticulously kept and continually upgraded, all through Nora's efforts. Moreover, she has been constantly tabulating and preserving the events and memorabilia of their long life together. We are all the beneficiaries of this practice.

CHAPTER 17

Reflections

I've saved this chapter to look over my shoulder a bit and reflect on some of the experiences and thoughts I've had in researching, interviewing, and writing about Leroy Webb, his family and friends, his horses, and his country.

Much has been written about the evolution of this country during what I call its "formative years." Immediately following the Civil War, the nation was less than one hundred years old and an uncoordinated mosaic of regional differences, ethnic inequities, an undisciplined economy, and a somewhat blurred vision of where we were headed. On the positive side, America was blessed with a core of people, mostly hybrid, who possessed the capacity to grow and achieve. This, blended with a land of unparalleled natural resources, resulted in a societal success seldom before seen on this earth. During these formative years, between 1865 and 1965, we went from a people clustered primarily east of the Mississippi River residing in fewer than thirty states to a people residing in fifty states covering over three times as much land.

The path wasn't easy or without sin. Native Americans were dislocated, land distribution and ownership were often skewed, railroad development frequently favored the few, and natural resources were often exploited.

The balance sheet, however, favored the positive over the negative. The

Political correctness should not be at the expense of historical correctness.
—Frank Vandiver

resultant society reached a level of prosperity and relative equality of un-matched magnitude. I believe the evolution of the American cattle industry, the ranches, and those who developed, owned, worked, and perfected them is a representative microcosm of that progress. When the great migration from east to west began after the Civil War, the sacrifices required to perfect this expansion were many. The description of hardships of our predecessors in traveling long distances through uncharted lands, seeking a better life, and building on what they found may seem like platitudes to many of us who never experienced it. I am one who will probably never fully appreciate it, but the people I've gotten to know did raise me up an appreciative notch or two. Tom Brokaw correctly called the World War II era "The Greatest Generation." To Brokaw's greatest generation I would add the old settlers and cowhands who left their mark on the American West before, during, and after the Civil War. Many of the cowboys I've interviewed sandwiched their service in that conflict between long years of cowboying, and I would imagine the skills developed in their early years prepared them well for such a war.

My generation was the benefactor of many sacrifices made by the previous generation during the 1930s and early 1940s. We entered our teens in a time of prosperity, relative peace, and, more importantly, were raised by parents who had endured the dust bowl, the depression, and in many cases, combat on foreign soil. We all agreed that these parents were able to inculcate a few of their values to those of us who reached early maturity in the 1950s—a gift which was unique and probably not fully realized until we reached adulthood. My friends and I agree that we benefited from growing up in Lubbock, Texas. It was and is a marvelous place, known not for its beauty (flat and few trees) but for its people. I can't think of a better place to have been raised during the 1940s and 1950s. It is identified now for that phenomenal Bell Ranch purchase, for being the home of Buddy Holly (a grade school and high school classmate of mine), for Texas Tech, for feedlots, and for cotton farming, but the people have always made its effects long-lasting.

I have identified a core of people in this writing endeavor, with Leroy Webb as the perfect central theme. I couldn't have picked a better individual.

As I "sunset" my efforts with this biography, I feel the title, *The Last Cowboy*, remains applicable. Commencing with my grandfather's early cowboy days through those of Leroy's, we've traveled from open range and unclaimed grasslands to fenced pastures to feedlot beef to corporate processing to selected distribution to fast food restaurants and whatever lies ahead in the twenty-first century. There has been a true metamorphosis in the cattle business which would support the "last cowboy" premise.

I read with interest a book by Patrick Dearen entitled *The Last of the Old-Time Cowboys* (1998). Dearen had interviewed seventy-six old-timers whose cowboying span has covered most of the twentieth century. The consensus seemed to be the same, namely that "we're a dying breed." As one old cowboy put it, "We've gone out of the cowboy stage. There's ropers and bull riders and what-have-you, but we've run out of cowboys." This, of course, is somewhat an overstatement as I've interviewed and known younger cowboys who are excellent professionals, both in and out of the saddle. Nonetheless, there is a difference. The transition of cowboys begins with the defenders of the Alamo, Sam Houston, and others responsible for the acquisition of the Texas and New Mexico lands; carries on to the administration of James K. Polk's Treaty of Guadalupe Hidalgo in 1848; and moves

- to the demise of the buffalo in the 1870s, taking pressure off the prairie;
- to free grass and trail drives in the nineteenth century;
- to barbed wire fences, windmills, and enhanced rail transport at the century's turn;
- to pickups and horse trailers which move horses quickly to the workplace;
- to the "saga of the sorghums," or feed grains, such as milo, sudan and hegari initially raised during the mid-twentieth century and their subsequent use in the feedlot finishing of heavy beef;
- to assembly line beef processing, packaging, and marketing (such as practiced by Iowa Beef Processors, IBP, which I observed personally during my environmental practice);
- to the high-speed computer's role in commodity information transfer and trading transactions.

Today, the livestock industry is big business. As a ranching expert, Harold Oppenheimer, explains, "It involves railroads, trucks, chemical companies, farm equipment, packing companies, grocery chains, retail stores specializing in leather and other by-products, and veterinary supplies and drugs." He states that virtually every stock on the major exchanges is directly or indirectly related to the livestock industry. (Mednick, 1996, p. 207) The recent exponential growth of the "fast food" industry has made this even more ap-

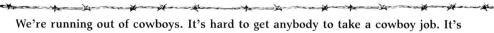

We're running out of cowboys. It's hard to get anybody to take a cowboy job. It's too lonely and too far out.

—Bruce King
Former governor of New Mexico

parent. These are the major contributing factors which have forced such a transition. Future years will bring more dramatic changes in the cattle industry. Animal biotechnology now includes DNA injection into embryos and other genome technologies which have the potential of enhancing cattle handling, breeding, and beef quality. (Womack, 2002)

To what extent have expanding domestic and export demands for beef contributed to changing the era of range cowboying that Leroy and his friends experienced? When one considers the inherent inefficiencies of the pre-1950s, by spending weeks rounding up mavericks and errant steers, moving cattle overland from horseback, and range feeding cattle all the way to processing and distribution, the then "cowboy hours" required to produce a pound of beef to the consumer far exceed that which we have today. If one believes the Malthusian Theory proposed in 1798 that the population explosion will overwhelm our food production capacity, then efficiencies matter. Thomas Malthus (1776-1834) so far has been proven wrong, as technological and scientific advances and their corresponding efficiencies have accommodated the population growth, particularly in the United States. This means, however, that many aspects of the cowboy's way of life as Leroy experienced it will never again return.

Leroy Webb and most of his cowboy friends understand this, but all agree that none of the recent technological advances, including helicopters, four-wheelers, robotics, and computer spreadsheets, can gather cattle in rough country, selectively breed and upgrade horses or cattle, wean, cut and brand calves and yearlings, or replace the intangibles such as the bonding between horse and horseman coupled with the solitude, freedom, space, and openness the cowboy experiences.

There will always be good cowboys, good rodeo performers, big ranches, western movies, boots and big hats, but some could possibly become more symbolic than real as we move into the future. The large ranches described herein are breaking up into smaller tracts, many owned by non-cowboys and "wanna-be" cowmen for playgrounds, bragging rights, and leisure living. This is not necessarily a criticism, but in my opinion, a fact of modern life. The indelible truth remains, however, that the real American cowboy, from the era of the 1850s to the present, is a unique, indelible, and irreplaceable part of our heritage. As I researched materials for this book and interviewed authentic old-time cowboys such as Leroy Webb and his friends, it became apparent that these grassroots characters and hands-on foremen and managers have been the major players in the creation of this heritage. Capital in-

There's been a lot of things that have changed, but there's a lot that's still the same. Nothing will replace the versatility of the horse.

—Dub Waldrip, General Manager,
Chappell Spade Ranch

fusion from absentee European and American entrepreneurs was critical, as was the expansive spirit of all levels of cattlemen and capitalists, but the common denominator for all these elements basically comes back to the sweat of the range cowboy.

It's an interesting culture. Larry McMurtry pointed out that two of his three favorite cowboy authors, Walter Prescott Webb and J. Frank Dobie, read and wrote their way out of the actual cowboy life. (Only the third of his favorites, J. Evetts Haley, died as both a rancher and a historian.) I engineered my way out of ranching and agriculture after seeing it break my dad both financially and physically (but not spiritually) in the 1950s, but it always draws us back. Even McMurtry uses a metaphoric style in writing his novels by "herding a few desirable words into a sentence, then corralling them into small pastures called paragraphs, then spreading them across the spacious ranges of a novel." (McMurtry, 1999, p. 54)

It's infectious to all of us who have been exposed, however slightly. Explanations are not necessary—that's just the way it is. So, I return to my prologue premise that Leroy Webb in a chronological sense is "the last cowboy," and I repeat my appreciation for having the privilege to partner with such a man and his friends as we traveled together through each chapter of this book.

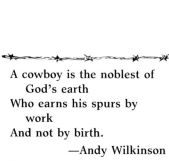

A cowboy is the noblest of
  God's earth
Who earns his spurs by
  work
And not by birth.
      —Andy Wilkinson

Photograph by Gray Hawn

Further Acknowledgments

I have received a huge benefit in getting to know Leroy, his family and friends. I would be remiss, however, if I didn't add some layers of a few special people who guided and encouraged me in this venture. My wife, Gwen, and daughters, Kelly, Kristy, and Katy, as a family made it easy for me as a starter. I've been blessed living around four women for a good portion of my life. My wife, Gwen, is a University of Texas graduate and partner for over forty years. Our three Aggie daughters, now all married, are all pretty good at riding horses, as is my oldest grandson, Davis Sharp.

I've had the opportunity throughout my travels to hang around some

Great support from the Ford women.

184

Gray Hawn photographing cowboys on the Ford Section 4 pasture, Deaf Smith County, Texas.

professional writers who gave me direction. Then along came some long-time friends who offered some additional flavor. Gray Hawn, a world-class photographer, went out to the Bar Y Ranch with me to photograph Leroy in his native habitat, which adorns the cover of this book as well as a few photographs along the way. Gray is a self-taught photographer who has that intangible talent of extracting the natural purity of people and scenery through her photography. She is the last person to have photographed Princess Grace of Monaco before her death, has photographed U.S. presidents, Texas governors, and many other prominent people throughout her career. Yet, her common touch puts her in immediate communication with lonely old cowboys, allowing her to capture their legitimate image.

Veryl Goodnight, whom I consider one of the world's finest sculptors, particularly of horses, also accompanied us and has given me an even higher appreciation of the horse and animal world, as has her husband, Roger Brooks. The two have taken

Veryl Goodnight and Roger Brooks. Unveiling of The Day the Wall Came Down, *Berlin, Germany (July 2, 1998).*

Riders in the Sky—Joey, Too Slim, Ranger Doug, Woody Paul (2002).

an interest in the subject matter of this book, and their roots from the Old West are deep, as is their sense of history and western lore. Veryl's sculptures of horses jumping over the Berlin Wall, "The Day the Wall Came Down," are classics. Only two are in existence: one at the George Bush Presidential Library at Texas A&M, and the other in Berlin, a gift to the German people from the United States. The sculpture depicts four mares and one trailing stallion jumping over the partially destroyed wall which had divided East and West Berlin.

Cowboy or "western" music is another byproduct of the early American West and cowboys. I grew up on this music, but its popularity did not really prevail with the later generations until it received a revitalization by a singing group called "Riders in the Sky." My wife and I brought this group to Austin when they first were formed in the late 1970s. (They were affordable then.) Since that time, they've become members of the Grand Ole Opry in Nashville, performed all over the world, and have won a Grammy along the way. Douglas Green (Ranger Doug), Fred Labour (Too Slim), Paul Chrisman (Woody Paul—King of the Cowboy Fiddlers), and more recently, Joey Miskulin have done a marvelous job of disinterring and perfecting the harmonious western melodies so popular during the 1930s and 1940s

(*Tumbling Tumbleweeds*, *Don't Fence Me In*, *Cool Clear Water*, etc.). Douglas Green is an outstanding historian and author. Fred Labour is a great children's storyteller and humorist. Paul Chrisman has a Ph.D. in nuclear physics from MIT and is basically "self-learned" on the fiddle. Joey Miskulin is a multi-instrumental studio musician who has played with many performers, including Roy Rogers. All are my friends, and Douglas Green's *Singing in the Saddle* adds a musical dimension to Leroy Webb's era of range cowboying.

I've have the advantage of being associated with two families/business partners who operate the Ford lands in Deaf Smith County, both as owners and as lessors. Jim McGowan and his wife, Lucy, are second- and third-generation ranchers and farmers, as is Ted Eicke (whose wife, Rene, is first-generation but a good farm and ranch hand). These people know the cattle and feed business and gave me good insight as to their perspective of the pre-Leroy, Leroy, and post-Leroy generations of cowhands and cowboys. I had the opportunity to take Leroy to the Ford place while he was leasing the Hampton Ranch and introduced him to the Eickes and McGowans. There was a lot of common ground for discussion.

The Ford place, part of the old XIT Ranch, has been a home for mother cows, feeders, stockers, grain sorghum and wheat production, as well as the Davis/Ford families, for the past seventy-five years. Prior to that, this land had seen buffalo herds, stagecoaches, XIT cattle and cowboys, and maybe even the footprints of Coronado. My father and brother John are buried up on "Section 4" (a section of native grass which will never be broken out). So, it's a special place to me, as are those who currently work it.

The last layer of expertise I've solicited is that of former U.S. Senator Joe Tydings and his wife, Kate Clark. Joe Tydings served in the U.S. Senate under John F. Kennedy and Lyndon B. Johnson, is the son of Senator Millard

Joe Tydings and wife Kate Clark (2001).

Tydings, who served under Franklin Roosevelt, and the grandson of Joe Davies, first U.S. ambassador to the Soviet Union. I met him over a decade ago doing environmental trial work for various clients and found him to have an extraordinary sense of history—almost encyclopedic. He has a real appreciation of the western expansion phase of America's development. Senator Tydings has added significantly

*Jim
McGowan
and Ted
Eicke gath-
ering some
yearlings
on Section
4, Deaf
Smith
County,
Texas.*
(Photograph
by Gray
Hawn)

*Eicke and
McGowan at
the end of the
day.*
(Photograph by
Gray Hawn)

Grandfather, G. C. Davis—Pioneer, cowboy, great mentor.

Grandmother, Harriet King Davis—school-teacher, wife, mother, saintly person. And (left) mother, Lucile Davis Ford—intellectual, spiritual, extraordinary mother (circa 1912).

to the bibliography from which I have drawn historical information for this book and has provided selective editing. His wife, Kate, served in the White House in the previous administration as a social and communication assistant and is a marvelous critic and editor. Joe and Kate are good friends and traveling companions, great sources of information, and excellent editors. Our family is most appreciative of all they've done for the Ford family.

My last reflection is directed toward the two generations of the G. C. Davis family which preceded me: my grandfather, grandmother, and mother (previously acknowledged), and my dad, J. Frank Ford, who gave my siblings and me a profound appreciation for cowboy and western lore—an infection which is probably not subject to cure. When I say "not subject to cure," perhaps I'm reflecting on what Lawrence Clayton noted in his introduction of the revised J. W. Williams' book: "We know that as long as cattle roam pastures, ranchers will need cowboys. . . . As long as the ranch continues to be an element of life in the American West, and perhaps even if this way of life disappears entirely, some of us will continue to remember this golden day of life in the West." (Williams, 1999, introduction)

*Three generations: two cowboys,
and one engineer (clockwise
from top left):*

G. C. Davis, 1914

J. Frank Ford, Sr., 1926

Davis L. Ford, 1954.

Appendices

Special Letters,
Articles,
Memorabilia

I have included several appended materials, primarily discovered among Leroy and Nora's personal memorabilia. There are countless newspaper clippings and journal articles about the Webb family and Leroy's cowboy, rodeo, and horse breaking accomplishments, some of which I have excerpted because of their historical value, although many have no source citations. I've also included old land grant maps and personal letters applicable to this story, as well as historical information about the Maverick Club and Cimarron Rodeo, which have been a part of Leroy and friends' lives for more than fifty years. Frank Atmore, whose family has been associated with Leroy for many decades, wrote a history of his family and the Cimarron country, which I have included, again for historical purposes.

Team roping on the open range.

APPENDIX I

Letters, Etc.

Leroy

By Howard Powers, 1992

We went to Colorado
In the year of '61.
We went to see the mountains
And to camp and have some fun.

The mountains were fantastic
With the peaks still capped with snow.
The mountain streams were crystal clear
And flowed into the lakes below.

We toured the Garden of the Gods
And drove up to Mt. Evans.
We saw some peaks that looked like
They reached into the heavens.

We held our breath at Royal Gorge
And stared down to the river.
Big Thompson Canyon was awash
And caused the ground to quiver.

Then in the news I chanced to see
That there would be a show
In Greeley, so we had to see
Those Quarter Horses on the go.

Now, facts grow dim as years go by
And memories begin to blur,
But there are things that we recall
And of this one I'm more than sure.

Time came to show the reiners
And I guess there were a few
That ran the pattern that was set
To show the judge what they could do.

Then came a gorgeous yellow stud
They called him Skipper's Smoke.
It made the chills run up your back
The way that horse was broke.

He came in like a freight train
Stuck his old tail down so low.
He left his skid marks in the dirt
Then waited for the cue to go.

He did a pair of figure eights
That were so smooth and pure.
His rollbacks were so doggoned fast
They ended in a blur.

The cowboy that was riding Smoke
Sat him like he was born
To spend his life astride a horse
And did his teething on the horn.

A big black hat perched on his head
It must have had a four-inch brim.
His red top boots with his pants tucked in
Now these were all a part of him.

Yeah, we went to Colorado
In the year of '61.
We went to see the mountains
And to camp and have some fun.

Yeah, we went to Colorado
And I say this not to joke.
The thing that I recall the most
Is Leroy Webb and Skipper's Smoke.

1101 N. 11th Street
Yukon, Oklahoma 73099

1957 or 58
Leroy was driving a truck for a feed company. At that time, they were Team-Tying. Team-Tying is where you head & heal steers. Once he's caught the header gets off and ties both back feet with a square knot. Leroy, could tie a square knot faster than you could see. He came over an introduced himself and asked me if I needed a partner. He didn't have a horse at the time, so I let him barrow one of mine. Whenever he had time off he'd come to the ranch & we'd rope together.
That is how we became the best of friends. And we still are to this day.

We was at Cimarron Fourth of July. Leroy and I roped and tied a steer in 14 flat. Which was a good time for tying. I was fixen to rope with another guy, and I had to head. A guy said to Leroy, "Jack's fixen to beat you himself." Leroy said, "Don't worry about it, Jack can't even tie a square not in 14 (seconds) flat!"

GETTEN A LEG UP!
I had my leg broke at a show in Belen, NM
I needed to get on my Jr. Mare to warm her up. I couldn't get that mare to stand still so, I had Leroy hold her for me. Out of orneriness, Leroy kept saying, WHOA, WHOA, & moven her away from me. I said "Leroy, if you move this horse again I am gonna rap this crutch around your neck." I bet there was 8 or 10 people standing around dying laughen at us.
Later that day, I needed to have my Sr. Mare shown in the cutting contest at this show. I asked Leroy, "You wanna show my mare?"
"Ahhh, hell, Jack, I don't know anything about cutting!"
"You cut a cow before, just go in there and drop you hand and cut a cow."

...He won the cutting contest.

1960
SPREADEN THE WEALTH

Leroy & I were coming back from a show in Colorado. We had 9 studs, 3 mares and 1 gelding on. We were going up the La-Vita pass, a real narrow two-lane road, and the truck vapor locked. We were trying to figure out what to do. Leroy came up with the brilliant idea to have me a' foot, back behind the truck to look out for traffic, so he could back it down the mountain. I told him, "You can't do that, you'll wreck it, and we'll scatter a million dollars worth of horses all over this highway!" Leroy said, "It don't make a damn if we wreck it, it'll be the best set of horses these hills ever seen!"

DEAFMAN WITH A LEAD-FOOT

We hauled horses to shows in an old Semi. Leroy would scare me to death driven so damn fast. He'd say, "Don't worry I've wrecked 2 or 3 trucks, but this one, I can drive. I just put my feet up on the dash and try to relax. Over the years I made boot prints in it just trying to get my grip. He so damn hard a' hearing, I finally would just tap my finger on that speedometer. Needless to say, he figured it out but, nothing's changed.

THE FACTS

He's one of the best cowboys I ever saw. Great cowboy-bronc-rider. He can ride some bad boogers. Not only that he is a fine man & a gentleman at that.
The best friend I got.

1101 N. 11th Street
Yukon, Oklahoma 73099

FRED LAMBERT OF THE CIMARRON
SOUTHWEST AUTHOR

P. O. Box 332
CIMARRON, NEW MEXICO

Gone is the smoke from an old forty-five,
    The buffalos' thundering roar;
The screching brakes of the Overland stage
    Are stilled for evermore.

        Gone are the shouts of the teamsters,
            The rattle of pick and spade;
        Gone is the fear of the Ranchero
            Of the Apache's stealthy raid;

The Santa Fe roars o'er glittering rails,
    The highways are filled with cars;
Cross country planes soar overhead,
    Almost thrusting aside the moon and stars.

        Now folks of the West are friendly folks,
            Peaceful,with manners mild;
        Gone are the days of the old forty-five
            The days when the West was wild.

" Fred Lambert
of the
Cimarron "

APPENDIX II

Articles/Clippings

Pawnee Eagle Is Grand Champion

(Source Unknown)

Beautiful horses are always associated with the great San Luis Valley and one of the finest of the breed is the stallion quarter horse Pawnee Eagle, owned by Leroy Webb, former Alamosan, now living in Monte Vista.

Pawnee Eagle was named Grand Champion stallion at the Southwestern International Livestock Show in El Paso, Texas, recently.

The handsome animal won the honor of being all-round Quarter Horse Champion at the same show.

Webb's horse also won first in the Western Riding and placed in the Roping and Pleasure.

The sorrell stallion made a total of 12 points in this one particular show.

A week prior to the El Paso show, Pawnee Eagle was named All-round Quarter Horse Champion of the Amarillo, Texas, show. . . .

Chipper's Susy Captures '69 Ski-Hi Futurity Race

(Source Unknown)

Chipper's Susy, owned by Leroy Webb of Monte Vista and ridden by D Martinez captured the Ski-Hi Futurity Sunday to highlight the last day of racing action.

The horse, trained by Bill McCall of Pueblo, covered the 350-yard distance in 18.46 seconds. A blanket was presented to the winner by Germers of Alamosa. . . .

Webb Quarter Horse Champion of Champs

(Source Unknown)

"Champion of Champions" was the title earned by Skippa Chip, a quarter horse, owned and trained by Leroy Webb of Monte Vista.

He won first in halter class, first in calf roping, first in reining and second in steer roping, at the Colorado State Fair in Pueblo. . . .

Skip's Princess Wins 1963 Trophy Saddle

Rocky Mountain Quarter Horse Association Newsletter, Fall/Winter 1963

Skip's Princess, owned by Hank Wiescamp of Alamosa, Colorado, and trained by Leroy Webb, won the R.M.Q.H.A.'s 1963 All Around Don King Trophy Saddle.

Skip's Princess won her points by placing first in Aged Mares, first in Senior Reining, and third in Senior Calf Roping. She had a total of forty halter points and twenty-nine performance points.

In second place was Shiek's Image, also owned by Hank Wiescamp and trained by Leroy Webb. Shiek's Image had a total of eight points in halter and twenty-one and one-half points in performance—winning the Junior Reining. . . .

Webb Horse "Pawnee Hawk" Qualifies for World Champion Quarter Horse

Leroy and Nora Webb of Monte Vista have qualified with the American Quarter Horse, Pawnee Hawk, for the second annual World Championship Quarter Horse Show in Louisville, Ky.

The show, which will take place Nov. 7 through Nov. 11, is sponsored by the American Quarter Horse Association, Amarillo, Texas, and the Ponderosa System, Inc., Dayton, Ohio.

Pawnee Hawk

Webb's Pawnee Hawk is among some 1,200 American quarter horses which have qualified for this prestigious show to be held at the Kentucky Fair and Exposition Center.

Pawnee Hawk is the leading junior horse in the nation in heading, heeling and calf

Monte Vista resident one of nation's Top Quarter horse trainer-breeders

(Courtesy *Monte Vista Journal*, October 14, 1971)

Jack Kyle, National Quarter horse judge, has said that Leroy Webb of Monte Vista is in his opinion the top quarter horse trainer in the nation. Webb, who was born on a ranch in Cimarron, N.M., left home and began working full time with horses at the age of 14.

He was recognized at the Albuquerque State Fair by the son of Hank Wiescamp, one of the nation's top quarter horse breeders. Wiescamp hired Webb in 1960 and for nine years the name of Leroy Webb continued to gain recognition among horse breeders and owners all over the nation as a top trainer and breeder.

Leroy, his wife Nora and their son Hurley moved to Monte Vista five years ago and began to build a ranch which brings in horses to be trained from all over the United States. . . .

It has just recently been announced that Webb's "Pawnee Eagle" won the Rocky Mountain Quarter Horse Association All-Around Champion for 1971. The saddle will be presented at the Denver Stock Show. This particular honor is one of the highest to be awarded. . . .

roping. The horse stands 15-2 hands, weighs 1,280 and is a four-year-old. He is bred, owned, trained and shown by the Webbs. He will be standing to outside mares in the San Luis Valley, Webb said.

Webb will enter Pawnee Hawk in calf roping, heading, heeling and halter at the show, and hopes to capture the World Championship. In all there will be events in which World Champions will be chosen during the 12 performances. . . .

Leroy Webb

(Source Unknown, 1974)

Leroy Webb is my name and Monte Vista, Colorado, is my present home, but I was born and raised on cattle ranches in Northeastern New Mexico. When you are brought up on ranches like Waite Phillips' in Philmont River, and the W. S. Ranch, you are riding horses before your memories begin. When school started, we rode horseback to the main road to meet the school bus and our spare time was filled with ranch chores . . . milking cows, looking after the hogs, gathering eggs, working those ranches . . . all the work was done out on the open range.

Our horses were broke as we did our chores. Often we would leave camp with green broncs, and after a few days of working them while performing our duties, we could get them pretty well started.

At fourteen, I made the big decision to leave school to break horses and punch cattle. Starting out wasn't very easy but I got plenty of experience working on spreads like the W. S. Ranch, Cimarron, N.M.; the Circle Dot, the Xs at Kent, Texas; the Fort Union, Watrous, N.M.; and the Matadors at Matador, Texas. After that, I went to Driggins Land and Cattle Co., Santa Rosa, N.M., the C.S. Ranch, Cimarron, N.M., the S at Big Lake, Texas, and Lamy, N.M. I'm sure I have missed a few but I am positive that I learned plenty.

Roping came very naturally to me but it was all done out on the open range. In the mesquite country of Texas you couldn't afford to miss a loop or you might have to tear down a lot of brush before you got the second chance. Roping became my favorite event, but

my showing experience started in a funny way. At that time my job was with Shelby Hays Ranch, Leyba, N.W., and the owner, Mr. Hays, liked the way a colt was handling for me. He wanted the colt to be shown in the reining class at the New Mexico State Fair and he asked me to do it. As you might imagine that could be sort of a problem for a fellow that had never seen a horse show . . . let alone ride in one. My ace in the hole was a good roping buddy, Jack Kyle, of Santa Rosa, N.M., who I knew could give me all the answers to my questions. Jack is one of the finest horse trainers in the world in my opinion, and he gave me, and "Ole Parma Pete," a few pointers on what to expect at the fair. I'll make the story short here by saying that we did OK because in a large reining class in the New Mexico State Fair of 1959 we placed second, but the important thing was that I got myself hooked on this showing stuff! After all, it was just what I had been doing all my life . . . "putting a handle on a horse," and it was not half as tough.

About this time, my wife and I got our first registered Quarter Horse mares, both palominos, of Shoemaker breeding. We were real lucky getting started with the right kind . . . those that have ability plus conformation. A horse's worth will always be based on his ability to get the job done in my book. From our start in 1959, we have grown to thirty broodmares and five stallions on four hundred acres of fertile, level, irrigated land. We raise horses, alfalfa, brome grass, and oats. The farm is located in the San Luis

Valley of Colorado and is known for its high protein feed and is ideal for growing out big, stout, healthy colts.

The first AQHA Champion to my credit was Skipper's Smoke in 1962. Then came Skip's Princess, Skippette, Skip's Ink, Skip's Trauma, Skip's Tres Bar, Skip Sir Bar, Skip's Three Bar, Silver Son, and Pawnee Eagle. During this time I was awarded the Rocky Mountain Quarter Horse Association All Around Year End Award five times, and was awarded the Golden Spread All Around the one time I tried for it.

I have had the pleasure of riding some exceptionally great horses but my favorite, and I want to say the most outstanding all around horse that I have put a saddle on, is Pawnee Eagle. His disposition, character, size and ability left nothing to be desired. This horse won AQHA points in nine events, fifteen All Around awards, and four saddles during a six month period. The fact that he was home-bred made it all the sweeter for me, but to have him named All Around of the Rocky Mountain Quarter Horse Association in 1971 had to be my most satisfying moment, especially the "owner-trainer, Leroy Webb" part. Pawnee Eagle got us off to a great start with the fine get he put on the ground. We were very disappointed when one of his most promising colts was refused registration as a stallion by the Association because of too high a white stocking. This colt was registered as a gelding, sold to Mr. Tommy Manion of Springfield, Illinois, and later sold to Fred Chandler of Atlanta, Georgia. The whole quarter horse world now knows this great individual, sired by Pawnee Eagle . . . he is the famous halter gelding "The Untouchable." Everything finally came out for the best and promoted our breeding program and Pawnee Eagle way beyond our expectations. Pawnee Eagle has been sold to Pawnee Eagle, Ltd., of Houston, Texas, and is standing at the Sam Wilson Ranch of Pattison, Texas.

Our replacement for Pawnee Eagle is Pawnee Hawk, a full brother to The Untouchable, whom we feel will be a worthy replacement. We are real proud of this bay, 15-2 colt, who has four perfect stockings and a blaze, knows how to move, and we feel he will do it all.

In addition to standing Pawnee Hawk, we have two Skipper W bred studs, one Shoemaker stallion and a home-bred stallion, Spanish Bar Lad, and all are producing very well. A yearling colt, another full brother to The Untouchable, is sure to be an eye-catcher.

As to the future, we plan to break as many outstanding Quarter Horses as possible, for breeding good-looking horses that "can do it all" is our ambition, and we like to have these kind to work with. We specialize in show horses and breeding stock and take a few outside horses for training. In the future we will limit our showing and concentrate more on our breeding program.

Having been successful enough to win the AQHA high-point calf-roping mare and later the AQHA high-point steer roping stallion awards, I am sure that training rope horses will always be my favorite hobby.

It was in 1952 that I met and wed my lovely wife, Nora. We have one son, Hurley, who is now 19 years old. Nora is a gal that can do what has to be done on the ranch, knows how to keep us happy, is always ready for the unexpected visitors, and is in the right place at the right time. I am sure that none of the good things that have happened to us would have been at all possible without the devotion, love, and help of my wife and son.

. . . Leroy Webb

Leroy Webb Wins
Merritt Champ

(Source Unknown)

Leroy Webb, Monte Vista, was named winner of the King Merritt Memorial Championship Stake, at the Wyoming State Fair held in Douglas, Wyo.

Webb, riding Pawnee Eagle, his quarterhorse stallion, placed high in the reining, calf roping heading and heeling and working in the cow-horse class to win the stake.

The King Merritt Memorial Championship Stake was established several years ago in honor of King Merritt, well known rancher in Wyoming. King Merritt was also a champion steer roper in the 1940s....

Plus prize money, Webb will be awarded a hand-tooled trophy saddle during the National Stock Show at Denver.

Roping with:

LEROY WEBB

Trainer of Silver Son
Winner of 1969
Performance Horse Award

by
Loren R. Whittemore

Courtesy *Rocky Mountain Quarter Horse*, January 1970

Silver Son, P141,471, a 1960 Palomino stallion owned by H. J. Wiescamp of Alamosa, Colorado, was the winner of the 1969 Performance Horse Trophy Saddle Award. Trained and shown by Leroy Webb of Monte Vista, Colorado, Silver Son accumulated the necessary points to win by placing first in Aged Stallions, Sr. Working cowhorse, Sr. Roping, Team Roping Heelers, Team Roping Headers and third in the Sr. Reining and Sr. Western Riding classes.

Because of horses like Silver Son the name Wiescamp has earned and will always have its own special notch in the Quarter Horse world. The ability to prove just how versatile and adept these

horses are to work in every performance class has also earned Leroy Webb an enviable place of prominence in the eyes of the Quarter Horse world as well. Riding Wiescamp horses, Leroy has won the RMQHA All Around Year End Award for the years 1962, 63, 68 and of course again this year. In addition to these he won the All Around Champion Saddle awarded by the Golden Spread Quarter Horse Association in 1967. He has also won trophy saddles at Santa Fe, N.M.; Lubbock, Texas; the Colorado Springs-Woodland Park Saddle Award in 1968; the San Luis Valley amateur roping award; and this year's CC&B (Casper-Cody-Buffalo, Wyo.) All Around Saddle.

All of these accomplishments have definitely earned for Leroy the respect and admiration of his fellow contestants. Even though he performs in just about every performance class, there is one that holds his basic affection—roping. Because of his extensive experience and devotion to roping, we asked him about any observations he might have on the subject.

The basic question was, "What is the most common error or problem you feel young or inexperienced ropers who are just breaking into the game seem to have?" Leroy thoughtfully stated that to him it seemed their biggest problem actually lay with their horses and was caused from rushing them too much. He feels that most young ropers can rope pretty good from practicing on the ground before they start, but when they are in the arena they are trying too hard and pushing themselves and their horses too fast. Each one seems to try to run each calf out of the box and tie him in ten seconds. This is especially an error in registered roping when time is not the only basic factor. They should be giving the judge time enough to see their horses work.

He feels that many ropers try to crowd their horses too much and as a result the horse gets nervous and "shook up." In practice they shouldn't try to rope each calf as quickly as possible. It is better to let the calf get lined out and in this way teach the horse to follow straight behind. If the roper does try to rope each calf immediately the horse will soon get to setting up and stopping just as soon as he leaves the box. When a horse does this, even if a roper does catch his calf, the premature stopping motion will throw him off balance and cause him to lose time getting off and to the calf. This Leroy feels has cheated many ropers out of the money many times and registered ropers out of time enough for the judge to really watch their horses work.

Leroy likes to follow the calf out for at least three good jumps before throwing his rope. It takes about that long for a horse to get into position behind the calf and really start rating him. It also enables the roper time enough to get into the rhythm of the motion and action and gives far greater control of the rope.

This is also very important if you want your horse to be an all around type roping horse.

At eighteen Leroy was working for the well-known Matador Ranch in northern Texas. At its peak in the later 1800s when the Matador owned and controlled some 2,000,000 acres spread over several locations in North Dakota, Montana, Canada and 1,000,000 acres of it along the Canadian River there in Texas. The Matador was estimated to have run around 40,000 head of cattle. With Albert Mitchell as the ranch manager the herd became well-known for its top quality Herefords. Even in the early 1950s when Leroy worked for them they ran one pasture alone that had 100,000 acres in it. At this time they still operated as they had throughout the years with the cowboys working out from a chuck wagon. Trying to work the area as they went they would move every few days. They did this year round with the exception of July and August, when they quit because of the heat.

Leroy gained much of his proficiency at roping while working on the Matador. They worked all ages of stock from baby calves, which they roped and drug to the branding fires, to some 4 or 5 year old animals that had eluded earlier round-up crews. The latter gave heading heeling practice. . . .

This year's winning of the performance horse award marks an impressive accumulation and combination of a lot of years experience, about 20,000 miles travel to shows each year alone, a top hand, and some mighty good horses. But as in all things there must be change in order to have progress. Recently Leroy has gone on his own in order to spend more time on his irrigated pastures and to develop facilities to take in and train horses. It is with confidence that the RMQHA as well as the Quarter Horse industry as a whole will be looking forward to seeing the accomplishments and the names of Weiscamp and Webb in their own rights for many years to come.

JACK and *LEROY*

**Two elements in Quarter Horse history–
Jack Kyle and Leroy Webb—reunite at a
third, New Mexico's Tequesquite Ranch, which
has registered horses with AQHA for 54 years.**

Courtesy *The Quarter Horse Journal* (March 1997)

"LEEroy, quit talking and watch the road!"

The truck temporarily jumps out of the dual ruts that serve as a road on this part of New Mexico's Tequesquite Ranch. Outside, it's dark, but Leroy Webb is driving with the interior lights on in the truck. His hearing aid works better if he can see your face when you're talking.

Jack Kyle is riding shotgun, and though he and Leroy have spent scant time together in the last 20 or 30 years, they have fallen back into the familiar roles they shared first as friends, then as co-workers hauling Hank Wiescamp's show string back in the '50s.

Leroy runs his cattle on part of this ranch once owned by Albert Mitchell, a leader in the Southwestern ranching community, four-term AQHA president, and a salvation to AQHA during the Association's rockiest years. (See "Legends," September 1994.) One of Leroy's fondest memories is of Mr. Mitchell and Jack Casement, Warren Shoemaker, Coke Roberts, etc. holding court at the New Mexico State Fair. They were sitting on bales of hay back in the barn area, discussing the future of the Quarter Horse. Leroy hung back like a mouse in the corner, just happy to be on the fringe of such great horsemen. He wouldn't have had the courage to stick around and eavesdrop if he hadn't have been with Jack.

Jack had inspired Leroy to come show a horse at the fair. Despite never having seen a horse show before, Leroy won his first reining.

When Jack accepted a job with Hank Wiescamp across the state line up in Alamosa, Colorado, he talked Leroy into going with him. They spent a show season hauling a semi-load of good horses to AQHA shows. Their friendship sometimes seemed like "you and me against the world," because they won so much that most competitors dreaded seeing them pull into a show.

Those who know the duo from their glory days in the show ring assume that Leroy is the elder. His hair turned white and most of his hearing left him decades ago, but on horseback he seems much younger than 68. More ruggedly handsome than the Marlboro man, he has manners that would make his mother smile. After years in Colorado, showing horses for Wiescamp, and then the public, Leroy and his wife returned to New Mexico. They live in Cimarron, although they spend a lot of time at the Tequesquite Ranch, now that their cattle are there.

Jack only stayed at Wiescamp's one season, then showed horses on his own back in New Mexico. He left his beloved New Mexico after his wife died in 1978. Now 70, he lives in Yukon, Oklahoma, to be near his grandchildren, which also puts him closer to the pulse of the reining horse industry. His specialty now is starting young futurity prospects, and raising a select number of foals. Last year, horses he bred won the NRHA Super Stakes for his daughter, Jackie Krshka, and the Congress Futurity for Tim McQuay.

The two cowboys hadn't seen each other in several years when they reunited last April to work Leroy's calves.

Now, as dawn sneaks up from the east, they arrive at the pens up on the plateau. Four or five other pickups and trailers converge, and within minutes everyone is horseback, awaiting instructions.

Leroy's never been comfortable telling people what to do. His instructions sound more like suggestions, but his willing crew responds. Jack and Leroy take off for the southern fenceline. Jack is riding one of Leroy's horses, and giving Leroy a hard time. "I know now why you invited me out here," said Jack. "You need me to train this horse for you."

Soon the cold air is filled with the shrill bugling of 160 calves temporarily out of reach of their morning meal. It's enough to make you envy Leroy's hearing loss.

The top job on the crew's hierarchy is dragging calves to the branding fire. Jack and one other cowboy receive the honor of roping one of the milling calves by its back feet, dallying and delivering it a short distance to the ground crews. Like an assembly line, each person on the ground has a responsibility: One holds the head, another the feet. One strategically places the brand. One vaccinates. With a hot iron, another cowboy sears the buds, which would otherwise grow into horns. The "knife man" notches the ears and castrates the bulls. This is Leroy's job, one he handles with surgical precision, although he is far from typical surgical conditions.

Jack repeatedly enters the herd, throws a loop, yanks the slack straight up above his head, turns under the rope, dallies and drags. He rarely misses, even after the easy catches are out of the way, and he's having to rope around those already worked, in search of the less eager. His arm has to be burning with the intensity of the branding irons when he finally lets someone else do the heeling honors.

Leroy actually has more help than he needs—-a compliment to his popularity, and to the ranching tradition known as "neighboring." Besides area ranchers and their hired hands, the deputy from Leroy's hometown, Cimarron, drove all night after his shift in order to work calves. He helps Leroy at home, too, and since he will never accept any pay, Leroy has started giving him a calf every year. "That used to be work a little," said Leroy. "The way the market is now, I'm not doing him much of a favor."

"Cowboys always amaze me," said Leroy, now back in the truck and heading to a lower pasture. "These fellas aren't going to get a dime for being here. But look how hard they work! There's no grumbling. I just wish the weather had turned out better."

Indeed, the cold and constant wind has added a degree of difficulty to the early morning's activities.

As Leroy drives down the long switchback to lower ground and the next pasture, he and Jack reminisce about just how cold it could get in Alamosa, Colorado. They travel back in their memories to an equally cold early morning when they rode out with Hank Wiescamp to gather a herd of sale horses, which they'd ride through the ring that afternoon.

Leroy's mind is back in Alamosa when Jack snaps, "LEEroy, if you don't slow down, your truck's gonna breed that rig in front of us!"

Leroy just smiles. Nothing seems to rattle him. "I always did make Jack nervous with my driving," he admits, "but I never did get us in a wreck."

Then they're back in the '40s, remembering the mountain pass Wiescamp's semi wouldn't negotiate until they started unloading horses. Their stories are so compelling you can easily imagine Jack standing on the road's narrow shoulder, his hands full of lead ropes attached to some of the finest show horses on the circuit, now nervously milling as Leroy grinds gears up the hillside . . . But now, back to branding.

While they gather the next pasture, the weather changes, but not the way Leroy had hoped. The skies are overcast, the wind is relentless, the dust as blinding as smoke from a brush fire. This area has been drought-stricken so long that fire is a real possibility. Weaning weights are down, and so are cattle prices. Ranching just really doesn't look very glamorous at this minute.

No one can communicate without yelling, and then they get dirt in their mouths. The work drags on for hours. Leroy and Jack, the elders in the group, keep roping and cutting, although Leroy is suffering more from guilt over the working conditions than from the work itself.

By two o'clock, the cowboys can break for lunch. Leroy jumps in the truck, totally covered in dirt. As he relaxes for the first time in hours, his face smooths out, and white lines appear on the bridge of his nose and around his eyes—the only clean places on his face.

Back at the Mitchell dining hall, the cozy place they'd left at four this morning, Leroy constantly apologizes for the weather and the dirt. The cowboys aren't grumbling. Some are even laughing. Leroy says that even though they've got another bunch left to work, there's no way he'll ask these guys to go back out.

He doesn't have to ask. Either the wind has affected their minds, they think an awful lot of Leroy, or the cowboy image is real. Soon the whole crew is back battling the wind. This will make for a great story—the kind of day they'll all still be talking about years from now.

Jack gets back on Leroy's horse. Leroy sharpens his knife.

Warren Shoemaker recalls

His First Palomino

The horse was named Chief, and he was spoiled and dangerous before Warren turned him into a well-known trick horse.

By Maggie Crais
(Courtesy *The Western Horseman*)

Warren Shoemaker, at age 78, is one of the Grand Old Men of the Quarter Horse industry, and his Bar O horses out of Watrous, N.M., have played an important role in the development of the modern Quarter Horse. As a youth, Warren especially liked palominos, and he went on to raise a lot of them. Although the first palomino he owned wasn't of the quality that the Shoemaker horses be-

came noted for, Warren is still proud of the animal's accomplishments.

He got him in a trade with a neighbor, Jim Leftwich. Warren and Jim had traded a lot of horses to one another, and it was a game between them—see who could trade the meanest horse and get the best of the deal. One day Jim saw Warren in Las Vegas, N.M., and said he needed help in gathering a few cows for sale off the place he leased north of town. "When you come, bring a tradin' horse; I've got a good one for you this time," Jim said as they parted.

Warren knew what that meant, and decided to bring a horse named Buck, a snakey mount that would always try to buck off his rider when he least expected it. Warren rode Buck for the gather, and left his rear cinch home; using a rear cinch on Buck was an invitation for disaster. Jim rode the horse he wanted to trade, and Warren got excited when he saw it was a palomino; he'd always wanted a palomino.

Warren and Jim gathered the pasture, cut out a few strays along with the cattle that were to be sold, and branded a few late calves. It wound up being a long day, but after the work was done they got down to horse trading. Jim said he wanted "boot" in the trade, but Warren said no, he didn't have any money, so just make it an even trade. Jim kept after him—he knew Warren wanted the palomino, and finally Warren said, "I'll give you my pocketknife to boot."

"Okay," Jim said. "I'll trade."

Warren thought he'd made a good trade. Jim had ridden the palomino all day, so there couldn't be much wrong with him. But of course he had watched Buck closely all day, too. Buck hadn't acted up, and Warren knew what was wrong with him.

They pulled their saddles off, and Warren handed Jim his reins, and Jim handed Warren his; but when Warren started to take a rope off his saddle to put around his horse's neck so he could change bridles, Jim suggested that they not change. He said they could just get their own bridles back when they saw each other in a few days. Of course, Warren "smelled a rat" immediately, but nothing more was said.

Warren started to saddle the horse and found out what "the booger" was right quick. The horse took off running

sideways, got ahead of Warren, who had to turn loose, and lit out for the horizon. Jim stood by laughing. "Well, saddle that horse and get after him," said Warren. "Get that sonuvagun so I can go home."

Still chuckling, Jim grabbed his saddle and threw it on top of ol' Buck, making sure to snug up both the front and rear cinches. He stepped aboard and Buck fired like a rodeo horse; Jim would almost get thrown off one side, regain his seat for a second, then fight to keep it; when the bucking finally stopped, he regained his composure and started out for the palomino; it was nearly dark when he brought him back to Warren.

Two gates, several miles apart, separated Jim's place from Warren's and Warren knew when he got off to open the gates, he'd be afoot again, so he talked Jim into riding with him. When Warren got home he just jerked the bridle and saddle off the horse and boogered him on in the corral.

Warren named the horse Chief, and decided he was just spoiled, so next morning he went out to work with him. He cornered the horse and finally got the bridle on him, but before he reached for the saddle blanket he slipped a catch rope around Chief's head; the catch rope was attached to a second rope, which was tied to a stout post.

When Warren started to put the blanket on him, Chief jerked away and ran, and Warren encouraged him a little by waving the blanket after him. The horse hit the end of the 60 feet of rope and fell hard on his side. Warren got him up and fooled around with him some more, then reached for the blanket again, and Chief took off a second time, hitting the end of this rope and jerking himself over backwards.

Warren never had much trouble saddling Chief after that, but he still had to watch him. Throughout his life, the horse would still try to catch Warren asleep and pull some type of stunt. But

Warren knew the horse was smart, and figured with the right kind of handling, he could teach him anything. Warren had watched Leonard Stroud train a few trick horses for rodeo acts, and thought this might be a good way to use Chief.

He spent a lot of time with the horse after that, and one of the first things he taught him was to lie down and roll over on his back. Chief would also sit up and bow with his right foot out front and his nose on the ground. When he was told to "say his prayers," Chief would put both knees on the ground and tuck his nose between his legs. Warren had a brush with a wooden handle—he'd give it to Chief and hold one boot in front of him, and Chief would shine it. All of these tricks were done on voice command.

Warren made a block 12 inches high and 12 inches square, and trained Chief to get on top of it and bow. After several years of this Warren would get on top of Chief and then get him to perform the stunt. He made a board walk 4 feet off the ground and 16 feet long; it was 8 inches wide, with a 16-inch approach, and Chief would walk the entire length, go off the other end, then walk back to the board, put his front feet on top of it, and bow to the crowd.

Chief would pick up Warren's gloves, hot, or the bridle, and bring them to him. He'd pick up a red or blue scarf, whichever one Warren asked for; and he could answer "yes" and "no" questions by shaking his head (Warren would shift his weight slightly to the right when he wanted "yes," and slightly to the left when he wanted "no").

After Warren had been training and showing his horse for about a year, Leonard Stroud came to Las Vegas to perform at the Cowboy's Reunion Rodeo. Warren was proud of Chief, and told Leonard all about him; so Leonard decided this was one horse he had to see.

Leonard had a horse that could jump a convertible in his performance, and after watching Chief go through his tricks, Leonard asked Warren if his horse could jump,

"Yeah, he'll jump a little bit," Warren told him.

"Well, let's see him jump," Leonard said.

Warren wasn't too anxious to give Chief an opportunity to take him for a bronc ride, so he told Leonard, "I don't know anything about riding a jumping horse. You take him and jump him."

Leonard got on Chief and got a good run at the 2x4 Warren had pushed through a crack in the fence, and was holding on the other end. Warren still laughs at the incident and says, "Boy, that old horse cleared the board by about a foot and a half, and ol' Leonard lost a stirrup. Chief saw him lose it and hit the ground buckin'."

The show was on. Leonard had a lot of items tucked in his shirt pocket, and Chief succeeded in throwing cigarette papers, Bull Durham, and Brown Mule all over the place. When Chief decided he had bucked enough, Leonard stepped off him and said, "Trick horse, hell! Take him down there to my buckin' string."

Warren used Chief for everything. He was an everyday horse, a rope horse, a bulldogging horse, a trick horse. Horse trailers didn't exist in those days, so when Warren went to a rodeo he either rode Chief or led him. He limited himself to shows in a 50-mile radius and got paid $50 a day for Chief's performances. Sometimes Warren won extra money roping calves. But aside from the money, which Warren sure could use, he enjoyed the performing. He knew he had a good act, and liked for people to enjoy the things he had worked so hard to achieve.

Chief died some years later of sleeping sickness after he had been retired and put out to pasture. Warren said it was like losing an old friend.

APPENDIX III

Historical Records

At the Foot of Baldy Mountain

By Frank Atmore

Dick Atmore was definitely a man of amazing figures with 90+ years of ranch life, 64 years of marriage, and four younger generations of family to his credit. Along with the rest of the Jackson family, he earned his final resting place in the shadow of the mountain where they had all lived difficult but interesting lives.

Dick's story began many years ago in such faraway places as Milton, Illinois, where his grandmother was born (1831) and Sheffield, England, birthplace of his grandfather (1834). The two were married in 1866 and traveled to New Mexico by ox cart. Their first stop was in the Maxwell/Springer area where Bridget Mahon Jackson established a boarding-house. Next, they moved to Baldy Town where she boarded and fed the workers in the gold mines. Because she was a hard worker and good manager, she was able to save enough money to purchase approximately 1,700 acres of the original Lucien Maxwell land grant property that stretched along Ute Creek below Baldy Mountain. John and Bridget moved their family into a homesteader's cabin on the land; and old logs lying in disarray continue to show the outline of the old dwelling. The original cattle barn is still used today for a machinery shed.

Ranching wasn't easy for the Jacksons and their seven children; and sometimes family relationships were strained to the breaking point. A few years after the youngest child, Alice, was born in 1879, the boys banished their dad from the ranch because of his drinking problem. Bridget longed for a nice home; and her boys had the log walls built by 1885. However, as a result of a disagreement between them, their mother died before the house was completed some 14 or 15 years later. The house had running water piped from a spring but no electricity. In fact, electrical lines were not strung along Ute Creek until the 1940s. The dwelling contained six rooms; and all of the walls, both those outside and those dividing the rooms, were made of hand-hewn logs. Many years later, Dick and his Uncle Jack added a stone fireplace; and Jack lived in the "big house" until his death in 1938.

Throughout the history of the Jackson/Atmore Ranch, Bridget's descendants had a difficult time keeping the land as a single unit. Each time a member of the older generation died and willed a part of the ranch to several living children, the land had to be repurchased; and this happened at least two or three times. On another occasion, Jack suffered financial reverses and was forced to sell the ranch to the Gallaghers in Moreno Valley. However, they defaulted on the payments, and Jack was able to regain the property.

During the time the Jackson family was making history at the foot of Baldy Mountain, Rodney Clem was born in East Orange, New Jersey (1877). He apparently joined the Atmore family, a traveling musical group, as they journeyed across the country. By 1905, he was in Northern New Mexico where he changed his name to Rodney Atmore and asked Alice Jackson, Bridget's youngest daughter, to marry him. They built a nice log home on the property Alice had inherited from her mother and raised their five children there. Their original place has now been expanded into the Bear Lodge. Rodney adjudicated water rights for the ranch, served as Justice of the Peace in the Territory before it became a State, served as Ute Park Postmaster from 1908 to 1910, and established the first school district in Colfax County in 1915.

Richard, or Dick as he was known by the residents of Ute Park, was the oldest son of Rodney and Alice, and he was hired by his Uncle Jack to work the ranch. In February, 1932, Dick married Doris Ellen Lane; and they lived behind the "big house" in the log cabin which had been the schoolhouse in the town of Franklin located near the Philmont-Baldy fence line. Following Uncle Jack's death in 1935, Dick moved his family (they had boys named Frank and John) into the "big house." Dick and Jerry (aka Bear) formed the Atmore Brothers Ranch partnership. The inheritance taxes amounted to $600 which, toward the end of the Depression, seemed like an exorbitant sum of money! Still one more legal tangle had to be settled when Alice died in 1945. With Bear living on their mother's place and Dick occupying their uncle's property, the boys bought their sisters' shares, combined the two Jackson properties, and later purchased 290 additional acres from the New Mexico Game Department to straighten the west boundary of the ranch. Dick and Doris made the final repurchase in 1979 when Jerry died.

Ranching proved to be a very long and hard life for the Atmores; but Dick and Doris worked side by side to run the ranch, keep the records, and raise their boys. Because wild animals lived all around them, Doris kept a close eye on the boys while they were young; and she was very good at handling a gun—just in case her family needed protection. Even though each day was filled with work that needed to be done, the family managed to find time for fun. Doris at the piano, Dick with his accordion, and Mr. Lane, her father, with his violin, made a wonderful trio. They were in constant demand as entertainers throughout the area. The men always branded calves on the second Sunday in May. Other fellows came to help, and Doris spent the entire weekend preparing food, feeding the cowboys, and cleaning the kitchen. "It was a great way to spend every Mother's Day," she always said. Added to her many responsibilities at the ranch was her job as Ute Park Postmaster for 21 years. Through her efforts, the Ute Park office was changed from 4th to 3rd class in 1967.

The many years of hard work and the mounting discomfort of Dick's artificial hips made the Atmores realize they could no longer handle the ranch operation by themselves. Frank and John were living in Utah; and the family decided John would be the one to return to the ranch and assume responsibility for working the cattle, irrigating the fields, cutting the alfalfa, and mending the fences. John came back to New Mexico in 1979.

Age and failing health continued to take a toll on the two who had been so active in earlier years. In 1997, the Atmore family sold the ranch to Robert Funk, and the property became the Express Ranch. Dick and Doris moved to the lower altitude of Cimarron to spend the last three years of their lives. Frank and Lannie retired and moved into the "big house" which was the family home for generations, and John and Shirley bought a home in Cimarron where they stay when they aren't back at the ranch. And Dick and Doris? They are resting in the Jackson Cemetery at the foot of Baldy Mountain on land which belonged to their family for 130 years.

How We Got Where We Are!
(or where did we come from?)

The Caldwells and Sammons
By Hope Coslett Pees

Caldwell–Sammon Roundup,
June 11-12, 1994

James Martin "Bud" Caldwell was of Scottish descent. His father, Joshua Caldwell (born March 14, 1832, and died November 17, 1863) was killed during the Civil War. Joshua had married Sarah Alexander who was said to be French (or perhaps part French). Sarah Alexander Caldwell is buried in the Hart Cemetery in Bentonville, Benton County, Arkansas.

According to Marianne Bevill, a Culwell descendant who lives in California, one of the Caldwell men was said to have had such a thick Scottish brogue that some members of his own family couldn't understand him. Marianne has the Culwell family Bible which had belonged to Thomas and Elizabeth Culwell.

Joshua's father was James Coldwell (the Caldwell name was spelled variously as Caldwell, Culwell, Coldwell and Colwell). James Coldwell was born January 10, 1803, in North Carolina and died in Arkansas on October 8, 1880. He is buried in Goshen Cemetery, Washington County, Arkansas.

James' first wife was Almedia Nixon (born January 15, 1809; died December 18, 1836). They were married May 23, 1837. After Almedia's death, James married Nancy Lamar (who was apparently a widow).

James Coldwell's father was Thomas Culwell, who was born October 24, 1773, in North Carolina. His wife, Elizabeth (do not know her maiden name), was born in Maryland. Except for James, whose name was spelled as Caldwell and Coldwell (which is on his gravestone), the other family members were Culwell.

Several Culwell/Coldwell/Caldwell family members moved to Texas about the time of the Civil War, and some of the descendants of these families still reside there.

James Martin Caldwell was born in Bentonville, Arkansas, September 3, 1854. According to his obituary printed in the *Springer Times*, "His father was killed in the Southern Army of the Civil War, while he was eleven, and their home burned five times during the war, causing him to undergo many hardships and be refrained from attending school; however, he put in much time studying while in camps by the light of the campfire. He moved into Texas when quite young, but later went back to Arkansas where he was united in marriage with Miss Martha Brown, July 4th, 1877. After his marriage he again crossed the plains in a covered wagon, this time coming into New Mexico and entered into the cattle business. After several years he sold his cattle to Pat Garrett, who killed Billy the Kid, and moved to the Cherokee Nation, Indian Territory. Then finally with a train of seventeen covered wagons he tracked back west to settle in this community where he has lived since 1897." James and Martha were married by John R. Maxwell, Methodist minister. John Maxwell was the husband of James Caldwell's sister, Mary A. Caldwell.

Two of James and Martha's sons, Berlin and Count, married two daughters of Robert Walker "Bob" Sammon and his wife, Maria de los Santos Leal. Elizabeth Clifford Sammon married Berlin, and Bessie Sammon married Count, thus forging a close alliance between these two families.

Bob Sammon's family was probably of English descent or perhaps Irish (further research is required to determine this, however). The earliest Sammon of whom we know anything is a JAMES SAMMON who owned land in Isle of Wight County, Virginia, and later lived in Sussex County, Virginia. His will is dated January 31, 1765, Albemarle Parish, Sussex County, Virginia. Although he and his wife, Phillis Avey or Ivey, undoubtedly had other children, the names of only two are known: Avey (daughter) Sammons and William Sammons.

Our ancestor, William Sammons, married Rebecca Avey or Ivey. They had land in Halifax County, Virginia, and Lunenburg County, Virginia; they later lived in Greenville District, South Carolina. William's will is dated August 5, 1804, Greenville District, South Carolina.

William and Rebecca's son John Sammon(s), who married Elizabeth "Betty" Walker, is our ancestor. This family lived in Greenville District, South Carolina, and their son John Sammon Jr. ultimately moved to Gwinnett County, Georgia; there are still descendants of John Sammon living in Lawrenceville, Gwinnett County, Georgia.

John Sammon Jr. married first Elizabeth Harrison, and after her death, he married her sister, Mary B. Harrison. These Harrison women were the daughters of Clement King Harrison and Elizabeth Williams.

John and Elizabeth had only one daughter, Elizabeth Sammon. John and Mary B. had several children, among whom is our ancestor, Robert W. Sammon, who married Susan Elizabeth Thrasher. They were the parents of Robert Walker Sammon and Mary Laura Lelia "Lollie" Sammon (there was also a son who died soon after birth).

Descendants of Lollie Sammon and Frank Medlock live in North Carolina (and some of the grandchildren, great-grandchildren, etc., have moved elsewhere).

Phew! So many names! So many dates! So many places!

At any rate—our Caldwells and Sammons "hooked up" in New Mexico and here we are. Here being at the first Caldwell-Sammon Roundup—and may there be many more!

History and Descendants of William G. Richards

About 1863 or 1864 two men arrived in the little settlement of Trinidad on the Purgatoire River in the southern part of the Colorado Territory. They were not then known to each other nor were they men of similar background, but the near future would bring them into an association that would grow closer with time.

One, a young man in his twenties, came south as a freighter from Denver, where he had been among early gold-seekers along Cherry Creek in 1858. William G. Richards was a native of the Hoosier State, having been born in Indiana February 25, 1838. At age twelve he had gone with his parents to the plains of Kansas, which was then a part of the vast unorganized Territory. Eight years later he struck out on his own, lured by gold into the mountains far to the west but still within the boundaries of Kansas Territory set up in 1854. The Cherry Creek settlements which he saw were tiny places still awaiting stimulus of a major gold find. Richards did not strike it rich, rather he was freighting out in Denver when the famous Gregory Lode was discovered. He was still in freighting work two years later when the Colorado Territory was organized in 1861 and he came down to Trinidad near the New Mexico line.

The other was an old man nearly seventy-five years old. Born in Spain in 1791, Andres Lehan had been brought to California at the age of two by two well-to-do aunts. Three ships made the arduous voyage around the Horn together, bringing the two women and the little boy, among others, to the town of Los Angeles in the Spanish King's empire. A short time later his parents came over, and the family group, sometime prior to 1810, made the slow journey inland from California to New Mexico. Andres' father sent him all the way back to Spain at the age of nineteen to find a bride, but he returned, much to his father's chagrin, without one. It was the young man's opinion that if the Taos country was good enough for him and his people, it certainly was good enough to provide him with a wife. And that it did in the person of a young woman named Abiquill.

The vast Southwest was detached from the Republic of Mexico and became a part of the United States when war was concluded by the Treaty of Guadalupe Hidalgo in 1848. In the same year Andres Lehan was drawn back to California by the gold rush. He left his wife and family in New Mexico and headed westward with a little train of four burros. His trip was a financial failure, and he returned to Abiquill. There a daughter, Manuelita, was born to the Luhans in 1854. Still attracted by the call of gold, Andres Lehan put his wife and children and belongings in a wagon sometime in 1860, and headed north for Denver, but success evaded him the second time. The Lehans then started south again and came into Trinidad about the same time that young Richards appeared there.

William G. Richards left Indiana at the age of twelve years with his parents to the plains of Kansas. Eight years later he struck out on his own, coming to Denver. (On his way he hunted along the Purgatoire River.) He freighted out of Denver to Trinidad. (This country looked so good he came to settle in 1865.) He married Manuelita Luhan, daughter of Andres Luhan, on March 11, 1866, at Trinidad. She was sixteen and he was twenty-eight. To this marriage eleven children were born, seven boys and four girls.

Manuelita Luhan Richards met a tragic death in 1891, leaving a baby to be raised by the rest of the family. This baby was John Richards, one year old. William C. Richards lived with his daughter Mary Richards Ballou until his death. He passed away April 13, 1921.

In 1938 there were 107 descendants, but there are many more now. We had reunions in 1948, 1954, and July 1979.

Children of William G. Richards and Manuelita Luhan Richards

William A. Richards was born in 1868. He left home as a young man and was never heard from again. As far as we know he had no family.

Lupe Richards Carson II was born in 1870 and married Kit Carson II, son of the scout Kit Carson. They had eleven children: Josephine Carson Beach, Amanda Carson Crane, Charles Christopher Carson (died as an infant), Allen Carson, Julia Carson Waddell, Anita Carson Budnick, Nettie Carson, Christopher Carson III, Ophilia Carson (died as an infant), and Margarete Carson (died at the age of nine years). Lupe passed away in 1957. All of the children have died except Kit III.

Rebecca Richards Lopez was born in 1872 and died in 1963. Seven children were born to her: Billie Lopez, Lottie Lopez Holloway, Joe Lopez, Albert Lopez, Alice Lopez Russell, Anna Lopez Berry, Elfido Lopez Jr., and Wanda Lopez Adams. All are living except Billie and Albert.

Mary Ann Richards Ballou was born in 1874 and died in 1955. She married Plato Ballou in 1900. They bought the Cordova ranch fifty miles south of La Junta. Mary Ann had five children, two children by a former marriage and three Ballou children: Cleo Marion Ballou Denton, Mary Mathilda Ballou Autry (Tillie), and Alma Amanda Ballou Morrow. Two died; Cleo, Tillie, and Alma are living.

Alexander A. Richards was born in 1876 and died in 1964. He married Virginia Cordova and four children were born to this union: Emiliano (Millie) Richards, William Auguetine (Billie) Richards, Susie Frazier, and Josephine Richards Hawley. All are living.

James Richards was born in 1878 and died in 1967. He married Josephine Beach. Nine children were born to this union: Phobie Kathrine Hinrechf, Jimmy Richards, Tommy Richards, Alex Richards, Amanda Milo Wilson, Evelyn Richards Whoeke, Bobby Richards, Wilford Richards, Faithy Richards Bradley, and Buddy Richards. All are living except Jimmy and Wilford.

Samuel T. Richards was born in 1881 and died in 1971. He married Blanch Karney and they had five children: Alex Richards, Elizabeth Richards Petterson, Edith Richards Horn, Virginia Richards Ekholm and Mary Richards McDonald. All are living except Elizabeth.

Thomas Richards was born in 1883 and died in 1969. He never married. He lived on the Richards home place at Higbee until his death.

Dave Richards was born in 1885 and died in 1978 in Nevada. He left home when he was fourteen and married a widow with two girls.

Amanda Richards Cordova was born in 1887 and died in 1918 in childbirth. She married Juan Cordova and four children were born to this union: Tommie Cordova, Iola Cordova Webb Bernal, Emlie Cowling, and John (Juano) Cordova. Iola Cordova married Bud Webb and they had four children: Donald, Leroy, Shirley, and Janet. Iola's marriage to Bernal produced two children. John (Juano) was one-and-a-half when his mother died and Mary Ballou, his aunt, took him to raise. Juan Cordova and Alexander Richards's wife, Virginia, were brother and sister.

John M. Richards was born in 1890 and died in 1949. He married Blanch Russell. One daughter was born to this marriage, Leona Richards Knickerbacker, who is still living.

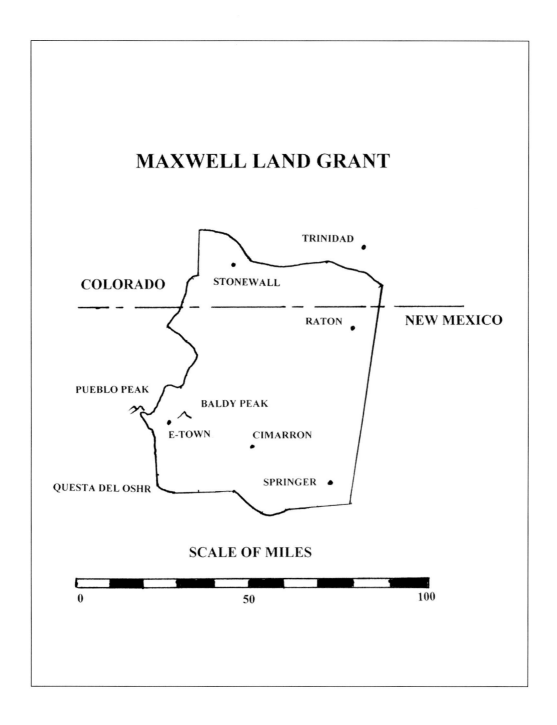

MAXWELL LAND GRANT

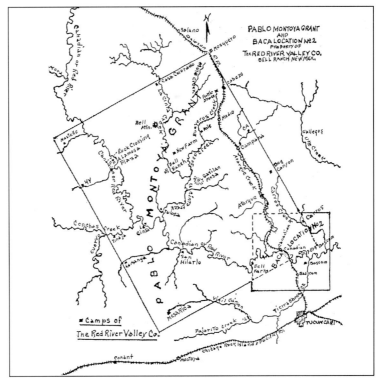

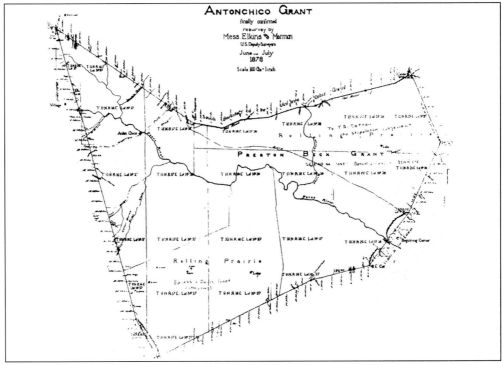

Pablo Montoya Grant (top) and Anton Chico grant.

APPENDIX IV

Cimarron Rodeo and
Maverick Club

Certificate of Comparison

United States of America,
State of New Mexico } ss,

It is Hereby Certified, that the annexed is a full, true and complete transcript of the

CERTIFICATE OF INCORPORATION

of

THE MAVERICK CLUB
(No Stockholders' Liability)

(No. 15673)

with the endorsement thereon, as same appears on file and of record in the Office of the State Corporation Commission

In Testimony Whereof, the State Corporation Commission of the State of New Mexico has caused this Certificate to be signed by its Chairman and the seal of said Commission, to be affixed at the City of Santa Fe on this 12th day of June, A. D. 1929.

Hugh H. Williams
Chairman

Attest:

Jose D. Fernandez
Clerk,

MAVERICK

RODEO

Mon., July 4, 1949

AT

CIMARRON, NEW MEX.

50th Reunion of the 1949 Maverick Rodeo performers (1999)

MORNING SHOW

ALL ENTRIES TO BE MADE BY TIME OF EVENTS FIRST CALL.

1. 10:00 A. M. — PARADE AND FLAG CEREMONY

2. INTRODUCTION OF OFFICIALS

3. BOY'S HORSE RACE
   For boys 14 years of age or under. Starting from 5/16 chute.
   Three prizes, $10, $5 and $3.

4. BEST DRESSED COWGIRL
   On the track in front of grandstand. Three prizes and hard work
   for the judges.

5. CALF ROPING — First Section
   Rope and tie down—Contest rules—Three Prizes $50, $30, $20. Entry $7

6. SHETLAND PONY RACE
   Children 8 years of age or under on genuine Shetlands.
   Three Prizes $5, $3, $2.

7. BAREBACK BRONC RIDING
   Contest Rules. Three Prizes $40, $20, $15. Entry $7

8. BARREL RACE
   (A) FOR BOYS — A timed event for smooth-handling horses.
   Three prizes, $25, $15, $10. Entry $5.

   (B) FOR GIRLS — A timed event for smooth-handling horses.
   Three prizes, $25, $15, $10. Entry $5.

9. COW PONY RACE
   Quarter Mile Race for cowboys on cow ponies with stock saddles.
   Three Prizes $25, $15, $10. Entry $5.

12:00 TILL 1:00 — CHUCK WAGON TIME

Visit Kiwanis Club refreshment headquarters under the grandstand.

AFTERNOON SHOW

ALL ENTRIES FOR AFTERNOON EVENTS TO BE MADE BY 1:30

10. WILD COW RIDING
    Three Prizes. $40, $20, $15. Entry $7.

11. GIRL'S HORSE RACE
    Cowgirl race from the 5/16 chutes. Three Prizes of $10, $5, $3

12. SADDLE BRONC RIDING
    Contest Rules. Three Prizes $50, $30, $20. Entry $7.

13. WILD HORSE RACE
    No Holds Barred. First to saddle and circle track.
    Three Prizes $30, $20, $10. Entry $3.

14. CALF ROPING — Second Section

15. PONY EXPRESS RACE
    Teams of four cowboys on cow ponies, each to run half way around the
    track. Batons carried and passed on. Three Prizes $25, $15, $10.
    Entry $4 team.

16. RELAY RACE
    One rider and three horses. Rides one lap on each mount.
    Three Prizes $25, $15, $10. Entry $5.

17. WILD COW MILKING
    A free-for-all. Three Prizes $25, $15, $10. Entry $5 team.

18. MAVERICK STAKES
    Feature race of the day. An open race from 9/16 chutes.
    Three Prizes $40, $25, $15. Entry $5.

JUMBO BARBECUE BUFFALOBURGERS

50c Each

PLEASE NOTE: THE MAVERICK CLUB ASSUMES NO RESPONSIBILITY FOR PERSONAL INJURY OR PROPERTY DAMAGE

PRICES: *Cars 25c each; Adults $1.00; Children 25c*

26TH ANNUAL MAVERICK RODEO
CIMARRON, NEW MEXICO

1949

79TH
MAVERICK CLUB

1923   2002

RODEO
JULY 4, 2002
CIMARRON, NEW MEXICO

SOUVENIR PROGRAM

79TH MAVERICK RODEO

THE LONGEST RUNNING OPEN RODEO IN THE WEST

79TH MAVERICK CLUB RODEO
1923   2002

CIMARRON, NEW MEXICO

EDKER WILSON, STOCK CONTRACTOR
$4.00 Central Entry System Charge

MAVERICK CLUB ROPING
JULY 3
CIMARRON, NEW MEXICO

ENTRIES OPEN AT 9:00 A.M.
START AT 10:00 A.M.

9 - 7 - 5 -for $30.00
PROGRESSIVE AFTER ONE HEAD BUCKLE TO
HIGH MONEY WINNER OF EACH ROPING.

THESE ROPINGS FINISH ON JULY 3RD.

ALL PROCEEDS ABOVE EXPENSES
GO TO CHARITABLE ORGANIZATIONS

9. OPEN TEAM ROPING
Limit 50 teams - Entry fee - One for $30.00 - Enter on 4th
$500.00 added money Sponsored by Cimarron West
Buckles - Sponsored by Dave Kennehe, Maverick Club

10. CENTURY ROPING
Team Age Total 100 years and more
Entry fee: One for $50.00
Buckles - Sponsored by Cimarron Storage and Cantrell Appraisals

11. SID MORROW MEMORIAL SADDLE BRONC RIDING
Limited to 10 - Entry fee: $50.00
$500.00 added money Sponsored by International Bank
Buckle - Sponsored by Pacheco Family

12. POLE BENDING (AGES 11-14)
Limited to 10 - Entry fee $15.00
Buckle - Sponsored by Chase Ranch.

13. MIXED RIBBON ROPING
Limited to 30 - Entry fee: $40.00
Buckles - Sponsored by: Wahoo Ink., and United Chevy

14. WILD HORSE RACE
Limited to 6 teams - Entry fee $60.00 per team
Enter on July 4th, by 9:00 A.M
Buckles - Sponsored by Crossroads Salon, PSA, and Colfax Trading Co.

15. CALF SCRAMBLE
FOR THE KIDS (6-12 yrs. old) ONLY.
SORRY PARENTS

16. BULL RIDING
Entry fee $50.00
$500.00 added money - Sponsored by B&B
Buckle - Sponsored by Sam Minor Construction.

Must be entered and compete in 3 events to be eligible for
ALL AROUND
P.R.C.A. rules apply in all events
Entries may be called to:
WILSON CENTRAL ENTRY
PHONE: (719) 274-5707
(719) 274-5724
from 8:00 A.M. - 6:00 P.M. - June 26, 2001
On site entries July 3
and the morning of July 4

Money must be paid by 9 a.m.
July 4, 2001

Liability waiver must be signed by each contestant

For more information call:
Barney Gonzales (505) 376-2646

QUEEN'S BUCKLE
Sponsored by:
Buddy Morse

ALL-AROUND BUCKLE
Sponsored by:
Rick Enterprises

RODEO ADMISSION
$5.00 Per Person - Children ages 6-12 $2.00

PRINTED BY MARKUS PRINTING (505) 445-9016

Very Special Thanks To Our Added Money Sponsors

To Our Rodeo Sponsors
South Central Colfax County Hospital
St. James Hotel
Bennet & Barron
Philmont Scout Ranch
International Bank
Cimarron Art Gallery
Cimarron West
Zia Natural Gas
Farmway Feed
1st National Bank

RODEO DANCE
JULY 3
at the
Maverick Rodeo Grounds
9:00 P.M.
Adults $6.00 Per Person
18 & Under $5.00 Per Person
ROD TAYLOR AND THE ROUNDERS

RODEO PARADE 9:00 A.M.

1. GRAND ENTRY

2. BAREBACK BRONC RIDING
Limited to 15 - Entry fee $50.00
$500.00 added money if at least 10 entries - Sponsored By The 1st. National Bank
Buckle - Sponsored by ZZ Bar

3. JIGGS PORTER COMMEMORATIVE CALF ROPING
Limited to 30 - Entry fee: $50.00
$500.00 added money - Sponsored By South Central Colfax County Hospital
Buckle - Sponsored by CS Cattle Co.

4. PETE GENTRY MEMORIAL SENIOR BARREL RACE
Entry fee $30.00
$500.00 added money - Sponsored by Farmway Feeds
Buckle - Sponsored by AAA Pump Service by Pete Gentry

5. WILD COW MILKING
Entry fee $60.00 per team. Entry on
July 4th by 9:00 A.M. Limit 8 Teams
Buckles - Sponsored by Russell's One Stop Shop,
Cimarron Trading Co., and Kit Carson Inn

6. THIKE STOCKTON MEMORIAL JUNIOR BARREL RACE
Entry Fee: $15.00
Buckle - Sponsored by Northern New Mexico Gas Co.

7. TACK RELAY RACE
Entry fee: $50.00 per team
Buckles - Sponsored by Solano's, RBS, and Maverick Club

8. COW PONY RACE
Entry fee: $100.00 - WINNER TAKE ALL.
Buckle - Sponsored by Vermejo Park Ranch

MAVERICK LOGO & DESIGN BY: KEITH WALTERS © 1993

We are honored to present
The 79th Annual Maverick Club Rodeo Grand Marshall
National Cowgirl Hall of Fame Recipient Ruby Gobble

Ruby grew up on a ranch near Wickenburg, Arizona and was the youngest of five children. She was milking cows and riding desert burros at the age of 3. By the time she was 6 Ruby was playing the ukulele and singing western songs. Ruby could twirl a rope and when this little cowgirl was 12 her paint mare foaled and Ruby called the colt Tony (after Tom Mix's horse "Go Tony"). Ruby became best friends with Tony and broke him to ride and taught him to do tricks. Soon they were performing at rodeos around Arizona. They were making quite a name for themselves when tragedy struck. Tony died at the age of 5 of an infection caused by kick from another horse.

At 17 Ruby found another friend by the name of 'Taffy" and in 3 short months they were performing the same tricks for cheering crowds at rodeos.

Ruby's interests turned to calf roping in 1946 with the help of neighbor named Frank Mesilla. Ruby went every day until she got to the point of giving Frank a few tips on the art , including how to stay on a horse when he just about went over the top of her horse Sabado because Ruby taught him to stop quite well.

In 1949 Ruby was selected The Queen of Glendale, Arizona World's Champion Rodeo and traveled to Hollywood. While her abilities as a Horsewoman won her the trip she was depicted "The Glamour Girl of Rodeo" because she was beautiful, slim, and cool.

In '50 Ruby entered the Girl's Rodeo Association and spent the next 4 years winning awards and championships on a Buckskin named "Sabado". In '51 and '53 Ruby won the World Champion Team Tying Title and in '52 won the World Champion Ribbon Roping Title.

In 1952 Ruby was in Laramie and winning a calf roping competition. When Ruby roped the 4th calf in a row and Sabado started bucking and jumping around Ruby thought he was just happy that she did so well. In the picture below you can see that he even has ears pinned back. It turned out that the cinch hobble strap had broken and the rear cinch had slipped back

under his flank and caused all the commotion.

Ruby makes her home on the well known "Chase Ranch" where she and Gretchen Sammis raise Hereford cattle, horses, cats, and dogs. Ruby also drives a big bulldozer they call the " Monster" . The Village of Cimarron and the Maverick Club are proud to have Ruby as our friend and neighbor. Thanks Ruby.

RODEO RULES

All Contestants in all events will abide by current PRCA rules or ground rules established by the **MAVERICK CLUB**.

Although contestants are non-professionals, they may be barred for any of the following offenses:

Refusing to contest on any animal drawn or selected.
Being under the influence of liquor.
Rowdiness.
Mistreatment of stock.
Quarreling with judges or officials.
Failure to give assistance when requested by an arena director.
For any other reason deemed by the manager.

ALL AROUND COWBOY

A contestant must be entered and compete in three events, excluding all Junior events, to be eligible for **ALL AROUND COWBOY**. It is the responsibility of each contestant to notify the officials in the entry booth of his compliance with this regulation.

Buckles furnished by the **MAVERICK CLUB** for the winner of each event and the **ALL AROUND COWBOY**.

ST. JAMES HOTEL
1880

Corporate Sponsor

The Maverick Rodeo participants have been visiting The St James Hotel for the last 78 years.

Sharon and Roger Smith welcome you to join them for fine dining, comfortable lodging and refreshing sprits.

The St. James Hotel where the western tradition is still preserved after 122 years. Located on Hwy 21 in Cimarron near The Old Mill Museum in the Cimarron Historic District.

Endnotes

Chapter 1: What's Past Is Prologue

1. Fortunately, both the Webb and Caldwell families are serious chronologists and archivists, making my job much easier.

2. Count Caldwell, Nora Webb's uncle, gave an extensive oral account of many of these events shortly before his death in 1977. A portion of this interview is appended. The St. James Hotel in Cimarron, opened in 1880 by Henri Lambert, has been restored and is a wonderful place to visit. Room registrations for many of its famous guests such as Clay Allison, Davy Crockett II, Jesse James, Zane Grey, Buffalo Bill Cody, Wyatt Earp, and Doc Holliday are on display. Bullet holes in the ceiling are still visible from the era of the Colfax County War that took place there. It is a national landmark.

3. The history of Sam Houston is a story in itself. Few people realize the impact he made on both Texas and American history. His resistance to Texas' joining the Confederacy was particularly significant. He was against slavery, which was an extremely unpopular position at that time in Texas.

4. The American Wind Power Center is probably the most outstanding windmill museum in the country. Located in Lubbock, Texas, it covers over twenty-eight acres, and includes a museum, art and sculpture gallery, and outdoor windmill displays. More than sixty windmills are displayed in the exhibit hall, the oldest made in 1868.

5. I can understand this. As a young summer hand on the family place near Hereford, a part of the old XIT Ranch, I had to work on fences and windmills, tasks I ardently disliked. I preferred to be on a horse and, in my amateurish way, play the role of a "real" cowboy.

6. In my interviews with Don Webb (Leroy's brother) and Bill Hemphill (the old Matadors cowhand and wagon boss), both gave extensive accounts of the working conditions on the Matadors and Pitchfork ranches during the 1940s and 1950s: "Every cowboy had a bedroll, seldom went to town, and would spend months at a time under the stars. You rode to work on a horse."

7. Paul Engler, a most knowledgeable feedlot entrepreneur and president of Cactus Feeders in Amarillo, related to me his perceptions of cowboys over time and

the genesis of the feedlot business. He mentioned to me that he lost one of his best feedlot cowboys to a lesser paying job because he got tired of "opening and closing gates."

8. Charlie Ball has devoted his life to the feedlot industry, serving for many years as the executive director of the Texas Cattle Feeders Association (TCFA). Charlie served with me on several boards at Texas A&M and worked with my younger brother, John, who served as deputy assistant secretary of agriculture under President Reagan. His comments have been most helpful.

9. Letter from Charles E. Ball to Davis L. Ford, October 11, 2001.

Chapter 2: Roots and Beginnings

1. Kit Carson, whose oldest son married into Leroy Webb's ancestry, was very much a dominant figure in northern New Mexico history. Born in 1809, he spent his younger years as a trapper. By chance, he met John C. Fremont on a Missouri River steamboat in 1842 and became Fremont's guide on three expeditions throughout the American West. The two were close friends, and Carson's skills enabled Fremont to secure his place in history through the ultimate Americanization of California, first as a republic, then as a state in 1850. Carson, though uneducated, gained fame as an Indian fighter (speaking fluently in many tribal languages), Indian agent and ultimate friend to many tribes, scout for the Union army, and ranching partner with Lucien Maxwell in the Taos-Cimarron area. (Roberts, 2000) He married Josefa Jaramillo of Taos and had seven surviving children, the oldest of whom married Leroy's great aunt, Lupe Richards. Kit Carson died in 1868 and is buried along with Josefa in Taos.

2. Leroy and Nora Webb have preserved their roots through a vast collection of historical documents preserved at their ranch headquarters at the Singleton Bar Y. I was able to sift through these documents to trace the Webb ancestry back to the late 1700s.

Chapter 3: Saddling Up

1. In my interviews with Leroy over the period of a year (2000-2001), he would cite many such injuries. He downplayed them as it "went with the job." His physical endurance, even today, amazes me.

2. Robert Allen, a long-time resident of Raton, pointed out the difference of spelling; i.e. "Wootton" of Santa Fe Trail fame and "Wootten" of Red River Ranch lineage. There is still uncertainty as to these origins.

3. Strategically located railheads and railroad lines to central cattle markets were critical to ranchers during that time prior to construction of major paved roads and the interstates. (Truck transportation is now the preferred choice.)

4. Albert K. Mitchell was general manager of the Bell Ranch for fourteen years and was a nationally known figure in the cattle business. At the time of this writing, Linda Davis is managing the CS Ranch near Cimarron and is one of the most respected individuals in the cattle industry. (Raton Range, 1990) She is the recipient of the National Golden Spur Award, the New Mexico Cattle Growers Association

prestigious Cattleman of the Year Award, and countless other honors. (Home Grown News from Colfax County, 1992)

5. I had the opportunity to review an extensive pictorial history of the Long X and the Reynolds Cattle Company, preserved in the Texas Tech Southwest Collection. (Southwest Collection, Texas Tech University, 2001)

6. The headquarters of the Philmont Boy Scout Ranch is just a few miles south of Cimarron. It has a visitors' center and a museum and is a wonderful place to visit, particularly when Scouts from all over the world are there during the summer months.

7. The Cimarroncita Ranch is best noted for its girls' camp, which opened in 1929 and closed down in the 1990s. Fortunately, my daughter, Katy Ford, was able to experience the camp as a wrangler for Mike Burk before it closed. In my interview with Jimmy Rockinfield, I got an interesting insight into the history of the ranch and the camp. Rockinfield, currently in his forties, is a Texas A&M graduate and one of the most talented outdoorsmen I've ever met.

8. Frank Atmore and his younger brother, John, have a marvelous sense of history, not only of their ranch in the Ute Creek area but also of the surrounding country. They are fourth-generation New Mexico ranchers. I had the good fortune of knowing their parents, Dick and Doris Atmore, before they passed away. They and their ancestors are buried on the old Atmore Ranch.

9. Frank Sauble eventually bought a ranch northeast of Springer, which is still in the family and run by the grandchildren, Roy and Bill Sauble.

Chapter 5: The Matadors and the Pitchfork

1. Report of Proceedings, Third General Meeting of Stockholders, Matador Land and Cattle Company (1898).

2. *Dictionary of American Biography XXII*, pp. 416-417.

3. Fortunately, John Stevens recorded his memoirs of this era through the Southwest Oral History Collection at Texas Tech University in Lubbock. His interviews were taped in June and December of 1972 and in September of 1973. One of the interviewers was Ms. Curry (Fran) Holden, wife of a well-known history professor, Curry Holden, at Tech and long-time friends and neighbors of the Ford family. He related in great detail his recollection of the effects of World War II on ranch labor, his memories of Murdo and John Mackenzie, the old Matador cowboys, the recordkeeping methodologies (long before modern computer technology), mesquite brush control, wild cattle, and ranching techniques and management practices. (Southwest Collection, Texas Tech University, 1972, 1973)

4. Interview with Bill Hemphill, Roaring Springs, Texas, 2001.

5. Interview with Leroy Webb, Santa Rosa, 2001.

6. Ibid., 2000.

7. Linda Kane, *Lubbock Avalanche Journal*, 2001, *lubbockonline.com*.

8. The JA (John Adair Ranch) deserves special mention, although not a part of Leroy Webb's life. The JA Ranch centers around the story of Charles Goodnight, a real cattle pioneer and empire builder in the late 1800s, who established the Goodnight-Loving Trail between Texas and Colorado.

9. I was fortunate enough to know D Burns, his wife, Mamie, and their two

grandchildren who lived at the ranch with them, Ann and Burns Hamilton. During the early 1950s, while in Lubbock High School, I made many trips to the Pitchfork for quail hunting and social events. My parents were long-time friends with the Burnses, so I enjoyed the benefit of hunting on the Pitchfork and watching the cowboys do their work (Don Webb and Johnny Caldwell were actually working cowboys there during my occasional visits). Another benefit was that my girlfriend in high school, Ann Gordon, was a friend of D and Mamie's granddaughter, Ann Hamilton. So, we enjoyed several social weekends at the ranch. Unlike Don and Johnny, who were out with the wagon working eighteen-hour days, we were coddled high school kids enjoying the benefits of a leisure weekend in the ranch headquarters (the "big house"). Mamie Burns was the consummate hostess and believed in decorum within the confines of the big house that included East Coast formalities such as dressing up for dinner and very strict etiquette. We were served by a bow-tied waiter and were presented "finger bowls" at the dinner table. Being a typical Lubbock High School "bubba," I thought it was thin soup and began drinking out of my finger bowl as no spoons were visible—much to the horror of my girlfriend.

10. Interview with Don Webb, Raton, 2001.

11. Frank Farmer, "The Vanishing Cowboy," an interview with D Burns (Springfield, MO), *Sunday News and Leader*, (February 1968).

12. Interview with Don Webb, Angel Fire, 2001.

13. There is an excellent history of the Matadors and Pitchfork ranches, particularly in the 1950s era of the Webb brothers, documented by J. W. Williams. (Williams, 1971, 1999)

Chapter 6: In-Laws and Outlaws

1. Although the story of Pat Garrett's relationship with and final killing of Billy the Kid has been subject to significant fictional interpretation, Garrett's own account is deemed the most credible. I still remember stories from my father and my mother when he talked to Frenchy McCormick, the last resident of Old Tascosa, in the 1930s. She would see Billy the Kid hanging around town and thought he was was a sorry bum. She would have nothing to do with him. I also heard stories during my recent visit to the New Mexican village of Anton Chico, where Billy the Kid would occasionally visit (and where Pat Garrett was married in the local Catholic church). The consensus was the same as Frenchy's—a "no good bum."

2. I. C. Florsheim was a successful merchant in Springer. His son, Don Florsheim, was a World War II veteran and enhanced a large family ranching operation just east of Springer. My lifelong friend James Collins became acquainted with Don Florsheim in the 1970s, and we had the opportunity on several occasions to visit the ranch. I've never seen such organization and cleanliness in a ranch headquarters as in this operation.

3. Evelyn Marsh, Nora's "double cousin," has been an excellent source in tracing the Caldwell family history. She and her husband, Bernard, live in Austin near my home and have provided much of the information included in this chapter.

4. Fred Lambert was a friend of Count as well as his brother, Berlin Caldwell. Count's narrative description of his gun battle, audiotaped shortly before his death, is both interesting and historically valuable.

5. Fred Lambert's written tribute to Berlin Caldwell is a western classic. I've included the entire tribute in the Appendix.

6. Fred Caldwell, Fred Lambert's namesake, retired as a police officer and became a presiding judge in Colfax County, New Mexico.

Chapter 7: Bouncing Around

1. Harp McFarland is a delightful old-time cowboy, and very knowledgeable about the history of New Mexico and Texas ranching. Although older than Leroy, he had acute insight on Leroy's "bouncing around" years. He, as Leroy, was very laudatory in his comments about Bill Blakley, one-time owner of the Sawyer Cattle Company. It was through Harp that Leroy met Henry Singleton. Singleton purchased the San Cristobal Ranch in the mid-1980s, the first of many New Mexico ranches he acquired.

2. A "snubbing post" is a fixed post in the center of the corral, used to secure the horse during the breaking process.

3. "Wooled him around" means applying some saddle blanket or other material alien to the unbroken horse to get him used to something on its back.

4. Horse breaking has evolved over the years—from severe to more gentle. Regardless of this transition, good horse breakers never injured or hurt the animal. Everyone I've interviewed marveled at Leroy's innate ability to break horses skillfully and smartly. He has probably broken more horses over his career than any other living individual.

5. World champion ropers with whom I've talked rate Leroy's roping ability at the top.

6. Jack Kyle is an amazing person: World War II combat veteran, world champion cowboy, and member of the prestigious Cowboy Hall of Fame. He resides today in Yukon, Oklahoma, still breaking and training quarter horses. One has to get up mighty early to request any of his time.

7. Hurley, who was totally blind by the age of three, had a beautiful relationship with his parents and communicated with them perfectly—thus, a chapter dedicated to the memory of this marvelous young man.

Chapter 8: Rodeos

1. The Fords and Tydings watched the 2001 "Scottish Highland Games" at Braemer, Scotland (the original land of the Culwells or "Caldwells"), which provided a forum for competition between "clans," dating back to medieval times.

2. This organizational history is outlined in the Fredriksson book (1985) and enhanced based on my recent discussions with one of my reviewers, George M. Cowden. George has an extensive knowledge of cowboy and rodeo history.

3. Permits were issued to professional rodeo cowboys who earned a prescribed amount of competition money. It's the rodeo equivalent to professional licensing required for professionals in many fields, representing a minimum level of competence.

4. The annual Fourth of July open rodeo at Cimarron is a classic. With small-town atmosphere, steeped in history as the longest standing rodeo in the Southwest,

the rodeo features a delightful array of competitive events. One has to "work the crowd" a few hours before the opening to fully appreciate its flavor of "Americana." It's an experience that I treasure and one of the benefits of researching a book such as this. My wife and I attended the July 4, 2002, Cimarron Rodeo. I had the opportunity to meet Freddie Martinez, one of Leroy's favorite cowboys, who is still a performer in the "Old-Timer" events.

5. An open rodeo is one which originally was designed to allow cowhands from the area ranches to compete openly.

6. The Springer and Phillips names epitomize the heritage of the Cimarron area, as described in earlier chapters. The organization of the Maverick Club is a further example of the perpetual recognition of the area's traditions resulting from the vision of such families.

7. Bronc riding is a traditional rodeo event using saddles (saddle bronc riding) or no saddles (bareback bronc riding). It requires a tremendous amount of skill, physical fitness, and perception in anticipating the bronc's master plan for removing his human intruder.

8. All-around cowboy is a distinction awarded to a rodeo cowboy who wins a stipulated number of events.

9. The PRCA "rodeo card" is merely a registration requirement. The PRCA permit is required to be classified as a professional rodeo performer.

10. Leroy continued to compete in rodeos well into his forties and fifties, long after most of his colleagues had hung up their spurs.

11. Individual rodeo events are displayed and explained at the Cowboy Hall of Fame in Oklahoma City. Team roping is a popular rodeo event. It involves two ropers who rope the head and hind feet of the calf. The header ropes the head first, and the steer trails him before the heeler ropes the two hind feet. (One secured hind foot loses points.) It requires exceptional skill and coordination between two horses and two riders.

12. PRCA ProRodeo Online website: *www.prorodeo.com*.

Chapter 9: The Wiescamp Years

1. This Wiescamp quote reminds me of my granddad, G. C. Davis, who was a born trader. He told me many times that he could "go into town with a pocketknife and come out with a mule."

2. *New Mexico Magazine*, June 2001. Another important name in the development of the quarter horse is Coke Roberds. Roberds was working on a ranch in Texas near the XIT in the early twentieth century. His stud, Steel Dust, had some thoroughbred blood and became part of the original quarter horse breed. Before the quarter horse originated, the favorite horses of these cowboys were called "Steel Dusts." (Holmes, 1998)

3. *AQHA Official Handbook*, 49th Edition, January 1, 2001. This handbook is a comprehensive document which includes governance on recordation and preservation of pedigrees, educational programs, equine research, shows, and racing.

4. Wiescamp bought most of the Phillips Ranch mares when Waite Phillips gave his ranch to the Boy Scouts. (Wiescamp in jest told Phillips he should have kept the ranch and given the mares to the Boy Scouts.) Shortly after Wiescamp bought the

Phillips mares, he bought more outstanding mares from the Ghost Ranch, located north of Abiquiu, New Mexico (of Georgia O'Keefe fame), owned by New York philanthropist Arthur Pack. (Holmes, 1996)

5. *Western Horseman*, July 1980. Leroy and many of the cowboys I've interviewed believe Shoemaker, along with Wiescamp, were two of the top quarter horse breeders ever.

6. Leroy was the sole trainer and rider for twenty-six of these champions.

7. *Western Horseman*, "The End of an Era," September 1998.

Chapter 10: Ownership

1. "Alamosa Trainer Strikes Out on Own," *Pueblo, Colorado Star Journal*, February 15, 1970. This front-page article was the first of many newspaper and journal articles on Leroy Webb spanning from 1970 through today.

2. Ben Johnson was born in 1920 in Pawhuska, Oklahoma, and won the Rodeo Cowboys Association Team Roping World Championship in 1953. He and his father took strings of horses from Oklahoma to Hollywood on contract with John Ford. Johnson then became a stunt horseback rider for several western actors, getting the attention of both John Ford and John Wayne. He became an actor, appearing in many western classics, and subsequently was elected to the Cowboy Hall of Fame, where his portrait is on display in the Oklahoma City Western Heritage Museum. Johnson, one of my favorite character actors, won the Academy Award for his performance as "Sam the Lion" in *The Last Picture Show*. Ben Johnson died in 1996.

3. Pawnee Hawk was the subject of much publicity. His exploits were summarized in the Alamosa, Colorado Valley Courier, December 4, 1975.

4. The solitary life is one which typifies most of the old-time cowboys I've known (including my father). Although they love company and family, they're totally at ease with themselves during periods of solitude on the open range. Most find their horses, cattle, game, open country, and star-filled nights to be good companions.

5. Leroy later became friends with Waite Phillips' son, Choate. Choate would help work cattle with Leroy on his UU Bar lease. It was on the UU Bar that Choate spent his early years, and he loved the place. He was saddened when his father sold the UU Bar, so he welcomed the chance to return when Leroy got the lease, retracing many of the steps he had taken as a boy. Choate and Leroy remain good friends to this day.

6. Cattle raisers commonly lease grazing land from owners, typically on a one-to-five-year lease at a fixed annual cost per acre. Depending on the available grass (convertible to weight gain and the corresponding price which the animal will bring), the current lease price can range from one to five dollars per year per acre.

Chapter 11: Hurley

1. Unknown to his parents, Hurley could only detect a blur in the first few months of his life. Up to the age of three, he could detect movement and some imagery. But after that he was totally blind, seeing his parents, horses, friends, and nature only through his mind.

2. I find it incredible that Hurley could learn and perform his equestrian and cowboy skills considering his disability. It is a true credit to Hurley and his parents.

3. This obviously is a very personal issue, and I was reticent to even address it. It was only after my interview with Nora that she suggested I write a chapter in memory of Hurley. Leroy's only mention of Hurley during my extensive interviews with Leroy was his following comment:

> *Our one son, Hurley, died at an early age—a beautiful child. Hurts too much to talk about him—a special person—bless his heart.*

4. Robert Lee Brothers was a special kind of poet. He was a friend of the Ford family, and especially fond of my sister, Susan Ford Wiltshire. Brothers published several volumes of poems during the 1940s through the 1960s, including *Democracy of Dust*, *Threescore and Ten*, and *The Hidden Harp*. Susan edited a collection of his poems, *Prairie Laureate*, which was published in 1998. (Wiltshire, 1998)

I changed only one word from his poem "With Every Spring That Passes" quoted here. That change was "father" to "son." I found this poem to be particularly applicable to Hurley and feel sure that Robert Brothers would have given me such literary license.

Chapter 12: The Bell Ranches

1. "Comancheros" is a term applied to New Mexicans who traded with the Indians and had a good relationship, strengthened by their mutual dislike of Texans. (Robertson, 1980)

2. Few people realize the importance of gold discovery in Colorado and the impact it had on western migration to Colorado and New Mexico. The Colorado discoveries drew many more gold seekers than did those in California. (West, 1998)

3. I specifically recall when Keeney (Col. R. Leland Keeney and Ellwood interests joined by marriage), Arnett (Ellwood partner), Chappell (Ellwood and Chappell interests joined through marriage), and Hampton (personal friend of Arnett and Chappell) bought the separate portions of the entire Bell Ranch. This was big news in Lubbock, Texas—a town of fewer than 80,000 people and hardly known as a big-time financial center. My dad was glad to see Howard Hampton get in on this deal as the new Hampton acquisition was only about eighty miles from our Deaf Smith County place. Dad now had the opportunity to conveniently purchase Hampton's registered whiteface bulls for his breeding program and get in an occasional mule deer hunt.

4. Fort Bascom, remnants which still remain on the former Hampton Ranch, was a cavalry outpost, designed to protect local ranchers as well as those traversing northern New Mexico toward the Colorado Gold Rush areas from various Comanche and Apache tribes.

5. Howard and Val Hampton were collectors of western memorabilia and were generous in sharing such items with the public through donations to museums. The Hampton papers are filed in the Southwest Collection at Texas Tech. Documents signed by U.S. presidents and other rare papers are included in this file.

6. The National Ranching Heritage Center located on the campus of Texas Tech University is a first-class display of original ranch houses, barns, windmills, and other ranch improvements. Visitors can see the actual headquarters-type of facility the cowboys and cowhands of Leroy Webb's era (and before) utilized.

7. Colorado City, Texas, is the community around which many of the Texas Chappell Spade Ranch activities centered. Former mayor Jim Baum and the Heart of West Texas Museum are excellent resources in researching this ranching history.

8. The advent of barbed wire had an immediate and profound impact on the cattle business. Glidden and his partners became wealthy virtually overnight from this invention.

9. Frank Chappell, Jr. has been helpful to me in this venture. I had the pleasure of meeting Frank, who was Howard Hampton's neighbor in Lubbock, back in the 1940s. He has encyclopedic knowledge of the Chappell Spade Ranch history, as well as the Bell. He has reviewed this chapter in detail and made significant contributions and corrections. I am most appreciative that he has shared his knowledge with the reader and me. Frank Chappell at the time of this writing was eighty-one years old and living in his native Connecticut.

10. William M. Lane II was a wealthy investor and maintained the Bell Ranch operations and traditions following his purchase of the Keeney interests in 1970. He was killed on the ranch in 1978 when he drove his Suburban off of the ranch road (near Burro Hill) late one night when returning from the nearby village of Roy. His family interests still own 290,000 acres of the original Bell Ranch. ("Who Owns New Mexico," *Crosswinds*, June 1997) (Interview with Sam Arnett III, October 16, 2001, Lubbock)

11. The pioneer home of Mr. and Mrs. Sam C. Arnett, Sr., was moved to the Lubbock Christian College (LCC) campus. The eight-room, two-story house has been completely restored and serves as a home for LCC visitors and associates.

12. Sam Arnett, Jr.'s classmate during the opening years at Texas Tech was my mother, Lucile Davis Ford. Like Sam Arnett, Jr., she transferred to the University of Texas, receiving her master's degree there.

13. I grew up with Sam Arnett, Jr.'s son, Sam Arnett III (known as "Bobby" in those days). I did not know him well when we were youngsters (we were about the same age) but contacted him last summer to arrange an interview. He lives in Lubbock, stays in communication with his Clabber Hill Ranch (and another ranch just east of Lubbock, the V8 Ranch) and is engaged in other businesses. He was gracious to assist me in developing firsthand information of the family history as well as the Clabber Hill Ranch, which Leroy had worked and knows. Moreover, he directed me to Kelton's book, *Renderbrook* (1989), which provides an in-depth history of the Ellwoods, Keeneys, Chappells, and Arnetts and the Spade ranches.

Chapter 13: The Singleton Ranches, Bar Y and Beyond

1. Interview with Harper McFarland, Stanley, New Mexico, January 2, 2002. Harp, who managed the San Cristobal when Singleton purchased it, worked closely with the new owner over the next fifteen years. He described Singleton as an astute businessman and first-class person. He noted that Singleton was equally comfortable in a business suit or in boots and ranch garb.

2. Henry Singleton was chairman of Teledyne from 1960 to 1990 and lived in Los Angeles. He purchased the ranch from Buddy Branum, who had previously acquired it from the Blakley interests.

3. Leroy manages not only the Bar Y today, but also portions of the Hollywood River Ranch, the V. K. Jones Ranch, and the Latigo Ranch, all of which are included in the Bar Y operational unit (division).

4. According to Leroy Webb and Harp McFarland, Singleton purchased these ranches with negotiating skills developed over his many years as a business executive. His timing was perfect as the ranching business was not particularly healthy at the time and many of the New Mexico landowners were eager to sell. Most of these transactions were on a cash basis, another leveraging factor in favor of the buyer.

5. Howard Hampton sold a portion of the ranch he had purchased from the Bell split-up to Worley in 1965. This ranch lies just south of the Canadian River and contains the ruins of old Fort Bascom. Howard sold this portion of his ranch for tax purposes. It is now in the Singleton estate.

6. When Singleton was outbid on the Hampton Ranch, Leroy lost his lease, subsequently leasing a portion of the Mitchell Ranch.

Chapter 14: Cowboys I've Known

1. A pickup man in the rodeo is the one who pulls the cowboy off the bronc or bull when the whistle blows (if he's still on). They are critical to the safety of the rider and serve a very important (if less glamorous) role in the rodeo arena.

2. "Rawhide" is uncured leather, which requires skill and patience to work into leathermade goods. Don learned the trade from the gauchos when he was in Argentina and from a Chilean friend while in Montana. He does it for a hobby, "giving away more stuff than I sell."

Chapter 15: Horses I've Known

1. In reading about Monty Roberts, the "Horse Whisperer," it appears to me that Roberts developed his real insight into horses by watching them unobserved for days and weeks (wild mustangs). I sense that Leroy similarly has an intrinsic insight into horse psychology based on all the one-on-one time he's spent with them.

2. Leroy preferred geldings but said that studs often would make good riding and cow horses. Slightly tougher than geldings, they could develop similar manners if properly trained.

3. The credentials of many of the horses Leroy trained for rodeos, racing, and showing are appended. Of the thousands of horses he's ridden over his career, the ones he cited in this chapter are the horses that quickly came to mind.

Bibliography

Books, Pamphlets, Essays

Allen, J. B. *The Medicine Keepers*. Lubbock: Grey Horse Press (1997).

Alstad, Ken. *Savvy Sayin's*. Tucson, Arizona: Ken Alstad Company (1994).

Atmore, Frank. "History of the Atmore Ranch—Owned by Express Ranches." Unpublished (2001).

Baker, T. Lindsay. *A Field Guide to the American Windmill*. Norman: University of Oklahoma Press (1984).

Ball, Charles E. *The Finishing Touch, A History of the Texas Cattle Feeders Association and Cattle Feeding in the Southwest*. Amarillo: Texas Cattle Feeders Association (1992).

Barker, Elliot S. *When the Dogs Bark "Treed"* (1945).

Beck, Warren A. *New Mexico: A History of Four Centuries*. Norman: University of Oklahoma Press (1962).

Beebe, Lucius, and Charles Clegg. *The American West: The Pictorial Epic of a Continent*. New York: E. P. Dutton & Co., Inc. (1955).

Black, Baxter. *Cactus Tracks & Cowboy Philosophy*. New York: Penguin Books (1997).

Brown, Dee. *Hear That Lonesome Whistle Blow: The Epic Story of the Transcontinental Railroads*. New York: Henry Holt and Company (1977).

Burns, Mamie Sypert. *This I Can Leave You: A Woman's Days on the Pitchfork Ranch*. College Station: Texas A&M University Press (1986).

Carlson, P. H. *The Cowboy Way*. Lubbock: Texas Tech University Press (2000).

Chrisman, Harry E. *Lost Trails of the Cimarron*. Norman: University of Oklahoma Press (1998).

Clayton, Lawrence. *Watkin Reynolds Matthew, Biography of a Texas Rancher*. Austin: Eakin Press (1994).

Clifford, Craig Edward. *In the Deep Heart's Core: Reflections on Life, Letters, and Texas*. College Station: Texas A&M University Press (1985).

Dearen, Patrick. *Halff of Texas: Merchant Rancher of the Old West*. Austin: Eakin Press (2000).

———. *The Last of the Old-Time Cowboys*. Austin: Republic of Texas Press (1998).

DeBuys, William. *Enchantment and Exploitation: The Life and Hard Times of a New Mexico Mountain Range*. Albuquerque: University of New Mexico Press (1985).

Dictionary of American Biography. XXII, pp. 416-417.

Dobie, J. Frank. *Cow People*. Boston: Little, Brown and Company, Seventh Printing (1964).

———. *Tales of Old Times Texas*. Austin: University of Texas Press (1928).

———. *The Longhorns*. Boston: Little, Brown and Company (1941).

Duke, Cordia Sloan, and Joe B. Frantz. *6,000 Miles of Fence: Life on the XIT Ranch of Texas*. Austin: University of Texas Press (1961).

Ebsen, Wayne. *Outlaw: Ballads, Legends & Lore*. Asheville, North Carolina: Native Ground Music, Inc. (1996).

Edrigton, T., and John Taylor. *The Battle of Glorieta Pass*. University of New Mexico Press (1998).

Ellis, George F. *Bell Ranch As I Knew It*. Kansas City, Missouri: The Lowell Press (1973).

Fredriksson, Kristine. *American Rodeo: From Buffalo Bill to Big Business*. College Station: Texas A&M University Press (1985).

Fulton, Maurice G. *History of the Lincoln County War*. Tucson: University of Arizona Press (1997).

Garrett, Pat. *The Authentic Life of Billy the Kid*. Norman: University of Oklahoma Press (1954).

Green, Ben K. *Horse Tradin'*. New York: Alfred A. Knopf (1969).

———. *A Thousand Miles of Mustangin'*. Flagstaff, Arizona: Northland Press (1972).

———. *Wild Cow Tales*. New York: Alfred A. Knopf (1970).

Green, Douglas. *Singing in the Saddle*. Nashville: Vanderbilt University Press (2002).

Haley, J. Evetts. *The Heraldry of the Range*. Canyon, Texas: Panhandle-Plains Historical Society (1949).

Haley, Evetts, Jr. (Editor). *Cowboys Who Rode Proudly: Carrying Cattle...and the Methods of Handling Them*. Midland, Texas: The Nita Stewart Haley Memorial Library.

Haley, John H. *Windmills, Droughts, and Cottonseed Cakes*. Fort Worth: Texas Christian University Press (1995).

Henderson, Colonel Harry McCorry. *Texas in the Confederacy*. San Antonio, Texas: The Naylor Company (1955).

Hillard, George. *A Hundred Years of Horse Tracks: The Story of the Gray Ranch*. Silver City, New Mexico: High Lonesome Books (1996).

Holden, Frances Mayhugh. *Lambshead Before Interwoven: A Texas Range Chronicle, 1847-1878*. College Station: Texas A&M University Press (1982).

Holmes, Frank. *The Hank Wiescamp Story*. Colorado Springs: Western Horseman, Inc. (1996).

James, Marquis. *The Raven: A Biography of Sam Houston*. New York: Blue Ribbon Books, Inc. (1929).

James, Will. *The Drifting Cowboy*. Missoula, Montana: Mountain Press Publishing Company (1995).

Jenkins, M. E., and A. H. Schroeder. *A Brief History of New Mexico*. Albuquerque: University of New Mexico Press (1974).

Jones, Dave. *Practical Western Training*. New York: Van Nostrand Reinhold Company (1968).

Kelly, Charles. *The Outlaw Trail*. University of Nebraska Press (1938).

Kelton, Steve. *Renderbrook: A Century Under the Spade Brand*. Fort Worth: Texas Christian University Press (1989).

Lambert, Fred. *Bygone Days of the Old West*. Kansas City, Missouri: Burton Publishing Company (1948).

Larson, C. *Forgotten Frontier: The Story of Southwestern New Mexico*. University of New Mexico Press (1993).

Lattimore, Richmond (Translator). *The Iliad of Homer*. Chicago: The University of Chicago Press (1961).

Lavendar, David. *Bent's Fort, A Historical Account of the Adobe Empire That Shaped the Destiny of the American Southwest*. Garden City, New York: Doubleday & Company, Inc. (1954).

Lomax, John A. *Cowboy Songs and Other Frontier Ballads*. New York: The Macmillan Company (1920).

Martin, Gene, and Mary Martin. *Trail Dust: A Quick Picture History of The Santa Fe Trail*. Boulder, Colorado: Johnson Publishing Company (1972).

Matthews, Sallie Reynolds. *Interwoven*. College Station: Texas A&M University Press (1982).

McAfee, W. R. *The Cattlemen*. Alvin, Texas: Davis Mountain Press (1992).

McNeill, J. C. *The McNeills' SR Ranch*. College Station: Texas A&M University Press (1988).

McMurtry, Larry. *Walter Benjamin at the Dairy Queen: Reflections at Sixty and Beyond*. New York: Simon & Schuster (1999).

Mednick, Christina Singleton. *San Cristobal, Voices and Visions of the Galisteo Basin*. Santa Fe, New Mexico: Office of Archaeological Studies, Museum of New Mexico (1996).

Morgan, Sarah. *Dining with the Cattle Barons—Yesterday and Today*. Waco, Texas: Texian Press (1981).

Morris, John Miller. *A Private in the Texas Rangers: A. T. Miller of Company B, Frontier Battalion*. College Station: Texas A&M University Press (2001).

Murphy, Lawrence. *Lucien Bonaparte Maxwell, Napoleon of the Southwest*. Norman: University of Oklahoma Press (1962).

———. *Philmont: A History of New Mexico's Cimarron Country*. University of New Mexico Press (1991).

———. *Philmont: A History of New Mexico's Cimarron Country*. Albuquerque: University of New Mexico Press (1972).

Murrah, David J. *The Pitchfork Land and Cattle Company: The First Century*. Lubbock: Texas Tech University Press (1983).

Neugebauer, Janet M. (Editor). *Lambshead Legacy, the Ranch Diaries of Watt R. Matthews*. College Station: Texas A&M University Press (1997).

——— (Editor). *Plains Farmer*. College Station: Texas A&M University Press (1991).

O'Neal, Bill. *Historic Ranches of the Old West*. Austin: Eakin Press (1997).

Pearce, W. M. *The Matador Land and Cattle Company*. Norman: University of Oklahoma Press (1964).

Polk, William R. *Polk's Folly: An American Family History*. New York: Anchor Books (2001).

Remley, David. *Bell Ranch: Cattle Raising in the Southwest*. Yucca Tree Press (2000).

Report of Proceedings, Third General Meeting of Stockholders, Matador Land and Cattle Company (1898).

Roberts, David. *A Newer World: Kit Carson and John C. Freemont and the Claiming of the American West*. New York: Simon and Schuster (2000).

Roberts, Monty. *The Man Who Listens to Horses: The Story of a Real-Life Horse Whisperer*. New York: Ballantine Books (1999).

Robertson, Helen Holt. Unpublished Paper, furnished by the Courtesy of the Raton Public Library, dated 1983, Raton, New Mexico.

Robertson, P. D., and R. L. Robertson. *Cowman's Country: Fifty Frontier Ranches in the Texas Panhandle, 1876-1887*. Amarillo: Paramount Publishing Company (1981).

Robinson, Charles, M., III. *Men Who Wear the Star: The Story of the Texas Rangers*. New York: The Modern Library (2001).

Self, Margaret Cabell. *Horses: Their Selection, Care and Handling*. New York: A. S. Barnes and Company, Inc. (1943).

Simmons, Marc (Editor). *On the Santa Fe Trail*. Lawrence, Kansas: University Press of Kansas (1986).

Simpson, Harold B., et al. *Frontier Forts of Texas*. Waco, Texas: Texian Press (1966).

Taylor, M. F. *O. P. McMains and the Maxwell Land Grant Conflict*. Tucson: University of Arizona Press (1979).

———. *Pioneers of the Picketwire*. Pueblo, Colorado: Obrien Printing Co. (1964).

Texas Tech University Southwest Collection. http://libweb.lib.ttu.edu/web2.exe/form/A2kgamtl.OOO.

Thompson, Jerry (Editor). *Civil War in the Southwest: Recollections of the Sibley Brigade*. College Station: Texas A&M University Press (2001).

Tinkle, Lon. *An American Original: The Life of J. Frank Dobie*. Boston: Little, Brown and Company (1978).

Vigil, Arnold (Editor). *Enduring Cowboys: Life in the New Mexico Saddle*. New Mexico Department of Tourism: *New Mexico Magazine* (1999).

Webb, Leroy. Personal files. "History and Descendants of William G. Richards." Unpublished.

Webb, Walter Prescott. *The Texas Rangers*. Austin: University of Texas Press, Second Edition (2001).

West, Elliot. *The Contested Plains—Indians, Goldseekers, and the Rush to Colorado*. University of Kansas Press (1998).

Wilder, Mitchell A. *Old Ranches of the Texas Plains: Paintings by Mondel Rogers*. College Station: Texas A&M University Press (1976).

Williams, J. W. *The Big Ranch Country*. Nortex Press (first printing 1971) and reprinted Lubbock: Texas Tech University Press (1999).

Wiltshire, Susan Ford (Editor). *Prairie Laureate: The Collected Poems of Robert Lee Brothers*. Austin: Eakin Press (1998).

Articles

Barrett, W., J. Casey, D. Chacon, W. Kryloff, D. McKay, S. Montage, and M. Salazar. "Who Owns New Mexico—the Largest Private Landowners in the State." *Crosswinds*, June (1997).

"Davis Wins Cattleman's Honors." *Raton Range*, December 21 (1990).

Farmer, Frank. "The Vanishing Cowboy," an Interview with D Burns. Springfield, Missouri, *Sunday News and Leader*, February 18 (1968).

Haley, John A. "Herb Pate and Changing Conditions." Haley Memorial Library, Midland, Texas, obtained from Jim Bradshaw, Archivist, June (2001).

Hendrix, John M. "The Forks, Operating Under Second Fifty Year Charter." *The Cattleman* (1939).

"Linda Davis Earns Highest National Ranching Award." *Home Grown News from Colfax County*, September 25 (1992).

Nordyke, Lewis. "Hereford Empire, Ruler of Lone Star State's Pitchfork Domain is the Whiteface Bull." *Hereford Journal*, July (1959).

———. "Rugged Riders of the Pitchfork Ranch," *Saturday Evening Post*, No. 14, October (1959).

Perkins, Doug. "A Crown Jewel of Texas Ranching." *The Cattleman* (1983).

"Ranching Leader, War Hero Les Davis Dies at Age 81." Associated Press. Obituary, May (2001).

Reeves, Frank. "Cow Horses: How an Up-to-date Ranch Has Developed a Remuda of Top Cow Horses and How They are Used in Modern Ranching." *The Cattleman*, XLII, No. 4, September (1955).

———. "Pitchfork Ranch and Its Horses." *Western Livestock*, June (1958).

"Spring Work on the Huge Ranch Is Much Like That of the Old West." *West Texas Livestock Weekly*, March 10 (1960).

Voyt, Don. "The Pitchfork Ranch." *The Quarter Horse Journal*, XXII, No. 12 (1970).

Whittemore, Loren R. "Roping with Leroy Webb." *Rocky Mountain Quarter Horse*, January (1970).

Womack, James. "Biotechnology in Animal Agriculture." Engineering a New Century—National Academy of Engineering Regional Meeting, The University of Texas at Austin (March 5, 2002).

Index

Red River Valley Company, 132
Red River, viii
Renderbrook Springs, 137
Rendlebrock, Joseph, 137
Reynolds, Bettie Matthews, 42
Reynolds, George T., 41-42
Reynolds, Sallie Ann, 42
Reynolds, William D. (Will), 41-42
Reynolds Cattle Company, 41
Reynolds Long X Ranch, x
Richards, Alexander A., 214
Richards, Amanda, 19, 20
Richards, Dave, 214
Richards, James, 214
Richards, John, 214, 215
Richards, Lupe, 19
Richards, Manuelita Lujan, 19, 213-215
Richards, Rebecca, 19, 20
Richards, Samuel T., 214
Richards, Thomas, 214
Richards, William A., 214
Richards, William G., 17, 18, 19, 213-215
"Riders in the Sky," 186-187
Ridley, Wanda, 159
Rinestine, James, 158, 160
Ring Camp, 31
Rio Grande, 3, 4, 147
Rio Grande, viii
Roaring Springs, Texas, 58, 160, 167
Roberds, Coke, 110, 204
Rock Island Railroad, 132
Rockenfield, Elizabeth, 46
Rockenfield, George, 45
Rockenfield, Gretchen, 46
Rockenfield, Jimmy, 44, 45-47
Rockies, 40
Rocky Mountain Quarter Horse Association, 108, 116, 174
rodeos, 48, 84-85, 91-101, 108, 114, 119, 153, 157, 164, 166
Rodeo Association of America (RAA), 92
Rodeo Cowboy Association (RCA), 92, 99, 155
Rogers, Roy, viii, 65
Rogers, Will, 33, 43, 171
Rook, Monte, 160, 164
Roosevelt, Theodore, 55
roping, 164, 166, 169, 202; *see also* calf roping, steer roping, team roping
Rose, Matlock, 160, 164
Round Rock, Texas, 140
Roy, New Mexico, 137, 164
Royal Irish Regiment, 33

Russell, Charles, 78

-S-
Salinas, California, 92
Sammon, Bessie, 75, 212
Sammon, Bob, 75
Sammon, Elizabeth "Betty" Walker, 212
Sammon, Elizabeth, 71
Sammon, Elizabeth Clifford, 73, 212
Sammon, Elizabeth Harrison, 212
Sammon, John, Jr., 212
Sammon, Maria de los Santos Leal, 72, 73, 212
Sammon, Mary B. Harrison, 212
Sammon, Mary Laura Lelia "Lollie," 212
Sammon, Robert W., 71-73, 75, 212
Sammon, Susan Elizabeth Thrasher, 212
Sammon(s), John, 212
Sammon(s), Phillis Avey, 212
Sammon(s), Rebecca, 212
Sammons, Avey, 212
Sammons, William, 212
San Angelo, Texas, 82, 84, 123, 137
San Cristobal Ranch, x, 4, 81, 82, 146-147, 149, 165
San Jacinto, 4
San Luis Valley, 102, 103, 110, 164, 167
San Miguel County, 149
Sandia Mountains, 147
Sangre de Cristo Mountains, 6, 23, 40, 76, 147
Santa Anna, 4
Santa Clara, New Mexico, 23
Santa Fe Art Museum, 38
Santa Fe County, 149
Santa Fe, New Mexico, 2, 3, 150
Santa Fe Railroad, *see* Atchison, Topeka
Santa Fe Trail, 3, 5, 6, 7, 10, 23, 35, 42, 46, 76, 79
Santa Mia, New Mexico, 116
Santa Rosa, New Mexico, x, 85, 87, 154
Sauble brothers, 43
Sauble, Frank, 48
Sawyer Cattle Company (Bar S), x, 81, 82, 83, 146, 149, 165
Schriener Ranch, x
Scotland, 53, 54-55
screwworm, 15, 16
Scurry, Sally, 47
Sessions, Sam, 82, 96, 98, 160, 166
Seventh Cavalry, 168
Shane, 115
Sharp, Davis, 184

Gray Hawn, photographer and friend, at Monument Valley, Arizona (scene of John Ford's classic western movies, Stagecoach, Fort Apache, *and* She Wore a Yellow Ribbon).

Gray Hawn of Austin is an internationally renowned photographer whose work is displayed in the National Gallery in Washington, D.C., the Shakespearean Theater in London, and the Epcot Center in Florida. Her photographs have been published in more than forty magazines (including *Town & Country*, *Modern Bride*, *Ultra*, *Texas Monthly*), and her work is included in the Loan Collection of the Professional Photographers of America, shown worldwide.

Gray photographed the last formal portrait of Princess Grace of Monaco in addition to creating an official government stamp portrait of Prince Ranier and Princess Grace, and in 1998 she traveled to India to photograph royal subjects and other dignitaries. Her style is recognized by many famous clients, including President George W. Bush, Sophia Loren, President of Mexico Jose Lopez Portillo, Farrah Fawcett, Lucy Baines Johnson, President Jimmy Carter, Lady Bird Johnson, Baroness de Nadine

Rothschild, and Tommy Lee Jones. In 2000 her fine art watercolor prints of the White House were used as diplomatic gifts by President Bill Clinton and Vice President Al Gore.

Gray's photographic art has won numerous "Best of Show" awards, and her salon exhibitions have been acclaimed throughout the United States. In 1996 she was awarded the degree of Master Photographer from the Professional Photographers Association of America for her photographic accomplishments. Since 1990 she has produced and directed children's television documentaries, for which she has won numerous awards, including a national "Best Programming" award for children.

Jack Curtis, author of *100 Best Portrait and Wedding Photographers*, said this about Gray Hawn: "We may look back on her renaissance style and impressionistic feeling and recognize it as a new school of photography."